EDUCATION

THROUGH

OCCUPATIONS

IN AMERICAN HIGH SCHOOLS

VOLUME I

APPROACHES TO INTEGRATING
ACADEMIC AND VOCATIONAL EDUCATION

EDUCATION

THROUGH

OCCUPATIONS

IN AMERICAN HIGH SCHOOLS

VOLUME I

*APPROACHES TO INTEGRATING
ACADEMIC AND VOCATIONAL EDUCATION*

EDITED BY
W. NORTON GRUBB

TEACHERS
COLLEGE
PRESS

Teachers College, Columbia University
New York and London

Published by Teachers College Press, 1234 Amsterdam Avenue, New York, N.Y. 10027

Library of Congress Cataloging-in-Publication Data

Education through occupations in American high schools / edited by W.
  Norton Grubb.
    v. <1   > ; cm.
    Includes bibliographical references and index.
    Contents: v. 1. Approaches to integrating academic and vocational education
    ISBN 0-8077-3451-9 (alk. paper).—ISBN 0-8077-3450-0 (pbk. :
  alk. paper)
      1. Education, Secondary—United States—Curricula. 2. Vocational
  education —United States—Curricula. 3. Career education—United
  States—Curricula.   I. Grubb, W. Norton.
LB1628. 5. E38   1995
373. 19 ' 0973—dc20   94-46742

ISBN: 0-8077-3450-0 (paper)
ISBN: 0-8077-3451-9

Printed on acid-free paper
Manufactured in the United States of America
02 01 00 99 98 97 96 95   8 7 6 5 4 3 2 1

CONTENTS

PART III

THE PEDAGOGY OF CURRICULUM INTEGRATION

ACKNOWLEDGMENTS

All the chapters in this volume are based on educational practice—on the practices of enterprising teachers, administrators, and students who have experimented with different approaches to schooling. Our greatest collective debt is therefore to these individuals, too many to name individually and often unaware of their roles as pioneers, who have begun to reverse a century of policies that segregated the academic and the occupational, the theoretical and the applied, the "head" and the "hand."

Virtually all the essays in this volume originated in research supported by the National Center for Research in Vocational Education, at the University of California, Berkeley, though all of them have been newly written for this volume. (The exception is Chapter 5 by Marilyn Raby, which is based on her extensive experience both developing and consulting with academies in California and throughout the country.) From its inception at Berkeley in 1988, the National Center has been committed to a broader conception of occupationally oriented education, more closely integrated with academic foundations and available to a larger number of students. The essays in this volume provide a fuller version of this vision, one we have often labeled the *new* or *emerging* vocationalism. Of course, the views expressed in these essays are those of the authors and not that of the U.S. Department of Education, which sponsored the original research.

With great sadness, these volumes are dedicated to the memory of Charles Benson, who died unexpectedly in July 1994 as these essays (including one co-authored by him) were being completed. Charles was a professor at Berkeley and the director of a series of institutes that combined research with the improvement of policies and practices on subjects as diverse as school finance, programs for children and youth, and vocational education. He was the founding director of the National Center at Berkeley, and his vision—of an educational system that serves well all of our children; of one that draws on a variety of competencies and develops a full range of capacities—was instrumental in establishing the agenda of the Center.

Charles was also extremely influential in putting the notion of integrating academic and vocational education on the national agenda. His early testimony to Congress sparked considerable interest in this topic and, subsequently, the requirement that federal funds be used for curriculum integration was incorporated into amendments to the Carl Perkins Act. He then developed a network of urban schools and community colleges dedicated to curriculum integration—a good example of his insistence on putting theories and ideas into practice. At the time of his death he was particularly concerned about the direction that school-to-work programs were taking at that moment—specifically, that they were constructing work placements without much thought to reconstructing high schools in any important ways. Consistently, he concentrated on just the right issues: on the well-being of children and youth, and on whether developments in policy and practice would genuinely improve their prospects rather than merely respond to the fad of the moment. His wisdom and spirit suffuse the essays in this volume, and will remain with us.

RESOLVING THE PARADOX
OF THE HIGH SCHOOL

W. NORTON GRUBB

The high school is now an inescapably vocational institution. When pressed, most students will admit that they are there to get a job. They understand—most of them—that the economic consequences of dropping out of high school are dire. Some see high school as a route to college, of course, but this too is largely a vocational decision, since college is a prerequisite for the best paid, highest status occupations.[1] Indeed, over the last 20 years the economic differences associated with education have increased, so the consequences of choosing different education paths have become greater and greater: The average earnings of young, male high school dropouts (those aged 25–34) were 65% of those of high school graduates in 1991, with a comparable figure for women of only 60%—and the likelihood of employment among dropouts was only three-fifths that of high school graduates.[2] The decisions made in high school—to take or not to take college prep courses; to work either hard or lackadaisically; to develop some goal or to drift aimlessly; to stay in or to drop out—have increasingly serious consequences.

Yet the high school doesn't appear to be vocational in the least. The highest status courses dominating the curriculum—the courses of the college prep track—appear "academic," in the pejorative sense of being removed from the real world of jobs and other adult responsibilities. The standard ways of teaching present a sequence of topics experienced as "school subjects," as things to learn in school, with their importance for later performance as workers and as citizens and community members left unclear. The most explicitly occupational parts of the high school curriculum, the traditional vocational education courses, have declined dramatically in enrollments under the pressure of stiffer graduation requirements

(Clune, White, & Patterson, 1989), and in many high schools there is no coherent sequence of vocational courses left to take. Career-oriented guidance and counseling have all but vanished from most high schools, with the few remaining counselors overwhelmed by paperwork requirements, crisis counseling, and just a little bit of college counseling. Although the high school is crucial to the vocational futures of its students, it appears to be an entirely academic enterprise, with a veneer of social life and extracurricular activities to keep students just interested enough to keep coming.

Yet this kind of separation between what high schools do and what they look like, common as it is, is hardly inevitable. It emerged around the turn of the century, when formal educational preparation for high-status professions—law, medicine, the professoriate, engineering—was becoming increasingly necessary, and when the high school as preparation for college became codified in prescribed courses, college entrance exams, and the college prep track. The separation between preparation for the professions and preparation for other, presumably less intellectually demanding occupations may have seemed natural at the time—it did, after all, follow the Taylorist separation of management from execution, of "head" from "hand." It also allowed divisions between middle-class children and "the children of the plain people ... crowding our schoolrooms," as the president of the National Education Association declared in 1897. The separation was resisted, not only by the labor movement, fearing the creation of a second-class education for its children, and by John Dewey, striving for a less-divided conception of education, but more importantly by parents and students. With the lure of high-status professions, however, the academic courses and the college prep track remained the center of the comprehensive high school.[3]

Once established, the separation of academic and vocational purposes spun out its own logic in a series of dismal consequences. Even though academic courses remained the choice of most students, it was always clear that the majority would not go to college or enter the professions, so the content became slowly degraded for most students—particularly in the courses of the general track. The purposes of the curriculum—its original link to college preparation and then to professional occupations—became increasingly murky for the majority of students; the link to future work— the reasons why the competencies learned in school might be important in later life—became increasingly vague. The links to institutions outside the school, never strong to begin with, continued to erode as the rationales for working with employers and community organizations weakened.[4] And the need to differentiate students "scientifically," with some destined for the professions while the rest prepared for semiskilled and unskilled jobs, in turn led to the current apparatus of testing and tracking students.

As a result, many of the current complaints about the American high school can be traced to the changes that made the high school the first in a series of educational institutions with responsibilities for occupational sorting and preparation while masking these vocational purposes behind the appearance of academic content. The lack of focus in the "shopping mall high school" (Powell, Farrar, & Cohen, 1985), the disconnection between the world of school and life after and outside of school, the domination of "academic" instruction without any context or purpose from outside the school, the motivational problems that come from students being unable to see what the purpose of schooling is, the emphasis on the college-bound and the neglect of the "forgotten half" not bound for college (W. T. Grant Commission, 1988), the weakness of career-oriented guidance and counseling—all these issues, the subject of so much complaining over the past century, are due in part to the way in which academic and vocational purposes have been separated.

In the current search for reforming the high school—for *restructuring* schools, to use the term in vogue—one solution is simply to reverse the separation between academic and vocational purposes that took place at the turn of the century. As the chapters in these two volumes argue, focusing schools more carefully on broadly defined occupational purposes and integrating academic and vocational education provides a way to undo many of the weaknesses of the high school. To be sure, this is not the only way to refashion high schools: orienting them around social problems (like environmental issues, or urban issues), or even traditional combinations of academic subjects (like science and math, or the humanities), are other ways to provide the focus, the context, and the purpose now missing from the comprehensive high school. But the occupational focus presented in these volumes has the advantage of acknowledging the central occupational purpose of schooling and the crucial role of work in the lives of adults, rather than obfuscating vocational purposes behind an academic facade.

There are, of course, many different starting places for reforming schools (as Chapter 3 clarifies). For example, some reformers, enamored of the apprenticeship systems in Germany, have proposed opportunities for work-based learning (the subject of Chapter 9, Volume II), and some of them have implicitly argued that starting such programs external to schools is more promising than reforming schools as the first step. Other reformers have placed great faith in assessment mechanisms—for example, the creation of Certificates of Initial Mastery, or the establishment of job-specific skill standards, or "high-stakes" tests, still in the early stages of development—as ways of forcing schools to improve. Still others have placed their faith in parental choice, as Chapter 3 explores in greater detail, or in teacher professionalism, or in site-based management. It's difficult to argue that any one starting point is wrong, since many of these approaches have real potential for improving schools. However, some of them (e.g., parental choice or school-based management) emphasize a decision-making process without providing a vision of what education could be. Others, like reliance on assessment mechanisms, assume that schools can be forced to change if external incentives are right, even in the absence of any capacity to change. Many proposals neglect the issues of curriculum content and pedagogy that are the heart and soul of schools—and the links between any initial changes and possible revisions in content and pedagogy are long and tortured indeed. The proposals to integrate academic and vocational education, on the other hand, take issues of curriculum and pedagogy as central, and provide the vision that some other reforms lack.

The title of these two volumes comes from John Dewey, who declared in *Democracy and Education* that "education *through* occupations consequently combines within itself more of the factors conducive to learning than any other method" (Dewey, 1916, p. 309). He went on to argue why this would be the best approach to learning, and in ways that sound surprisingly modern (reviewed in Chapter 1). He intended to contrast education *through* occupations—the use of occupations as an "organizing principle," or lens, or context in which many subjects could be taught—with education *for* occupations, the kind of job-specific vocational education that he opposed, and the kind of occupationally oriented education that won out instead in American high schools. I like to think that the reforms envisioned in these pages are ways of returning to Deweyan ideals, ways of moderating the dualisms—between theoretical and applied, between academic and vocational, between "college-bound" students and the "non-college-bound"—that Dewey so opposed. These reforms are also ways of reforming the passive instruction so characteristic of the high school, by encouraging more contextualized, more activity-based, more cooperative forms of learning—as Chapters 10 and 11 stress. Dewey never had the opportunity to implement his vision, but we still do.

THE ORGANIZATION OF VOLUME I

Because the integration of academic and vocational education, in its fullest form, seeks to reverse a century of development within high schools, it is a complex reform, with many approaches and related elements. The essays in these two volumes examine integration from a variety of perspectives, each one emphasizing a different aspect. The chapters in Volume I, divided into three parts, describe the conditions that have generated interest in curriculum integration and define what integration is and could be. Volume II then takes up the problem of implementing these changes—a difficult issue not only because change in education is notoriously difficult to achieve, but also because integrating academic and vocational education requires undoing a division that has been in place for more than a century. A description of the chapters in Volume II can be found in the Introduction to that volume.

PART I: THE BACKGROUND OF INTEGRATION EFFORTS

In Chapter 1, on the historical and current sources of support for integration, I present a brief history of the idea of integrating academic and vocational education. While these ideas (including John Dewey's own support for "education through occupations") were not powerful enough to prevent the separation of the two during the twentieth century, they have been rediscovered in the various sources of support for integration—from the business community, from critics seeking to reinvigorate academic education, from critics of traditional vocational education, and from policymakers trying to reform the schools. The confluence of these disparate strands has meant a breadth of support for curriculum integration unmatched at any time in the past.

For at least the past decade, changes in the nature of work and the pressure of the business community to reform schools have been among the most prominent external pressures on the schools. In Chapter 2, Tom Bailey describes the changes in the organization and technology of work, clarifying how these changes in turn have led to pressures for the higher-order skills so often discussed. In turn, because these capacities are poorly taught with conventional schooling practices, these pressures have generated the need to reshape approaches to instruction, including the integration of academic and vocational content.

Schools have always been somewhat insular institutions, resistant to pressures from external forces, and if the business community were their only critic, then change would be unlikely. But there are several other currents of reform in American schools (analyzed in Chapter 3) that reinforce the pressures from the business community. While the variety of reforms is bewildering, they can be categorized into: efforts to professionalize teachers; curricular and teaching reforms; reforms that expand choice among parents and students; and restructuring efforts, most of which transfer greater control to the school level. Varied as these reforms are, however, we argue that each of them is consistent with the integration of academic and vocational education—and indeed that integration is one of the best methods of accomplishing the goals of these other reform movements.

PART II: APPROACHES TO INTEGRATION

Because the purposes behind integration are so varied, approaches to integration are varied as well. In Chapter 4, I present a continuum of eight approaches to integration, distinguished by their scope and ambition, by whether they depend on teacher collaboration or not, and by their relative emphasis on academic versus vocational content. This overview then allows me to provide a conception of integration—something that has often eluded reform movements.

The following chapters provide greater detail on the most promising approaches to integration. In Chapter 5, Marilyn Raby examines the *academy* model, a school-within-a-school with an occupational focus that has been widely replicated from its beginnings in Philadelphia and California. In addition to detailing the strengths of academies, the chapter also highlights some pitfalls—particularly the issue, common to many restructured schools, that academies can increase the likelihood of curriculum integration but not guarantee it.

In Chapter 6 I describe a number of schools that have adopted *occupational clusters* (or career pathways, or majors), in which students choose a broad occupational area that structures the curriculum during the last 2 or 3 years of high school. A number of state and federal initiatives (including the School to Work Opportunities Act) have promoted clusters. However, they appear to be among the most difficult vehicles for integrating academic and vocational education, partly because the ways in which they are implemented vary so much and partly because they require restructuring an entire high school (in contrast to an academy, which reforms only a small part). Nonetheless, for the same reason, clusters have greater potential for reshaping education for large numbers of students, and therefore it is important to understand their potential.

In Chapter 7, Ruth Katz, Lola Jackson, Kathy Reeves, and Charles Benson describe a number of occupationally oriented *magnet* schools. Like academies and clusters, these provide a broad occupational focus within which the integration of academic and vocational content can take place—a possibility that is often unrealized. However, even when magnet schools do not provide much integration, students themselves may be able to do so, and they can pursue the "two track" strategy of preparing both for employment and for further education after high school.

In Chapter 8, Mayo Tsuzuki describes the way *senior projects* have been adopted in several schools. This kind of approach is somewhat different from the others presented in this section, since it need change only a part of the senior year. However, many schools adopting senior projects have found that they need to reshape other aspects of their curriculum to prepare students adequately for a senior project, so this approach becomes a lever for indirectly reforming more of the high school. It is also a change that can be readily adopted without the massive changes required with clusters or magnet schools.

In discussing school reforms, it is all too common to leave students as afterthoughts—to be more concerned with the administrative and curricular details of change than with the ways in which students receive them. As a corrective, in Chapter 9 Amy Heebner draws on extensive interviews with students in magnet schools in which the integration of academic and vocational content is being attempted in order to clarify the benefits to students by presenting these benefits in their own words. What they report includes: greater interest in their classes; the sense of community possible in smaller, magnet high schools; and the ability to pursue a "two track" strategy of preparing for both employment and postsecondary education. While the students she describes were all enrolled in magnet schools, their views are remarkably similar to those reported by teachers in career academies and in schools using clusters. Such reports cannot constitute a full evaluation of curriculum integration, of course, but they do point to some of the benefits that such reforms can generate.

PART III: THE PEDAGOGY OF CURRICULUM INTEGRATION

The movement to integrate academic and vocational education is partly an effort to combine content that is usually taught in different subject areas. One of its great promises, however, is that it also can be a lever for changing teaching methods. In Chapter 10, Cathy Stasz, Kimberly Ramsey, and Rick Eden describe the conscious efforts to teach what they call *generic skills*— the capacities for problem solving, higher-order reasoning, and teamwork that many employers as well as educators have called for—in both academic and vocational classrooms. While teachers can change their instruction methods independently of other reforms, efforts to integrate academic and vocational education can provide the motivation and the context that facilitate the teaching of generic skills.

In Chapter 11, Sue Berryman reviews the thinking behind current efforts to *contextualize* instruction—that is, to teach both content and capacities (including generic skills) in a context where they are used. As an approach to teaching that more actively engages students, contextualized teaching holds the promise of enhancing the motivation of students, as well as enhancing their ability to apply what otherwise seem to be purely theoretical and "academic" ideas. Like the teaching of generic skills, contextualized teaching can be accomplished without integrating occupational concerns; but occupations, broadly construed, provide a natural way for contextualizing instruction in high schools. Like other teaching reforms, the methods of contextualizing instruction must be self-consciously mastered and incorporated into teaching, even in settings—like work-based learning—where the context seems the most obvious.

CONCLUSIONS: REFORMING THE HIGH SCHOOL

To summarize some of the benefits of curriculum integration, at one level, integration can be viewed as a way of reforming occupational education— of making it more general, better connected to related academic disciplines, better able to impart the higher-order competencies that are variously referred to as generic skills (in Chapter 10) or *SCANS skills* (Secretary's

Commission on Achieving Necessary Skills (1992a). At another level, some forms of curriculum integration provide students with more information about the relationship of their education to their occupational futures, and— particularly in schools where students have to choose an occupational focus or "major"—provide a new form of career-related guidance.

Valuable as these two contributions are, the greatest promise of curriculum integration is that it can reshape the high school in fundamental ways, for all students rather than for a subset labeled *vocational,* or *at risk,* or the *non-college-bound.* In this form, the movement to undo the divisions of the last century have the potential to realize John Dewey's vision of "education *through* occupations."

NOTES

1. High school students rank vocational goals higher than they do intellectual, personal, or social goals. However, both parents and teachers rate intellectual goals the highest, and rank vocational goals third and fourth, respectively—creating a potential conflict in how all of these segments view high schools (Goodlad, 1984, Chap. 2). A record number of college freshmen in fall 1993 cited vocational reasons for attending college: 75.1% cited being able to make more money, up from 49.9% in 1971, and 82.1% cited its value in getting a better job, up from 71% in 1976 (Higher Education Research Institute, 1994).

2. High school dropouts here are those with 9–11 years of schooling (National Center for Education Statistics, 1993, Indicators 30 and 32). For all ages, the earnings of dropouts compared with high school graduates fell among men from 73% in 1967 to 63.7% in 1988, and among women from 68.7% to 60.4%, based on consistent Current Population Survey data reported in Grubb and Wilson (1992).

3. Lazerson and Grubb (1974) provide some rudimentary numbers: Enrollments in explicitly vocational courses did not appear to increase after federal support for vocational education was granted in 1917, or with increased federal funding in the 1960s.

4. The movement for federal support for vocational education originally envisioned that the dominant form of vocational education would be a form of cooperative education—that is, on-the-job training combined with school-based learning in continuation schools—and it drew some of its inspiration from the German apprenticeship system, which was then (as now) a work-based system. However, many educators used the German experience to justify the school-based system that developed here; enrollments in continuation schools were always far smaller than in school-based vocational education, and over time school-based programs completely dominated coop programs and continuation schools.

PART I

THE BACKGROUND OF INTEGRATION EFFORTS

1

"THE CUNNING HAND, THE CULTURED MIND"

Sources of Support for Curriculum Integration

W. NORTON GRUBB

In the beginning, the division between academic and vocational education did not exist. During the nineteenth century, the establishment of public education was based on the ideal of the common school—where students of every background would learn together, with a curriculum common to all. The subjects varied only slightly; the dominant philosophy of mental discipline argued that the same curriculum—the subjects we now consider the standard academic curriculum—was appropriate for every kind of future. As late as 1893, a committee examining the high school declared that "every subject which is taught at all in a secondary school should be taught in the same way and to the same extent to every pupil so long as he pursues it, no matter what the probable destination of the pupil may be, or at what point his education is to cease" (National Education Association, 1893).

The first introduction of more overtly occupational material into the high school still espoused a single curriculum. The manual training movement of the 1880s developed graduated exercises in woodwork and metalwork, not to give students the specific skills necessary for employment but to train them generally in the uses of tools and the manipulation of materials, to round out their education, to "train the mind by training the hand." In its pedagogy, manual training also followed academic orthodoxy. Its graduated exercises in wood- and metal-working, designed to teach ever more complex skills with various tools and materials, followed the familiar teaching method I call "skills and drills," in which complex competencies are divided into sub-skills, with drill taking place for each contrived sub-skill rather than practice being encouraged on an intrinsically valuable task.[1]

Manual training was novel in insisting that the curriculum include more occupationally oriented content. But because its goal was still the development of mental capacities rather than job-specific skills, any notion of separating vocational exercises from academic learning was anathema. As one of the leaders of the movement for manual training proclaimed:

> Hail to the skillful, cunning hand!
> Hail to the cultured mind!
> Contending for the World's command,
> Here let them be combined.
> (Woodward, 1887)

While the manual training movement smoothed the way between the academic curriculum of the common school and the differentiated high school curriculum of the twentieth century, it never attracted many practitioners. Very few schools heeded its central lesson: that technical competencies were important because they provided an opportunity to learn more general capacities otherwise taught in academic subjects.[2] Instead, the pressures for more utilitarian forms of education, preparing students for immediate employment, led to a greater stress on job-specific skill training within the movement for vocational education. Business-oriented courses, already a small part of the high school curriculum (Weiss, 1982), were joined by programs in the trades and crafts, agricultural education, and home economics. In addition, as high schools came to include more lower class, immigrant, and African American students, the idea developed that common schooling was inappropriate. Instead, education ought to be differentiated according to the "evident and probable destinies" of students. Those destined for working class jobs—and most likely to be working- or lower class immigrants or African Americans—should be in vocational tracks, while those bound for managerial and professional positions—most often middle class and white—would be in academic programs.

The difference between manual training, with its emphasis on general learning for all students, and vocational education, with its insistence on job-specific skill training designed for the "evident and probable destinies" of different students, emerged again in the views of John Dewey and in several debates between Dewey and others. Much of Dewey's writing criticized the dualisms that dominated education, in his time as now—the separation of individual and society, of body (or activity or experience) and mind, of "learning" and "doing," of play and work, of academic education versus vocational education. He argued that academic and vocational education should not be separated, and in fact that vocations and broadly occupational themes are the most appropriate ways of focusing instruction: "Education *through* occupations [not *for* occupations] consequently combines within itself more of the factors conducive to learning than any other method" (Dewey, 1916, p. 309). Dewey gave several reasons:

> The crucial position of the question of vocational education at present is due, in other words, to the fact that it concentrates in a specific issue two fundamental questions:—Whether intelligence is best exercised apart from or within activity which puts nature to human use, and whether individual culture is best secured under egoistic or social conditions. (p. 320)

The first of these is, in modern parlance, the question of whether teaching should be contextualized or decontextualized, and of course Dewey argued strenuously for contextualized instruction. The second is the question of whether teaching should concentrate on the learner as an individual or as a social being, and Dewey's argument was consistently in favor of social conceptions of both the learner and of the subject being learned.

Apart from securing opportunities for providing a social context for learning, Dewey argued that occupations were superior to any other method of organizing instruction for three reasons. First, "An occupation is the only thing which balances the distinctive capacity of an individual with his social service." That is, individual interests—in developing capacities and finding important adult roles, for example—and the community's interest in having well trained and productive workers can be balanced. This in turn implies that any unbalanced conception of vocational preparation—for example, one in which students are lured into "uncongenial callings"—is inappropriate. For instructional purposes, the balancing of individual and social aspects implies that occupations can be used both to teach the skills and capacities necessary to gain access to worthwhile occupations and to teach about the social context of those occupations.

Second, Dewey argued that a vocational focus would help avoid passive, didactic teaching based on contrived materials. He declared that education through occupations

> is a foe to passive receptivity. It has an end in view; results are to be accomplished. Hence it appeals to thought; it demands that an idea of an end be steadily maintained, so that activity cannot be either routine or capricious. Since the movement of activity must be progressive, leading from one stage to another, observation and ingenuity are required at each stage to overcome obstacles and to discover and readapt means of execution. (Dewey, 1916, p. 309)

In other words, using occupations to focus instruction would foster active learning, an integration of experience ("doing") and reflection ("learning"), problem solving, and the "impasse" approach to learning of constructivists and Piagetians (Prawat, 1993). In addition:

> A calling is also of necessity an organizing principle for information and ideas.... it provides an axis which runs through an immense diversity of detail; it causes different experiences, facts, items of information to fall into order with one another. The vocation acts as both magnet to attract and as glue to hold. Such organization of knowledge is vital, because it has reference to needs; it is so expressed and readjusted in action that it never becomes stagnant. No classification, no selection and arrangement of facts, which is consciously worked out for purely abstract ends, can even compare in solidity or effectiveness with that knit under the stress of an occupation; in comparison the former sort is formal, superficial, and cold. (Dewey, 1916, pp. 309–310)

Thus, materials drawn from occupations can avoid the contrived nature of "school-like" curriculum materials, as well as reaching out and organizing a large number of subjects.

> An education which acknowledges the full intellectual and social meaning of a vocation would include instruction in the historic background of present conditions; training in science to give intelligence and initiative in dealing with material and agencies of production; and study of economics, civics and politics, to bring the future worker into touch with the problems of the day and the various methods proposed for its improvement. Above all, it would train power of readapting to changing conditions so that future workers would not become blindly subject to a fate imposed upon them. (p. 318)

Finally, Dewey declared that "The only adequate training *for* occupations is training *through* occupations" (p. 310). He feared that conventional schooling (and conventional vocational education) would narrow the education of those preparing for lower skilled jobs and deny them opportunities for developing their full range of capacities; but the broader conception of "education through occupations" would avoid such a restriction. In current terminology, an integrated education could avoid the kind of tracking, particularly of college-bound from non-college-bound students, that has marked the high school.

In fact, Dewey provided a clear example of what he meant by "education *through* occupations"—an example remarkably consistent with schools that have recently integrated academic and vocational education through academies and clusters:

Gardening [agriculture], for example, need not be taught for the sake of preparing future gardeners [farmers], or as an agreeable way of passing time. It affords an avenue of approach to knowledge of the place farming and horticulture have had in the history of the race and which they occupy in present social organization. Carried on in an environment educationally controlled, they are means for making a study of the facts of growth, the chemistry of soil, the role of light, air, and moisture, industrious and helpful animal life, etc. There is nothing in the elementary study of botany which cannot be introduced in a vital way in connection with caring for the growth of seeds. Instead of the subject matter belonging to a peculiar study called botany, it will then belong to life, and will find, moreover, its natural correlations with the facts of soil, animal life, and human relations. (p. 200)

Despite his support for "education through occupations," Dewey consistently criticized overly specific training—"trade training"—since it not only narrowed the scope of education and created inequities for some, but also because it "defeats its own purpose" as changes in industry take place and narrowly trained individuals find themselves unable to adjust. In a battle over vocational education in Chicago, Dewey opposed vocational education on the grounds that it had become overly narrow and occupation-specific, creating a second-tier education for working class youth and subordinating their interests to those of employers (Lazerson & Grubb, 1974). Similarly, a famous debate between Dewey and David Snedden clarified the different uses of vocations in the schools: while Snedden argued for relatively job-specific education, Dewey pressed again for a broader education than "specialized skill in the management of machines at the expense of an industrial intelligence based on science and a knowledge of social problems and conditions" (Kliebard, 1986).

However, Dewey's arguments had virtually no effect on high schools. While the Dewey School incorporated occupations into the elementary grades, it did not extend to the high school level where it might have provided an alternative to job-specific vocational education, and it had no real imitators that might complete what Dewey barely began (Leversee, 1990). Vocational education ended up developing along the lines advocated by Snedden, quite different from what Dewey espoused—more utilitarian and job-specific, more focused on narrow skill acquisition, increasingly disconnected from academic education. Reflecting Dewey's fears about creating "undemocratic" distinctions among students, other practices—ability grouping or tracking, and the introduction of testing as the basis for differentiating students—reinforced these divisions as well (Kantor, 1988; Lazerson & Grubb, 1974). The advent of federal aid for vocational education in 1917 reinforced the differentiation between vocational and academic education, different in their content, their goals, and their students.

Still, even as academic and vocational education continued to separate, doubts arose about the wisdom of this division. The first major review of vocational education—the Russell report of 1938, the result of a committee appointed by President Roosevelt—criticized vocational education for promoting a narrow conception with overly specific training, and for encouraging a dual structure segregating vocational education from academic education, amounting to a "caste system" linking social class to curriculum (Russell, 1938). The committee recommended that vocational education be made more general and flexible, that it become better connected to the academic curriculum to provide "a broad range of basic abilities of value in a whole related family of occupations."

Following a similar pattern, President Kennedy appointed a committee to examine vocational education in the early 1960s. Its report focused more on increasing the amount of vocational education and on making it more up-to-date and responsive to labor markets, a reaffirmation of vocational education as job-specific training. However, it also introduced the idea of clusters of occupations, and argued that high school programs "should be designed to provide education in skills and concepts common to clusters of closely related occupations" followed by specialized training at the postsecondary level. In this sense, subsequent federal legislation—the 1963 Vocational Education Act and its 1968 Amendments—attempted to make vocational education somewhat more general (Advisory Committee on Vocational Education, 1968; Panel of Consultants on Vocational Education, 1963). While the cluster concept made little difference in practice, it has resurfaced in current efforts at curriculum integration (as Chapters 4 and 6 clarify).

One other effort to reconstruct vocational education is worth mentioning: the movement for career education in the 1970s (Grubb & Lazerson, 1975; Marland, 1974). This effort critiqued the low status of occupational concerns in schools and called for integrating academic and vocational education as a way to create a more unified and relevant curriculum. It urged that there be more cooperation among teachers, with all teachers having greater knowledge about the applications of their disciplines in the work world. However, the proponents of career education were maddeningly imprecise about both goals and methods; aside from a few references to "fusing" or "interlocking" academic and vocational education, there was little advice about how curriculum integration should be achieved, and virtually no attention to the retraining of teachers. The insistence that all of education be reoriented around careers struck many as overly utilitarian. While career education intended to reshape all aspects of schools, its most insistent goal was to teach students about careers so that they could make better occupational decisions—and its real legacy was a single course in career education in many high schools and middle schools. Even that practice waned during the 1980s, a telling saga of what can happen when a reform movement becomes encapsulated in a single course peripheral to the conventional academic curriculum.

In retrospect, then, criticisms of separating vocational from academic education have been common, but they have had remarkably little influence. The redirection outlined by the Russell report was lost in the ferment of World War II, and the efforts of federal legislation after 1963 to support program improvement were unsuccessful in connecting vocational education with academic education. The career education movement, which had begun by trying to reform all schooling, ended up simply as another course—one about careers—in the overly crowded high school curriculum. While the integration of academic and vocational education has been an ideal for over a century, its implementation has been noticeably absent from schools.

CURRENT STRANDS OF SUPPORT FOR INTEGRATION

What distinguishes the current "movement" to integrate academic and vocational from previous efforts is the variety of support it has received. Critics outside the schools—the business community in particular, often seconded by policymakers—have been joined by those inside the schools; critics of both academic and vocational education have come around to the position that each might be strengthened by the other. To be sure, the variety of voices creates its own problems in defining precisely what integration should accomplish. But support from many sources has created what earlier advocacy did not: a number of schools experimenting with integration, federal legislation providing both financial support and legislative requirements, and a larger community understanding the potential benefits. At least four distinct groups have contributed their voices.

THE BUSINESS COMMUNITY

During the 1980s the business community[3] discovered a new "crisis": a shortage of basic skills in the work force, as well as workers unequipped with problem-solving abilities, with the capacity to continue learning as they progress through more demanding jobs, and with other skills often labeled "higher order thinking skills." (Chapter 2 provides greater detail about the changes in work that have prompted these criticisms.) Business representatives called for a broader education than traditional vocational training; as the Committee for Economic Development (1985) declared, "Business, in general, is not interested in narrow vocationalism. It prefers a curriculum that stresses literacy and mathematical and problem-solving skills"(p. 15). Other business groups that stressed the pace of technical change in the workplace also favored more general competencies over job-specific training. As the Panel on Secondary School Education for the Changing Workplace (National Academy of Sciences, 1984, p. 13) concluded,

> The education needed for the workplace does not differ in its essentials from that needed for college or advanced technical training. The central recommendation of this study is that all young Americans, regardless of their career goals, achieve mastery of this core of competencies up to their abilities.

One response to these views was the "New Basics" espoused by *A Nation At Risk* (U. S. Commission on Excellence in Education, 1983), which articulated a common program of English, math, science, social studies, and computer science as an antidote to the "rising tide of mediocrity threatening our very future as a Nation and a people" (p. 2). But subsequent reports have stressed that a conventional academic curriculum might not be appropriate. One of the clearest statements has come from the Secretary's Commission on Achieving Necessary Skills (SCANS) (1991) of the Department of Labor, which surveyed the requirements of high-performance work and outlined five necessary competencies: the ability to identify and allocate resources; interpersonal skills; capacities related to acquiring and using information; understanding complex systems; and the ability to work with a variety of technologies. Not only are these competencies quite different from those taught in standard academic courses but they also require a different approach to teaching:

> SCANS believes that teachers and schools must begin early to help students see the relationship between what they study and its applications in real-world contexts.... We believe, after examining the findings of cognitive science, that the most effective way of teaching skills is "in context." Placing learning objectives within real environments is better than insisting that students first learn in the abstract what they will then be expected to apply.... Reading and mathematics become less abstract and more concrete when they are embedded in one or more of the competencies; that is, when the learning is "situated" in a system of a technological problem. (p. 19)

The SCANS commission also argued that *all* students should learn the SCANS competencies, not just those students in "special tracks labeled 'general' or 'career' or 'vocational education'." Two subsequent SCANS reports (1992, 1993) provided some suggested assignments for teaching the SCANS competencies within academic classes. By stressing the importance of teaching work-related competencies and capacities in some important context, the SCANS recommendations have clarified that the conventional separation between academic and vocational content is obsolete.

COGNITIVE SCIENTISTS

Other critics have attacked the academic programs of the high school—part of a long history critiquing conventional teaching for being arid, boring, disconnected from the real world and therefore "irrelevant," and too dominated by "teacher talk," with little opportunity for students to participate more actively.[4] More recently, these criticisms have been reinforced by those of cognitive scientists who have argued that most learning (including learning in and for the workplace) is quite different from the form it takes in schools.

Most learning takes place in groups and requires cooperation, while most school-based learning is an individual activity; learning in the real world often relies on both simple and complex tools, whereas school-based learning emphasizes thinking that is relatively independent of tools. Most importantly, schools emphasize relatively abstract forms of learning disconnected from the "contexts" of work, family, and community, while "natural" forms of learning—in apprenticeship programs, for example, or in families—take place in contexts that are both intrinsically important to the learner and that reinforce norms and interpersonal skills, as well as cognitive learning. (Chapter 11 provides additional details on the claims of cognitive scientists and others concerning conventional instruction.)

As in the case of criticism by the business community, the response isn't obvious. There are many ways to provide active forms of instruction and to "contextualize" instruction—some having nothing to do with the work setting that motivated the SCANS Commission and the metaphor of apprenticeship as a model for learning (Collins, Brown, & Newman, 1989). However, these criticisms of conventional academic instruction provide an argument for introducing vocations as contexts for instruction, in the ways that John Dewey espoused. They also provide a justification for the teaching methods associated with vocational education: At their best, vocational instructors have incorporated more participatory forms of learning, based on projects of intrinsic interest rather than on abstract tasks, providing more opportunities for student initiative and cooperative learning rather than the teacher direction and the "teacher talk" that dominates most classrooms.

A somewhat different attack on conventional instruction has noted, as did the business community, the deficiencies in basic skills of a wide range of students, including most of those in the general and vocational tracks. For example, a consortium of schools in the southeast, organized by the Southern Regional Education Board (SREB), has identified the general track—"a basically unplanned program of study that fails to prepare young people for either college or work"—as partly to blame for it, with another part of the blame placed on the undemanding "academic" courses offered vocational students (Bottoms, Presson, & Johnson, 1992). But simply replacing general-track courses with standard academic courses is unlikely to be much help, since conventional academic teaching provides information in ways that hold little meaning for the majority of students. Therefore, the solution within the SREB consortium has been to replace general courses with those that integrate academic and vocational content, making greater demands on students who would otherwise be able to "cruise" through high school without learning much of anything.

EDUCATION RESEARCHERS

Many of the past criticisms of vocational education have reemerged in the recent interest in integrating academic and vocational education. Evidence about the ineffectiveness of vocational education, central to the Russell report, mounted throughout the 1970s and 1980s (Grasso & Shea, 1979; Meyer, 1981; Reubens, 1974; Rumberger & Daymont, 1984; Stern, Hoachlander, Choy, & Benson, 1986). A typical reaction to negative findings was that of Stern et al. (1986), who called for integrating vocational and academic education rather than for training in specific entry-level jobs as a way of invigorating academic education:

> Through practical application, theoretical ideas can come alive for students. Vocational education should no longer be seen as another set of subjects competing for students' time. It should be a set of activities that help students use, understand, and appreciate what they are learning in other courses. This kind of vocational education will increase students' long-term productivity as workers by encouraging them to understand the theory underlying the work they do. (p. 50)

Vocational educators themselves have responded to these criticisms, as well as to the declining enrollments caused by increasing graduation requirements during the 1980s (Clune et al., 1989), by stressing the role vocational education might play in making education more real, more "relevant," for a large number of students:

> Many young people enter high school already turned off to the learning process. More of the same is not the answer. Motivating students not only to do better, but also, in many cases, to remain in school, is the critical task of education. Vocational education is frequently the catalyst that reawakens their commitment to school and sparks a renewed interest in academic skills....
>
> What is really required today are programs and experiences that bridge the gap between the so-called "academic" and "vocational" courses. The theoretical and empirical bases as well as the practical and applicative aspects of academic courses and vocational courses must be made explicit and meaningful. This calls for a joint effort between the academic teachers and vocational teachers. (National Commission on Secondary Vocational Education, 1985, pp. 2, 14)

POLICYMAKERS

Finally, policymakers at the federal level have added their own pressures for integrating academic and vocational education. The most prominent example has been the 1990 Amendments to the Carl Perkins Act, requiring that every program supported by federal funds "integrate academic and vocational education in such programs through coherent sequences of courses so that students achieve both academic and occupational competencies." Other sections support *tech-prep* programs combining high school and postsecondary education—an innovation that provides opportunities for integrating high school curriculum in preparation for more job-specific postsecondary programs, analyzed in greater detail in Chapter 10, Volume II—and allow resources for teaching students about "all aspects of the industry" they might enter, another effort to broaden the focus of vocational education. While Congress made no effort to define integration, this legislation in a way completes the logic of changes dating to the early 1960s. While earlier federal legislation tried to provide resources for program improvement, the definition of "improvement" was generally left to the discretion of state and local officials. The recent amendments define improvement as curriculum integration, providing the resources necessary for such changes, as well as pressure to do so.

Most recently, Congress has enacted the School-to-Work Opportunities Act of 1994. Modeled roughly after the German apprenticeship system,[5] with its reliance on work-based training, this legislation includes a school-based component, a work-based component (examined more completely in Chapter 9, Volume II), and connecting activities, including liaisons with employers and guidance to students. The school-based component explicitly requires curriculum integration, specifying that schools provide "career majors" with "a coherent sequence of courses or field of study that prepares a student for a first job and that integrates occupational and academic learning." Partly because of the wide publicity given apprenticeship systems in other countries, we can anticipate that this legislation will promote additional experimentation with integrated curricula.

THE HISTORICAL LEGACY:
WHAT DOES CURRICULUM INTEGRATION MEAN?

Because there are many strands of support for integrating academic and vocational education, purposes and goals are inconsistent. Those members of the business community encouraging "higher order" competencies have different changes in mind than do those wanting to eliminate the dismal courses of the general track. Proponents of reinvigorating academic instruction by contextualizing teaching often have conceptions of context that have nothing to do with occupational preparation, and their purposes are quite different from those of vocational educators seeking new roles in the aftermath of declining enrollments.

One consequence of having different purposes within one "movement" is that many approaches to integrating academic and vocational education exist. As a result, integration takes many forms: Chapter 4 in this volume describes eight distinct approaches, each with many variants, and Chapters 5, 6, 7, and 8 elaborate on some of these. A related consequence is that, because the purposes of different advocates are sometimes not carefully articulated, there remain unresolved issues about what integration means. In particular, there are five issues with varying answers in different approaches to integration, both currently and in the past:

1. *What is the occupational content of integrated programs?* Within traditional vocational education, occupational content has focused on job-specific skills and attempted to provide students with a series of manipulative and cognitive skills necessary for certain occupations. Current attempts to provide competency-based vocational programs articulate exactly what these competencies are, for example. In contrast, the manual training movement, Dewey's thinking about the role of occupations, and the SCANS Commission have stressed that occupational content should not be job-specific, but should be related instead to broader competencies—for example, to the generic skills examined in Chapter 10 of this volume—with job-specific skills learned either in postsecondary education or on the job.

2. *What is the academic content of integrated programs?* Some advocates focus on higher order thinking skills and have in mind complex problem solving and sophisticated academic competencies. Others concentrate on "basic skills," usually defined as reading for comprehension, simple writing, and pre-algebra math; programs following this conception tend to be remedial. Most integrated programs have emphasized reading, writing, math, and some science (particularly related to health occupations), while literature, history, and the social sciences have been ignored (this is the subject of Chapter 6 of Volume II). In turn, this suggests that academic content often has been used to reinforce vocational purposes— an emphasis reflecting the origin of many integration efforts among vocational educators—rather than as an approach in which vocational content is used in the service of learning "academic" competencies.

3. *For whom are integrated programs appropriate?* In the manual training movement, for example, an integrated curriculum was thought appropriate for all students; and John Dewey similarly argued that "education through occupations" was the most powerful approach for every

student. In contrast, partly because vocational education has focused on a subset of mid- to low-skilled jobs, it often has been considered appropriate for the "manually minded," or students who do not do well in standard academic curricula. The historical split between academic and vocational education, therefore, differentiated students as well as curricula. One potential effect of efforts to integrate vocational and academic education, then, is that students who are segregated in the conventional high school might be more often combined in relatively heterogeneous classes.

Currently, the same debate persists. Many academies have been established for "at-risk" students, and integrated curricula are often advocated for the "forgotten half" or the "middle 50%." Some programs to develop integrated curricula—including some versions of youth apprenticeship or school-to-work programs—intend them for non-college-bound youth, assuming that students bound for four-year colleges will continue to take the traditional academic curriculum. On the other hand, the School-to-Work Opportunities Act stresses the provision of programs for all students, "from a broad range of backgrounds and circumstances, including disadvantaged students, students of diverse racial, ethnic, and cultural backgrounds, students with disabilities, students with limited English proficiencies, and academically talented students." Of course, debates about the appropriate group of students often include assumptions about the abilities and interests of students: older assumptions that some students are "manually minded" and destined for vocational education have resurfaced in statements that the non-college-bound don't need or want the conventional academic curriculum.

4. *Is the integration of academic and vocational education a reform of vocational education or a way of restructuring the high school for a larger number of students?* The manual training movement, John Dewey's visions, and career education envisioned different kinds of change, to be sure, but each intended to reshape the entire high school. Similarly, many current approaches to curriculum integration—the academies described in Chapter 5, the schools based on clusters examined in Chapter 6, and the occupationally oriented magnet schools in Chapter 7—provide structural changes in high schools. On the other hand, some approaches to integration reshape individual courses, to improve the academic content available to vocational students, but otherwise leave the high school unchanged.

5. *Is the integration of academic and vocational education a change in curriculum or is it a change in teaching methods as well?* The manual training movement changed the content of instruction by incorporating woodshop and metalwork, but it continued the contrived exercises,

graduated from simple to difficult, of conventional academic teaching. Vocational education further changed the content, and also introduced more project-based methods of instruction in some programs, although it has retained the "skills and drills" methods of manual training in other places. Dewey was interested in changing both content and pedagogy, but the resistance he faced was related more to the kinds of teaching he espoused, and to his basic vision of education, than to his support for using vocational applications.[6] Currently, proposals to integrate curricula are highly varied: Some exist as off-the-shelf curricular materials that combine academic content with vocational applications and ignore any changes in pedagogy, while others stress changes in teaching methods without including much occupational content. However, integrating academic and occupational content provides a rationale for changing methods of teaching as well, as Chapters 10 and 11 clarify.

These issues are not academic, in the pejorative sense of discussions removed from the real world of practice. The answers to them affect virtually every aspect of classroom practice, as the examples in subsequent chapters clarify. They also will determine how successful the current movement for integration is—how widely it will be accepted, how well it will succeed in teaching students now leaving high school with inadequate preparation, how well it succeeds in teaching competencies like problem solving, the application of knowledge, and interpersonal communications. Without clarity about these questions, efforts to integrate academic and vocational are likely to remain peripheral rather than realizing their potential to reconstruct the American high school by eliminating the divisions created a century ago.

■
NOTES

1. The teaching method of manual training is usually linked to the Russian woodworking exercises called *sloyd*, presented at the 1876 Centennial (see Cremin, 1961, Chap. 1). This approach to vocational skills instruction is still present in many vocational courses, as well as in conventional woodshop and metalshop, where they still exist.
2. Even those schools that called themselves *manual training schools* during the 1880s and 1890s tended to promote specific skill training for immediate employment, not for more general education, and they disappeared after 1900 (see Leversee, 1990).
3. The business community does not always speak with one voice. The national commission reports that attract the most attention usually include representatives of the largest, most socially conscious corporations, often those competing actively in the international economy—corporations that can afford to do their own specific training and that must take the long-run view about the capacities of the labor

force. However, the small- and medium-sized firms that operate in subnational labor markets, and that often cannot afford to do their own training, are more likely to pressure educators for specific skill training. The recent surge in customized training and in state funding for specific training linked to economic development are good examples.

4. For criticisms in the 1890s that sound quite modern, see Cremin (1961). For more recent criticisms, see Powell et al. (1985), Boyer (1983), Goodlad (1984), Sirotnik (1983), and Sizer (1984).

5. The movement for vocational education at the turn of the century also drew on the German apprenticeship system. However, advocates in this country misconstrued the work-based German system, instead using the economic superiority of Germany as an argument for a school-based system of vocational education.

6. From a Deweyan perspective, the attempt to distinguish between content and pedagogy is artificial; for example, because of his concern with application and with following the interests of students, Dewey inveighed against teaching only the content of standard disciplines. Any applied or contextualized program that responds to student interests (appropriately defined) will differ in its content from any other. On the resistance of the schools to changing their basic approach to teaching, see especially Cuban (1993).

2

THE INTEGRATION OF
WORK AND SCHOOL

Education and the Changing Workplace

THOMAS R. BAILEY

Anxiety about the state of the economy has driven education reform for over a decade. As the U.S. economy lost its dominant economic position in the world, many began to blame the country's education system. Widely reported international comparisons suggested that young people in the U.S. scored below their counterparts in many European and Asian countries and seemed to confirm the notion that a deficient U.S. educational system created an increasing human capital disadvantage relative to the country's trading partners (Commission on the Skills of the American Workforce, 1990; U.S. Commission on Excellence in Education, 1983).

But the perception of declining international competitiveness is not the only cause for concern. Real wages and the average standard of living have barely risen since the early 1970s, and inequality in wages and earnings has been growing since the early 1980s (Levy & Murnane, 1992).

Although there have been a wide variety of explanations for these developments, many policymakers have continued to emphasize the weakness of the education system. Education policy has been a central component of the Clinton Administration's economic reform agenda. During the early 1980s, many commentators argued that the country's schools had deteriorated and that education reform was designed to recapture a bygone golden age (Bailey, 1992). By the early 1990s, a more common explanation was that the demands of the economy had outstripped the potential of schools to fulfill them. A system that had been adequate during the two or three decades after World War II was no longer effective in preparing the work force for the technologies and markets of the early 1990s. In order to return to faster productivity growth and higher standards of living, the U.S. would have to combine education reform with significant additional investments in education or human capital.

What kind of education system would be effective in meeting the needs of the emerging economy, and how do the educational needs arising from a system that meets this criterion relate to the types of reforms and programs discussed in the other chapters of this book? This chapter addresses these questions.[1] It does so by examining in more detail the changes taking place in the economy and workplace and exploring the educational implications of those changes. The first part of this chapter discusses direct empirical evidence that the skill demands of the economy have risen. The chapter then turns to an analysis of the changing nature of work, focusing mainly on two broad models. These are referred to as the *mass-production model* and the *high-performance model*, although other names are also used in the academic and policy discussions. There is a review of information on the spread of the high-performance model. One crucial element of the model is that it begins to break down traditional barriers and divisions within the workplace. Workers from different departments—such as planning, design, engineering, manufacturing, service delivery, and marketing—begin to work together. Indeed, traditional distinctions between conception and execution, or between first-level supervisors and workers, are often blurred. For these reasons it makes sense to refer to the more innovative sites as *integrated* workplaces.

The subsequent sections analyze the skill and educational implications of the economic and workplace changes reviewed in this chapter. The central conclusion, with respect to the goals of this book, is that the emerging and innovative forms of work do call for a different approach to education. That approach involves changes in the content of education and, most particularly, in its pedagogy. As with the integrated workplace, innovative education challenges tradition—such as the breakdown of subjects into departments and the distinctions between "head" and "hand," academic and vocational, theory and practice. The integration of academic and vocational education plays a crucial role in these innovations. Thus, the integrated workplace calls for an integrated education system.

EMPIRICAL EVIDENCE ON CHANGING SKILLS

Over the last several decades, controversy has developed over the changing skills requirements of the economy. The general notion that a more modern and technologically advanced economy needs higher skilled workers was challenged by those who argued that automation, and even microelectronics, had the potential to incorporate skills into the technology itself. According to this view, the economy needed a cadre of highly skilled engineers, planners, and managers, but the bulk of workers would simply be machine loaders, tenders, and watchers. Subsequently, some participants in this discussion argued that increased international competition, more rapid technological change, and a more varied and volatile product market implied that decisions and planning had to be decentralized and carried out by so-called *front-line* workers—those in manufacturing who were actually building the products and those in services who delivered the service. Organizations that relied on unskilled workers to carry out the orders of a small leadership group would be much too rigid and cumbersome to operate in rapidly changing contemporary markets. Flexibility and innovation were necessary to compete, and this required skilled workers at all levels (Bailey, 1989).

Much of the evidence that related to this controversy—whether or not skills requirements were changing—was developed in case studies of particular workplaces, and these have yielded a rich lode of insights and examples (Bailey, 1989). Unfortunately, proponents on both sides of the controversy can marshal case study evidence. In an extensive review of this evidence, published almost ten years ago, Spenner (1985) concluded that there was no strong support for either position. Research work over the subsequent decade has perhaps given additional support to the notion that skill requirements are rising, but problems of generalizability still thwart definitive conclusions and, in any case, many examples of low-skilled jobs can still be found.

Furthermore, direct measurement of skills has proved to be extremely difficult. Observation of work tasks is costly and may focus on the skills that are available rather than on those that are optimal for the effective performance of tasks. Moreover, there is no accepted conceptualization of skills, or widely used methodology for measuring them.

An alternative approach has been to use broad-based data of characteristics that do not necessarily measure skills directly but might reflect skill changes. Two approaches have been used. In one, analysts have measured the relative earnings of workers with various levels of education. If workers with higher levels of education begin to earn more relative to those with less education, then this suggests that employers are increasingly looking for more educated workers and are therefore willing to pay more to get them. The second approach depends on forecasts of the growth of different occupations. If those occupations that typically are filled by more highly educated workers grow faster than those filled by less educated workers, then we can conclude that the economy requires more educated workers and, assuming that education reflects skills, more skilled workers. The following sections review the evidence from wage and occupational trends.

CHANGING RELATIVE WAGES

Changes in wages earned by different groups of workers do suggest a steady increase in the demand for workers with higher levels of education. In 1979, full-time 25–34-year-old male workers with college degrees earned about 13% more than did similar workers who were only high school graduates. The earnings differential for these groups rose to 38% by 1987. For women in the same age group, the premium earned by college graduates rose from 23% in 1979 to 45% in 1987 (Levy & Murnane, 1992, Table 7). This increasing educational wage gap suggests that the demand for higher educated workers is rising relative to the demand for workers with less education. If the jobs that employers have to offer now "require" more skills, then employers would be willing to offer more money to attract adequately skilled workers.

Changing demand is not the only influence on wages. Changes in supply also will affect earnings levels. Indeed, in the 1980s there was a decline in the growth rate of college graduates, and this sharp drop in the supply could have driven up their wages even without any changes in demand. But this supply factor cannot explain the entire wage gap. This is especially true in manufacturing. If the rising wage gap had been caused primarily by a shrinking of the relative supply of college graduates, then manufacturing employers would have hired fewer college graduates and more high school graduates, but the data show a relative shift toward the higher educated group. The employment of full-time 25–34-year-old college graduates rose by 10% between 1979 and 1987, while their earnings rose by one-third. In contrast, the employment of high school graduates in the same age group in manufacturing rose by only 6% while their earnings fell by 11% (Levy & Murnane, 1992, Table 9). Thus, in their review of the large and growing body of research on the shifting patterns of relative wages, Levy and Murnane conclude that during the 1980s there was a steady rise in the relative demand for more highly educated workers.

SHIFTING OCCUPATIONAL STRUCTURE

Projections of occupational change frequently have been used in the controversy about changing skills requirements. Indeed, they have attracted a great deal of attention, probably because, unlike wages or abstract measures of skills, different occupations are easily associated with different skills levels. A doctor or an engineer needs more skills than does a fast–food worker. But the discussion of occupational projections has often been misleading and, given the methodologies used, does not in the end shed much light on the nature of changes in required skills.[2]

One problem has been that the data seem to support both sides of the controversy. Those who argue that required skills are not changing point out that most of the 10 occupations that are projected to add the most jobs to the economy by the year 2005 require few skills. With the exception of registered nurses and general managers, all generally require low skills. On the other hand, those who argue that skills are rising point out that the 10 fastest growing occupations are dominated by those characterized by middle-level skills—for example, paralegals, system analysts and computer scientists, physical therapists, medical assistants, operations research analysts, human services workers, radiology technologists, and medical secretaries.

Both of these types of "top 10" analyses are misleading and unnecessary. Data are available to study the whole occupational distribution, and an analysis done in this way suggests that overall, the new jobs that will be added over the next decade are disproportionately those that currently use more highly educated incumbents. For example, while occupations in which more than a majority of the incumbents in 1990 had some postsecondary education accounted for 38% of all employment, those occupations were projected to account for 55% of all jobs created by 2005 (Berryman & Bailey, 1992, Chap. 2).

On the other hand, using the current projection methodologies, if the overall distribution of occupations in the early 1990s is compared to the projected distribution of occupations in 2005, the changes in occupations of different educational levels are not dramatic. While 22% of employed workers in 1990 had four or more years of postsecondary education, the occupational projections suggested that their share would rise only to 24% by 2005 (Berryman & Bailey, 1992, Chap. 2).

While these changes are small, it must be emphasized that the methodology used to forecast them virtually precludes forecasts of large changes in the distribution of skills. The approach assumes that the skill and educational requirements within occupations do not change. All change is driven by changing proportions of occupations. Thus, skill increases would occur because engineers replace operators or because analysts replace secretaries. The methodology assumes that the jobs of operators and secretaries have not changed. The change in the overall distribution is therefore sensitive to the projected growth rate of jobs. Since job growth over the next decade is projected to be only moderate, then a forecast for a large change in the overall methodology would be highly unlikely.

The modest level of these changes can be easily understood by thinking about adding hot water to a bathtub of tepid water. Even if the added water is much hotter than the water in the tub, unless the flow of new water is very large compared to the stock of existing water, it will take a long time to have a strong effect on the water's overall temperature. Since the forecast methodology assumes no change in existing jobs (the temperature of the water already in the tub) and since the projections foresee only moderate job growth (the flow of water into the tub), then it would indeed be surprising to expect large changes in the overall skills distribution (the temperature of the stock of water in the tub).

What can be concluded from the wage and occupational data? At the least, they suggest a steady but moderate increase in the demand for more highly educated (and therefore presumably more skilled) workers. On the other hand, they are not strong support for the argument that there is a revolutionary or dramatic rise in skills requirements, although the methodology used for the occupational projections precludes such a conclusion. Moreover, these analyses provide meager guidance to educators because they reveal little about the types of skills increasingly needed. In order to gain both a better grasp of those skills and to develop more concrete knowledge of future trends in skills requirements, we need a deeper understanding of changes in the economy and the resulting shifts in the nature of work.

■

TWO WORK MODELS:
MASS PRODUCTION AND HIGH PERFORMANCE

For much of the last half century, schools have evolved in the context of an economy that provided large numbers of good jobs for semiskilled workers. Production was organized efficiently to produce large numbers of standardized goods and services. Producers in the U.S. excelled at this mass-production system, taking advantage of their access to huge and growing U.S. markets. But growing international competition, increasing demands by consumers for variety, quality, and constant style changes, and the acceleration of the pace of technological change all undermined the stable markets for standardized goods on which the mass-production system was based.

These shifts began to create advantages for what has come to be known as the *high-performance workplace.* There are no single, accepted definitions for the mass-production system on the one hand and the high-performance workplace on the other, but the basic concept is that workers at all levels in the high-performance workplace are expected to be actively and intellectually engaged in their work. In more traditional or mass-production settings, the jobs of production (or front–line) workers are limited, well defined, and passive. Workers are expected to perform a set of tasks and anything out of the ordinary is referred to managers or to specialized support personnel. Little initiative is required.

In contrast, in high-performance systems, workers are engaged in less well defined activities and are expected to be much more actively involved with their jobs, contributing their ideas and initiative to furthering the goals and objectives of their work group and organization. Rather than simply carrying out specific tasks and following well defined instructions, workers are expected to solve problems, to seek ways to improve the methods that they use, and to engage actively with their coworkers. This is, therefore, much more than simply increasing the tasks that a worker can perform; rather it involves a new type of behavior and orientation toward the job. Indeed, it sounds very much like the behavior that is already expected from professional and technical personnel.[3]

THE SPREAD OF THE HIGH-PERFORMANCE WORKPLACE

The argument is made throughout this book that a pedagogy based on the integration of vocational and academic instruction would better prepare workers for high-performance work organization, but many analysts have argued that few firms have adopted these types of innovative practices. A better understanding of the spread of high-performance work organization can help both to interpret the evidence and to develop a better sense of future trends in skills demands.

Although there has been a great deal of discussion of the spread of the high-performance workplace, the extent to which a shift has actually occurred remains controversial. *America's Choice*, the influential report by the Commission on the Skills of the American Workplace (1990), attracted a great deal of attention when it claimed that only about 5% of American firms had made any significant transformation.

Although the 5% figure is often cited, the methodology used by the Commission to arrive at this conclusion has never been made clear. Over the last decade, however, there have been a handful of more or less broadly based surveys designed to identify the diffusion of various work reform and employee involvement practices (Eaton & Voos, 1992; Freund & Epstein, 1984; Lawler, Ledford, & Mohrman, 1989; Lawler, Mohrman, & Ledford, 1992). In addition, there have been a variety of more focused surveys of particular industries, regions, and states.

In general, these surveys often found that a majority of respondents (82% of the respondents to the GAO survey of the 1986 Fortune "1000") reported adopting some work reform or employee involvement technique. The extent of adoption has also grown since the 1970s. Nevertheless, at least by the mid-1980s, only a minority of firms could be said to have made a significant organizational transformation. Results from the GAO survey suggest that "between 20 and 30% [of the respondents] have a substantial effort in place that uses a number of different kinds of approaches with a large percentage of employees." Manufacturing industries appear to rely more on employee involvement (Lawler et al., 1989, p. 59).

A 1992 survey by Osterman (1994) is also more or less consistent with these general findings. In a national survey of firms with 50 or more employees, and using a reasonably weak measure of whether a firm was "transformed" (high performance), Osterman also found that a quarter to a third of the firms had made significant changes.

While many firms are experimenting with new forms of human resource management, others are pursuing a more ominous strategy. In many cases, employers appear to be searching for greater efficiency by cutting staff, relying where possible on temporary employees, and in other ways reducing their commitment to their labor force. The two trends are not completely inconsistent. Firms may make a commitment to a small "core" of workers while they rely on a large group of "peripheral" workers to absorb fluctuations. But it is still hard to imagine a high-performance workplace in which firms run away from their workers, or at least from a significant share of them.

Thus, the precise nature and extent of trends in work organization remain obscure. Discussions in the business press and the case study evidence do suggest a trend toward innovative work organization and a substantial number of firms, although still only a minority, have already made significant changes. Furthermore, economic forces are providing increased incentives for firms to adopt many of the practices associated with high-performance work organization (Bailey, 1993). But this change is difficult, and there are counter forces.

This suggests a dual role for education, one responsive and the other active. To the extent that firms are moving toward high-performance work organization, there will be an increased demand for personnel who are appropriately educated. At the same time, the absence of such workers may also be seen by firms as an impediment to the adoption of innovative human resource and organizational techniques. Although there are many other problems that stand in the way of wider adoption of high-performance work organization, education reform may provide a necessary foundation for further work reform. The next section takes a closer look at the educational implications of emerging work practices.

EDUCATIONAL IMPLICATIONS

What are the educational implications of the spread of innovative human resource practices? The case studies in particular suggest that what such practices increasingly need is something that has been referred to as "advanced generic skills" (Stasz, McArthur, Lewis, & Ramsey, 1990; see also Chapter 10). This suggests that schools need to make sure that their students emerge with those skills. But the educational lessons from the changing workplace go beyond the *content* of education. Effective preparation for innovative work systems implies a transformed *pedagogy* as well, one in which the integration of academic and vocational studies, and of both theoretical and practical learning, can play a central role.

SKILLS (CONTENT)

What skills are necessary for workers in high-performance workplaces? First, case studies of innovative workplaces suggest that many production workers have an increasing need for the types of skills traditionally learned in school—literacy, arithmetic—and, at a higher level, specific technical knowledge. But these studies also suggest that current changes in work call for more than simply an increase in traditional education. On the job, diverse tasks have been combined in new ways and low-level workers have been given new responsibilities. Thus, educational reform should look beyond the quantity of education. The content and process of education need to be brought more in line with the types of activities students will be engaged in after they leave school.

Workers increasingly need to be able to operate more independently of their supervision and to work in a less well defined environment. This requires a greater facility for creative thinking, decision making, reasoning, and problem solving. Workers need to have a broader understanding of the systems in which they operate. Without this, they are much less able to make decisions about their own activities. Nor will they be able to monitor and correct the performance of those systems, or to participate in the improvement of their design. This was not an issue when workers were simply expected to follow instructions; their role within the broader operations of their organization was the concern of their supervisors and managers.

But even more than a broader knowledge of their context, workers need a more abstract or conceptual understanding of what they are doing. This is what allows them to carry out tasks or to solve problems that they have not encountered before or that they have not been shown specifically how to carry out or to solve. Thus, more than in the past, individuals will need to be able to acquire, organize, and interpret information. Workers will also have more direct interaction with their coworkers, and therefore will need more experience in general social skills, such as group problem solving and negotiation. These changes clearly involve more than an accumulation of the type of knowledge traditionally learned in schools. These skills, increasingly required by the high-performance workplace, are advanced generic skills (Stasz et al., 1990).

TEACHING AND LEARNING (PEDAGOGY)

But how should these skills be taught? With respect to this question, the innovative workplace has further lessons for educational reformers. There are strong parallels between traditional approaches to learning and teaching (approaches that have dominated education for decades and that, increasingly, are being questioned) and the characteristics of the mass-production system. Similarly, conceptions of the pedagogic systems within which students learn most effectively have important parallels to innovative production systems (Berryman & Bailey, 1992, Chaps. 3 and 4.; Brown, Collins, & Duguid, 1989; Raizen, 1989).

Table 2.1 draws parallels between traditional pedagogy and traditional (mass-production) work along five dimensions. Over the last decade, these traditional pedagogic strategies have been increasingly challenged by a different approach based on contrasting principles (see Table 2.2). These more effective pedagogic principles are consistent with the characteristics of the high-performance workplace. Given the similarities between

TABLE 2.1. Traditional Pedagogy and Traditional Work

	Traditional Pedagogy	Traditional (Mass Production) Work
1	Knowledge is fragmented. Material is presented in small segments that can be absorbed one at a time.	Jobs and tasks are narrowly defined.
2	Learners are passive. Teaching is seen as transmission of knowledge from the teacher to the student. There is a reduction in exploration, initiative, and learning from mistakes, creating dependence on the teacher.	Workers are passive order-takers in a hierarchical work organization.
3	Learning is based on teaching students the correct responses to given stimuli. This creates problems when students or adults encounter "stimuli" for which they have not learned the correct response.	Work is designed to be a set of routinized responses to limited, prespecified problems.
4	There is an emphasis on getting the right answer. Thus, there is little attempt to get behind the answer or to learn from mistakes. And there is little emphasis on the process of solving problems.	The focus of work is on getting the task done rather than on systematically improving the process through which the tasks are carried out.
5	Learning is decontextualized. In the past, many educators believed students would not be able to generalize material taught in a specific context--generalization required decontextualization.	Most workers do their tasks without knowledge of, or orientation toward, the functions and purposes of the organizations in which they work (their work was decontextualized).

TABLE 2.2. Integrated Pedagogy and High-Performance Work

Effective Pedagogy (Integration of Academic and Vocational Education)	*High-Performance Work*
1 Knowledge and curriculum are integrated. Traditional disciplinary boundaries and the typical organization of the school day have all been questioned.	Tasks and jobs (such as design, planning, production, repair, and maintenance) are integrated, either through broader job definitions or through cross–functional teams.
2 There is active learning (rather than passive), in which students are engaged in a process of discovery rather than being given information.	Workers are given more initiative and take more responsibility in a flatter organizational structure based more on trust and teamwork.
3 There is encouragement of a deeper understanding that allows multiple responses to stimuli that the learner has not already encountered.	Employees are expected to be able to solve problems in non–routine situations.
4 New approaches focus on the thought processes that generate learning rather than on the "right answer." Indeed, the possibilities of multiple responses to realistic, and therefore often ambiguous, situations are emphasized.	There is much greater emphasis on continuous improvement of the process of producing goods or services rather than on simply getting something produced.
5 New strategies call for learning in context. Researchers now agree that learning in context gives greater meaning to the material, and is therefore more effective.	Production workers as well as managers are expected to be able to understand their functions within the context of the broader functions and purposes of their organizations.

the characteristics of high-performance workplaces and innovative schools, students in these schools will experience an environment much like the one they would find in an innovative workplace.

The high-performance workplace is based on a rejection of many traditional distinctions, such as conception and execution, theory and practice, and supervision and subordination. New thinking about teaching and learning challenges the same distinctions, although somewhat different terms are used—such as head and hand, academic and vocational, or learning and work. The new, integrated workplace therefore calls for an integration of education that brings together academic and vocational studies and school and work.

■

CONCLUSIONS

Concern about the educational demands of the economy has helped sustain an education reform movement that is close to a decade old. In 1983, *A Nation at Risk* (U. S. Commission on Excellence in Education) warned that our society and economic well being were threatened by the deterioration of the schools. In 1990, *America's Choice* (Commission on the Skills of the American Workforce) argued that U.S. schools were inferior to those of the country's trading partners, especially in preparing "front–line" workers. If the problems were not reversed, the publication cautioned, standards of living would fall and inequality would rise; the country, it said, was headed toward a second-rate economic role on the world stage.

What does the evidence discussed in this chapter suggest about these concerns? The wage and occupational data and the case study information all suggest that there is at least a steady rise in the demand for more skilled workers. Recent research on the nature of work in high-performance work organizations, and on teaching and learning, also suggest that the traditional pedagogy that has dominated American education may not be effective in preparing workers for many human resource practices that appear to be successful in supplying today's markets from modern technology workplaces. And in this context, an education system based on integrating academic and vocational education, and which emphasizes innovations in both content and pedagogy, does appear to be more effective than are more traditional approaches. A more integrated education would do a better job of preparing the work force for the new, integrated workplace.

Critics argue, however, that the evidence does not suggest that the country is experiencing extremely rapid or revolutionary changes in its work organization. This is a reasonable point, although it is possible that with a more abundant supply of appropriately skilled workers, employers would have been quicker to move to innovative systems, and less likely to adopt other alternatives.

But improved education alone would sharply accelerate a shift toward high-performance work organization, or toward more skill-using approaches to production. Common business practices, labor market institutions, the structure of financial markets, the legal framework within which firms operate, and other factors all create barriers to change and innovation. Education reform may be necessary for significant economic restructuring, but it is not sufficient.

Just as the concepts of the integrated workplace and the integrated curriculum challenge us to break down traditional barriers and divisions at work and in schools, they should also suggest that efforts to reform those institutions should not be carried out in isolation. Reforms such as the integration of academic and vocational education can play an important role in strengthening the effectiveness of the work force, but they need to be incorporated into a broad strategy to restructure both schools and workplaces.

■
NOTES

1. This chapter is based on a series of projects funded by the National Center for Research in Vocational Education (Bailey, 1989; Bailey, 1992; Stasz et al., 1990; Raizen, 1989). In addition, the chapter relies on three publications that were not published by the Center, but were themselves based on projects funded by it (Bailey, 1991; Bailey, 1993; Berryman & Bailey, 1992).

2. For a detailed discussion of the occupational forecasts, see Berryman and Bailey (1992, Chap. 2) and Bailey (1991).

3. For a much more detailed discussion of the distinctions between mass-production and high-performance workplaces, and between the necessary skills and behavior of their respective workers, see Bailey, 1989 and 1993.

3

THE POWER OF CURRICULUM INTEGRATION

Its Relationship to Other Reforms

ERIKA NIELSEN ANDREW
W. NORTON GRUBB

American schools have always been susceptible to reform by commission as one of the few ways to move the great, sprawling variety of schools (Cuban, 1990). So it has been over the past decade. *A Nation at Risk* (U. S. Commission on Excellence in Education, 1983) triggered a first wave of reform when it blamed schools for the declining economy and weakening national security. In response, many other commissions issued their interpretation of the problem. The Education Commission of the States (1991) estimated that there were 300 task forces for education reform at work throughout the country during the 1980s.

A number of common themes linked the reports. We needed a restoration of educational excellence, higher standards, and equity for all to stem the "rising tide of mediocrity." To raise standards, a common core curriculum was needed for all students (Passow, 1989). Equity and excellence were two other common themes of the first wave. Task forces called for the elimination of tracking, for lengthening the school year, and for the recruitment and retention of more academically able teachers. The states responded to these goals with sweeping legislation. By 1986, 45 states changed graduation requirements, 42 states increased math requirements, 34 states changed science requirements, 18 states modified language arts requirements, and most states began reassessing the structure of the teaching profession, including credentialing and the compensation of teachers who excel (Passow, 1989).

But after the first wave, many remain unconvinced. Legislative mandates seemed to imply that student achievement would increase simply by demanding excellence and by providing equity in curricular requirements. It was a period of "more of the same"—more courses, more requirements, more tests, more teacher requirements, and more money for teacher salaries (Anrig, 1992). And reforms were implemented with a top-down approach—through legislative mandates, and detailed rules, standards, and requirements that could bring only limited changes but could not affect the classroom (Passow, 1989).

The late 1980s ushered in a second wave of school reform. This wave began as a rebuttal to prescriptive legislation and as a response to the first wave of reforms, which failed to create the desired "excellence" in schools. As early as 1984, Cross (1984) had predicted this outcome:

> The curriculum will be tidied up, goals will be articulated, standardized tests will control transactions from one level of schooling to another, prospective teachers will study a core of common learnings, and the teacher education curriculum will be restructured to include certain experiences in specified sequences. There is not much evidence that the current mania for tidiness will produce orderly schools in which students and teachers pursue learning with the contagious enthusiasm that is so essential for excellence. (p. 69)

The second wave marked the end of belief in the "one best system" (Tyack, 1974), and the beginning of educational change school-by-school. As a result, the current wave includes an abundance of reforms aimed at a variety of different goals. The second wave has also been noteworthy for its efforts to create change at the local level and within the classroom—a result of skepticism that external mandates can transform schools and create desired student outcomes.

However, one problem is that the reforms are so varied that it is often difficult to understand what they are trying to accomplish. Our first purpose in this chapter is therefore to clarify the nature of current reforms. One way to describe the variety of current reforms is to examine how ambitious each is. In Larry Cuban's (1988) classification, "first-order change" accepts the existing goals and structures of a system and attempts to correct only the deficiencies in achieving those goals. Many of the first wave reforms—recruiting better teachers, selecting better textbooks, or increasing staff development days—are examples of first-order change, often the result of outside pressure. "Second-order change" challenges the assumptions, goals, and purposes of schools; they generally are more fundamental, more likely to reach to the level of the classroom, and have more often developed in response to pressures within the educational system.

Another way to describe current reforms is to categorize them according to their basic approach. In our interpretation, there are currently four main approaches to school reform: teacher professionalizing, curricular and teaching reforms, choice mechanisms, and restructuring.

1. *Teacher professionalization:* Reformers in this approach view teacher change as the linchpin of school change. Bureaucratic norms and regulations that restrict teachers are the villains, and greater teacher autonomy, expertise, and professionalism are the solutions.
2. *Curricular and teaching reform:* Schools in this approach usually begin at the classroom level to redesign curriculum and instruction around a particular philosophy of learning, often advocating active, student-centered, project-driven methods. In some examples, reform may occur only within a single subject or across two subject areas. In the more comprehensive examples, such as Coalition of Essential Schools, or in some outcomes-based education, the entire school is redesigned around a new philosophy of learning.
3. *Schools of choice:* There are many conceptions of choice, ranging from school-level, to district-level (including intradistrict, interdistrict, and magnet plans), to state plans. Magnet schools have become popular for many reasons: they facilitate promoting racial desegregation, they provide choice to parents and to students, and they allow "focus schools" to develop (Hill, Foster, & Gendler, 1990).
4. *Restructuring:* While this conception of school change means different things to different people, restructuring usually requires moving the locus of control to the school level, to create student/teacher-centered schools.

Our second major purpose in this chapter is to clarify how efforts to integrate academic and vocational education are related to these other strands of reform. Unfortunately, like much else that takes place in vocational education, integration with academic education has been peripheral to integration reform taking place in mainstream academic education—paralleling the historical division between academic and vocational education. However, this division is unfortunate in our view. The efforts to integrate academic and vocational education have much to offer other reform movements. The most thorough of these reforms offer ways of reforming the high school that simultaneously highlight its occupational relevance and address its most serious failings. Curriculum integration offers a philosophy of teaching—more student-centered, more project-based, relying more on cooperative learning groups and less on individual work—that is similar to many other efforts to reshape instruction. In the current drive to contextualize teaching—to teach academic subjects in the context of their applications—occupational applications provide one way to contextualize that simultaneously clarifies to students why learning academic material is crucial to their futures. Certain models of integrating academic and vocational education provide one way of restructuring high schools, a way that acknowledges rather than obfuscates the occupational role of the high school.

Conversely, several mainstream reforms have important implications for the efforts to integrate academic and vocational education. They clarify, for example, the importance of teacher professionalism, and outline ways of making teachers (rather than textbook writers and other outsiders) more responsible for the content of education. They highlight the importance (as well as the difficulty) of teachers developing their own curricula, rather than taking materials "off the shelf." They also highlight the importance of local decision making and the new roles and responsibilities for all school members. Each arena of reform has something to learn from the others, then, and the current segregation of academic reforms from those taking place in vocational education should end.

■
TEACHER PROFESSIONALIZATION

There are several different beliefs at the heart of teacher professionalization. First, improved student achievement depends on improved teaching and therefore on an improved teacher work force (David, 1991b; Gheens Academy, 1991; Rochester City School District, 1989). Second, the creation of effective schools depends on a decentralized form of governance and mode of operation, so that teachers gain a sense of personal responsibility and accountability for student performance (Hill & Bonan, 1991). Third, better decisions about students should be made at the local level, particularly by teachers who are closest and "know" best (Darling-Hammond, 1988).

Proponents of teacher professionalization often challenge the dominant bureaucratic model of school organization. It assumes that knowledge can be translated into standardized rules and content, where teachers are functionaries for practices set by those outside the school, rather than well-trained and autonomous professionals using their own knowledge, judgment, and discretion. In contrast, proponents of teacher professionalism demand a realignment of teaching with the expectations of professionals: a systematic knowledge base, the presence of a collegial structure, a standard of ethics to guide practice, a systematic induction into the profession, and professional rather than external accountability. An institution designed to support these features would make teachers the ultimate authorities, and would promote collegiality to permit opportunities for ongoing communication, reflective practice, and joint planning.

Concrete examples of teacher professionalism include school-based management, which has typically created advisory committees that increase teacher control over budget, curriculum, and personnel (Clune & White, 1988); professional development centers, which are district-sponsored teacher academies that provide teachers with additional training to enhance their knowledge base; and professional practice schools, which incorporate the teacher training of professional development centers into fully functioning schools (much as teaching hospitals provide training within hospitals).

The various efforts to professionalize teaching are in theory applicable to all teachers, from any discipline. They are therefore compatible with efforts to integrate academic and vocational education. Indeed, such integration efforts—which have been most successful in cases where academic and vocational teachers have actively collaborated with one another—reinforce the need for professionalism because of the need for all teachers to collaborate with others and to develop local approaches to integration that fit local needs and resources. Furthermore, to the extent that integration efforts are also pedagogical reforms, the emphasis of teacher professionalism on more active, student-centered teaching is an important component of curriculum integration as well.

At the same time, we suspect that the movements to professionalize teaching have not yet drawn many vocational teachers into their efforts. As ways of increasing contact among teachers who have historically been separate from one another—particularly the case with vocational instructors, though it has been common among teachers in many academic disciplines as well—the various approaches to teacher professionalism provide another way of creating coherent educational institutions from the fragmented, classroom-bound approach of the current high school.

CURRICULAR AND TEACHING REFORMS

A second current approach to school reform has been to change the curriculum or the method of teaching, assuming that the problem with schools lies within classrooms. The majority of these reforms depart from the behaviorist interpretation of learning to arrive at a constructivist approach, with a corresponding antipathy toward the teacher-driven, didactic approach we call *skills and drills*. [1] In a constructivist approach, teachers must themselves be role models of active, meaningful learning; they need to construct their own lesson plans, considering both the content and the method of instruction. Since changing teaching methods usually requires greater control by teachers and new training (or retraining) for teachers, the efforts to reform curriculum and teaching overlap considerably with those of teacher professionalism.

Numerous state reforms also begin with curriculum and instruction. Many resemble California's State Frameworks, which suggest major themes, theories, and implementation strategies for each core discipline. Others, such as Maine's Common Core of Learning, are attempts to redesign the curriculum around expected outcomes. On a national level, in addition to the standards movement (addressed in the section below entitled "Restructuring"), professional associations, such as the National Council for the Teachers of Mathematics and the National Science Teachers Association, are working on new approaches for the core disciplines.

CURRICULAR INTEGRATION EFFORTS

In its most general formulation, curriculum integration is one response to many deeply rooted problems in education. Advocates assert that integration can stem the fragmentation in school organization and can also solve the problem of the never ending growth of information (Jacobs, 1989). It can also be a vehicle to help disciplines such as math and science reform their pedagogy away from skills, drills, and memorization toward higher order thinking and active learning by getting students to understand their applications (Cushman, 1992; Caine & Caine, 1991).

As with the integration of academic and vocational education, there are many different approaches to integration. While Robin Fogarty's (1991) description of ten possible ways to integrate the curriculum is one comprehensive sample, three major forms of integration emerge in different authors (Fogarty, 1991; Jacobs, 1989; Jenkins & Tanner, 1992). In *parallel* approaches, two teachers sequence their courses so that similar topics are covered at roughly the same time—for example, a history teacher covers a certain era while an English teacher presents a novel from that same era, so that teachers and students (one hopes) can examine that period of history from both perspectives. In *multidisciplinary units or courses*, similar concepts from two disciplines are combined in a unit, an entire course, or even a program; examples might include courses in the history and literature of a particular country or period; hybrid courses, like earth sciences; broad fields, like social studies; or topics like sociobiology or ecology. In the *thematic* approach, a theme, issue, or topic becomes the subject of study, investigated with all the disciplines that might shed some light on it. Themes can be concepts, like individualism or culture; problems, like the environment or war (or specific wars); historical periods, like the Renaissance or the medieval world; or skills and capacities, like argumentation or problem solving. A functionally equivalent idea is to develop activities, or projects, which then motivate learning from various appropriate disciplines; this approach is then heir to activity curricula and project-based learning, ideas often associated with Dewey. However, unlike the use of themes, activities and projects usually involve making something—building a house, for example, or creating an environmental park—and therefore tend to move out of the realm of conventional academic subjects into those considered more vocational, like construction, agriculture, and the like.

Schools that fit within the thematic example typically experiment with curricular integration in a few, isolated classes. For example, they may integrate two courses, like science and math or English and history. Notable examples are the Foxfire approach, begun by Eliot Wigginton, and the National Science Teachers Association's Scope, Sequence and Coordination Project.

COMPREHENSIVE CURRICULAR AND TEACHING REFORMS

Another approach to curriculum reform has been to push for systemic (or second-order) change by articulating a set of wide-ranging principles.[2] The Coalition of Essential Schools begins with the relations between the teacher and student; the Paideia Project first defines the expectations schools have; and outcomes-based education and performance-based systems begin with the outcomes we expect for students.

The Coalition of Essential Schools
The Coalition evolved from a study of high schools (Sizer, 1984). While schools that join the Coalition vary enormously, they share a commitment to the following nine principles:

1. The school should focus on helping adolescents learn to use their minds well. Schools should not be comprehensive if that limits the central intellectual purpose.
2. Each student should master a limited number of essential skills and areas of knowledge. Schools should emphasize student mastery and achievement, not mere "coverage of content."
3. The school's goals should apply to all students, and tracking should therefore be abolished.
4. Teaching and learning should be personalized. Therefore, decisions about the course of study, and teaching materials, and specific pedagogies must be in the hands of the principal and teachers.
5. The metaphor of the school should be student-as-worker, rather than the more familiar metaphor of teacher-as-deliverer-of-instructional services. A prominent pedagogy is coaching, to provoke students to learn how to learn and thus teach themselves.

6. The diploma should be awarded upon a successful final demonstration of mastery, or the Exhibition.
7. The tone of the school should explicitly and self-consciously stress values of unanxious expectation.
8. The principal and teachers should perceive themselves as generalists first and specialists second.
9. Total student loads per teacher should be eighty or fewer and teachers should have substantial time for collective planning with teachers. (Coalition of Essential Schools, 1988, p. 1)

Like other current reform efforts, it isn't clear how schools belonging to the Coalition are actually changing. Not surprisingly, the initial steps are often halting, and the directions Coalition schools take are quite varied because the principles themselves are so varied and subject to such different interpretations.[3] Nonetheless, the Coalition is a striking model of schools reforming themselves by starting with classroom changes.

The Paideia Project

The Paideia Project, based on the ideas of Mortimer Adler (Adler, 1982), has generated about 200 pilot schools nationwide. A national network and training center is responsible for establishing model schools, directing professional development, and providing technical assistance for the Paideia schools (Education Commission of the States, 1991). Schools can elect to implement the Paideia Principles school-wide or as a school-within-a-school.

Like the Coalition of Essential Schools, Paideia schools adhere to a set of guiding principles:

1. that all children can learn;
2. that, therefore, they all deserve the same quality of schooling, not just the same quantity;
3. that the quality of schooling to which they are entitled is what the wisest parents would wish for their own children, the best education for the best being the best education for all;
4. that schooling at its best is preparation for becoming generally educated in the course of a whole lifetime, and that schools should be judged on how well they provide such preparation;
5. that the three callings for which schooling should prepare all Americans are (a) to earn a decent livelihood, (b) to be a good citizen of the nation and the world, and (c) to make a good life for one's self;
6. that the primary cause of genuine learning is the activity of the learner's own mind, sometimes with the help of a teacher functioning as a secondary and cooperative cause;
7. that the three kinds of teaching that should occur in our schools

are didactic teaching of subject matter, coaching that produces the skills of learning, and Socratic questioning in seminar discussion;

8. that the results of these three kinds of teaching should be (a) the acquisition of organized knowledge, (b) the formation of habits of skill in the use of language and mathematics, and (c) the growth of the mind's understanding of basic ideas and issues;

9. that each student's achievement of these results would be evaluated in terms of that student's competencies and not solely related to the achievements of other students;

10. that the principal of a school should never be a mere administrator, but always a leading teacher in the school who should be cooperatively engaged with the school's teaching staff in planning, reforming, and reorganizing the school as an educational community.

11. that the principal and faculty of a school should themselves be actively engaged in learning; and

12. that the desire to continue their own learning should be the prime motivation of those who dedicate their lives to the profession of teaching.

Because a Paideia school is centered on great works and discussions of "essential questions"[4] teachers must work with their colleagues, must constantly learn in collaboration with their students and other teachers, must include more active learning, and must participate in training of the Paideia methods. In an evaluation of the project (Kanoy, 1992), a majority of teachers stated that the seminar training has improved their Socratic teaching techniques, their communication and listening skills, their ability to express opinions logically and concisely, and their ability to evaluate differing opinions. Paideia training is also credited with helping them develop collegial relationships and improving their ability to lead discussions.

Outcomes-Based Education

Outcomes-based education (OBE) originally began as an instructional approach and is now evolving into a more comprehensive reform involving the entire high school (Spady & Marshall, 1991). Often called *mastery learning, outcomes-based instruction,* or *the outcomes-driven developmental model,* OBE assumes that all students can learn at their own rates. In an OBE perspective, schools begin with the outcomes they want for all students and then work backward to construct the curriculum. Since all students learn at their own rates, teaching is organized to vary the length and sequencing of instructional opportunities for different students (Spady & Marshall, 1991).

However, the variety of practices that call themselves outcome-based vary widely, so that it becomes difficult to pin down precisely what different reforms are doing.[5] Although OBE has been endorsed by, among others, the Business Roundtable, the National Governors' Association, and the Education Commission of the States, it has also been criticized for "dumbing down" the curriculum, emphasizing values over content, and holding students accountable for goals that are so vague they can't be assessed.

So far, few of the efforts to reform education through curriculum and instruction have incorporated occupational concerns—though the future orientation of outcomes-based education and the recognition in the Paideia project of the need to prepare students for the "calling" of earning a decent living come the closest. However, the pedagogical concerns of these reforms—shifting from teaching methods we have called "skills and drills" to those that are more student-centered, project-based, "contextualized" approaches, in which teachers act more as facilitators than as didactic instructors and in which students must take more active roles in their learning—are precisely the goals of the best efforts to integrate academic and vocational education. By definition, such efforts try to integrate parts of the curriculum that have been independent, clarifying the occupational relevance of academic subjects as well as the potential for vocational subjects to lead back to the academic disciplines. Particularly in schools where academic and vocational teachers have collaborated actively, one consequence has been to transfer the teaching methods commonly associated with vocational education to academic instructors. A greater reliance on cooperative learning (where students work in small cooperative teams), on project-driven approaches and discovery methods, on student-directed activities and student participation rather than on teacher-dominated classrooms, on learning in a specific context rather than decontextualized learning, and on the teaching of generic skills (described in greater detail in Chapter 10) has always been more common in vocational education, and so efforts to integrate academic and vocational education have the potential to change teaching methods in ways consistent with other current reforms.

Integrating vocational subjects specifies a particular way of contextualizing teaching, and of creating projects for students to work on—ways linked to the occupations that students see around them, and to which they may aspire. The integration of occupational concerns into the reform of teaching therefore provides a natural way of linking schools with students' futures, rather than continuing to pretend that high school has nothing to do with the adult responsibilities all students will face.

■ SCHOOLS OF CHOICE

The choice movement points to school bureaucracy as the villain. The lever for change is to give power to parents and students to choose among different schools under the assumption that their choices can lead to school improvement (Finn, 1990). While ideas about choice have been around since the 1960s, the practice was first introduced to encourage voluntary deseg-regation (Metz, 1986). Others argue that choice makes it possible to match student interest with the program characteristics best suited to an individ-ual student. Similarly, by creating a school composed of students, parents, and school people with the same values and interests, teachers will be more committed, parents will be more supportive, and students will thereby per-form better (Association for Supervision and Curriculum Development, 1990). And finally, choice has been advocated as a way to extend the oppor-tunity to choose—now available only to wealthy families who can afford private schools—to poor families (Fliegel, 1990).

One difficult issue in all choice plans is the link between choice and school improvement. In theory, the decisions of parents can force the closing of poorly performing schools while allowing effective schools to expand and innovative schools to develop. In practice, however, this places an enormous burden on parents to distinguish effective from inef-fective schools, to make choices based on effectiveness (rather than on loca-tion or extra-curricular activities, for example), and to choose on the basis of their children's interests rather than of their own predilections. In addition, the response of existing and potential schools—the supply side of the "market"—poses other problems: Whether poor schools will "go out of business" and good schools emerge is unclear. As ways of resolv-ing at least some of these problems, while retaining the attractive ele-ments of choice, some large school districts have established reforms— *controlled choice plans* and *magnet schools*—that provide some public solutions to these problems rather than leaving them to the operation of markets.

CONTROLLED CHOICE

Controlled choice plans require students to select a school to attend with-in a district. There are usually restrictions; for example, individual choices may not be allowed to upset the racial balance in a school. This type of plan tends to be expensive because of transportation costs and costs for dis-seminating information so parents can be fully informed. Some intradis-trict choice plans lead to new schools created from the ground up. The best known example is probably New York City's District 4, in East Harlem, where there are now over 50 programs in 23 buildings, with themes rang-ing from the Jose Feliciano School for the Performing Arts, and the Acad-emy of Environmental Sciences, to the Isaac Newton School for the Sci-ences and Mathematics. These programs are considered successful because teacher morale is high, vandalism and truancy are down significantly, and test scores have risen dramatically (Paulu, 1989).

MAGNET SCHOOLS

Magnet schools are selective schools with specific academic or vocational focuses. They were first introduced as competitive high schools in the 1950s. In the 1960s they were used as alternatives to forced busing, to prevent white families from leaving cities for the suburbs. From the 1970s to the early 1980s, the federal government encouraged magnet schools as vehicles for desegregation, through Emergency School Aid Act (ESAA) funds. More recently, magnet schools have appeared in the nation's largest districts as a reform strategy to meet the diverse needs of students. Some districts have a few magnet programs, while others (like Kansas City, Missouri) have turned the entire district into magnet schools. Some districts have initiated magnet programs using federal desegregation monies and emphasize racial desegregation as the goal, while others (such as the one in Dade County, Florida) are implementing magnet programs as a school reform strategy.

The focus of magnet schools also varies considerably. Some magnets are designed around a unique pedagogical emphasis. For example, the Brown School in Louisville, Kentucky, offers multiage and multigrade groupings, community experiences, and a child-centered instruction that enhances a self-directed learning style. Other magnet schools offer occupational majors in such areas as education and social services, computer science, or the arts. Of course, magnet schools need not have an occupational focus: some follow a selective college prep curriculum, or specialize in academic subjects like science and math. Others focus on a problem area, like the Environmental Sciences magnet in Kansas City.

The many self-evident advantages of magnet schools have increased enrollments in them, to perhaps 20% of all students in urban school districts (Blank, 1990). Apart from their value in allowing parents and students to choose a school compatible with their interests, magnet schools do appear to improve the educational performance of students. Furthermore, there is at least some evidence that performance is better the more thoroughly a magnet school adheres to its theme, implying that the extent of focus may be responsible for the success of magnet schools (Blank, Dentler, Baltzell, & Chabotar, 1983).

The efforts to develop choices for students within the public school system comes the closest of any mainstream reform effort to the efforts to integrate academic and vocational education—particularly the creation of academies (which are schools-within-schools), occupationally focused high schools, and schools with broad occupational clusters. Such alternatives provide students and parents with choices within the public school system, either within a single school with academies or in a series of clusters (the subject of Chapter 6) or within a district with a number of magnet schools (the subject of Chapter 7).

RESTRUCTURING

Restructuring is a relatively new conception of school change that has been used to describe reforms as varied as instituting choice programs, waiving regulations, empowering teachers, developing partnerships with businesses, promoting higher order learning outcomes, and shifting to school-based management. Despite this variation, restructuring generally requires a shift in control to the school level, to create student and teacher-centered schools. This approach, a direct response to the failure of earlier reform attempts imposed from the outside, focuses on five different "building blocks" of schools (Lieberman, 1990): curriculum and instruction; the structure of schools; a two-pronged focus on a rich learning environment for students and a supportive environment for teachers; partnerships and networks with other schools, universities, community agencies, and businesses; and a recognition of the need for parental and community participation. However, most schools currently engaged in restructuring have been able to focus only on one or two areas, with curriculum and instruction being the most difficult to change (National Governors' Association, 1991).

Given the confusion surrounding the term *restructuring*, the goals for the different projects vary. Many states with restructuring pilot projects have loose requirements for participating schools. In Washington state, for example, applicants were asked to design their own application forms using any medium or combination of media. Others have goals so broadly stated that they encompass every aspect of schooling; thus Maine's Restructuring Schools Project required schools to "reexamine their school's mission and seriously consider redesigning staffing, scheduling, curriculum, decision making, instructional tasks, activities and grouping" (Cox & deFrees, 1992). On the other hand, Philadelphia has a specific goal to create schools-within-schools, in which students get more personal attention from teachers and other adults, teachers experiment with different approaches to instruction, and schools involve their communities more intensively (Philadelphia Schools Collaborative, 1990). The Arkansas plan is equally specific, expecting that schools will experiment with performance-based assessment and use the Coalition of Essential Schools' nine core principles. As a final example, the New America's School Development Corporation (NASDC) has sponsored a research and development competition for new school designs, explicitly questioning all assumptions about current educational practice, including the length of the school day, traditional age and grade groupings, student/teacher ratios, and testing. While the private funding promised for its implementation has been relatively scarce, its existence is yet another signal of interest in reshaping schools in fundamental ways.

A final example of restructuring relies on an external mechanism—a system of national assessment—as the lever to initiate school change. The New Standards Project has proposed *mastery standards* for education instead of our current time-based standards. The mastery standards would be based on student performance of tasks requiring the kind of behaviors we want students to exhibit as adults. With mastery standards, the line between testing and curriculum would dissolve because, by using task-based exams rather than conventional multiple choice exams, teaching would have to change in order to prepare students adequately (Tucker, 1992). A related argument is that appropriate assessments can change education not simply through their demands on students but by placing teachers at the center of developing and scoring them (Resnick, 1992).

To be sure, the assumption underlying the New Standards Project—that new forms of assessment can be powerful enough to change all other aspects of schools—is controversial, and its success remains to be seen. The Project constitutes an example of restructuring in the sense that its ambitions for school change are ambitious—an example of fundamental, second-order change. But it departs from other examples of restructuring in its reliance on an external mechanism forcing schools to change—in opposition to the view of other restructuring efforts—that change must be local and collaborative.

The various efforts at restructuring attempt to address the deeply rooted failures of the high school: the chaos of the "shopping mall high school" (Powell et al., 1985), the disengagement of students, the ineffectiveness of conventional teaching, the isolation of teachers, and the inequities of tracking. Unlike the efforts to integrate academic and vocational education, most restructuring efforts have neglected the current inability of schools to help students think about future occupations and vocational consequences of educational choices, and the isolation of schools from the adult worlds of business and politics. While many restructuring practices reject the "shopping mall high school," they do not create schools with a specific focus or link with the outside world. Like most efforts to integrate academic and vocational education, restructuring requires local control—but the end to which local control is the means is usually unstated.

CONCLUSION

Although the starting point of different reforms varies, many similarities exist among them. Many attempt to eliminate the deep-seated dysfunctions of the "shopping mall high school"—including teacher ineffectiveness, student disengagement and passivity, and teacher isolation—in hopes of creating schools with a cohesive focus through proposing new responsibilities for both teachers and students. Many approaches to reform can be characterized by the following:

- They are student-centered, with more personalized instruction that makes room for meaning-making, active engagement, and a view of learning that comes from cognitive science.
- They see teachers as learners, either through action-based research, new teacher induction, redesigning schools, or simply through teachers spending time on their own education.
- They assume that schools should have a focus, encompassing an agreement about what distinguishes any particular school. The focus can be occupational (as in a health-oriented school) or discipline-based (as in science and math magnets), or problem-centered (as in magnets focused on environmental issues).
- They enhance teacher professionalism, reducing teacher isolation and increasing their discretion. To enforce quality, they rely on a student focus and external accountability rather than on constraints on what teachers do.
- They seek to improve morale among teachers and students demoralized by the constraints on their roles.
- They establish partnerships, either with universities, businesses, or networks of other schools, rather than attempting their reforms in isolation.
- They attempt to follow well-planned implementation processes, recognizing that implementation is just as serious a barrier to reform as is the lack of any vision for reform.
- They attempt change in several areas within the school and recognize the importance of second-order change by challenging assumptions, goals, and routines.

Finally, we return to the question of how the integration of academic and vocational education is related to other currents of reform sweeping secondary schools. To be sure, the notion of integrating academic and vocational education is not a unitary idea, since there are many different approaches (as outlined in Chapter 4). However, the more substantial approaches to integration share striking similarities with the four major approaches to reform we have identified.

TEACHER PROFESSIONALIZATION

The most substantial approaches to integration depend on teachers—vocational and academic—collaborating on the development of curriculum materials locally in order to devise programs that prepare students for occupations that are important locally and that draw on the interests of students and on the strengths of existing faculty. Indeed, those approaches that fail to initiate such collaboration—either because they use curriculum materials "off the shelf," or because they require existing teachers to reshape their courses without any new resources—are the most trivial examples of integration. However, the reliance on teacher collaboration at the school level also requires that teachers have the freedom and the authority to devise their own curricula and that they have the resources—intellectual resources as well as release time and money—to develop independent curricula.

It is therefore impossible to develop any of the more promising approaches to integration without giving teachers professional status and independence. Indeed, one of the most consistent barriers to integrating academic and vocational education has come from precisely the sources that most constrain teachers—from state curriculum requirements, from university entrance requirements that reinforce the standard academic curriculum, from teacher training programs, packaged curricula and computer-aided instruction programs that seek to standardize and "teacher-proof" teaching, and from time constraints.

CURRICULAR AND TEACHING REFORM

While the curriculum reforms now being instituted vary enormously, the majority of them are efforts to replace "standard" teaching—teacher-directed, didactic, with passive students receiving large amounts of unintegrated information, dominated by the approach we label "skills and drills"—with more active, student-centered, project-based approaches to teaching. Such approaches have always been more common in the best vocational classrooms (even if they have not been ubiquitous there), and one of the consequences of the most successful efforts at integrating academic and vocational education is that the methods of vocational instructors have rubbed off on academic teachers. Indeed, one advantage of integrating vocational material with academic approaches is that the focus on employment applications provides examples of, or contexts for, those capacities that are normally seen as "academic" in the worst sense of the term. While the integration of academic and vocational education is certainly not the only way to reinvigorate teaching, then, it is completely consistent with many of the curriculum reforms that are now taking place.

SCHOOLS OF CHOICE

Several approaches to integration create schools-within-schools—for example, the academies that have proliferated in California, or the *clusters* or *career paths* adopted in other schools—that focus on occupational areas; in other cases, entire schools can develop an occupational focus. This approach to integration then becomes a way of enhancing student and parent choice: one that creates magnet schools within a district, or clusters within a school (or schools-within-a-school in smaller districts), among which parents and students can choose. Of course, it is not necessary, within choice mechanisms, to have magnet schools, or schools-within-schools, defined by occupational areas; math and science magnets, humanities magnets, or magnets focused on social issues (the environment or urban problems) are all appropriate foci for schools of choice. Inevitably, however, some magnets or schools of choice are defined in occupational terms, and they then become opportunities for the integration of academic and vocational education.

RESTRUCTURING SCHOOLS

Restructuring seeks to return power to the local-school level, away from other bureaucratic levels. However, the purpose of restructuring—the end to which restructuring is the necessary means—is usually left unspecified, and therefore restructuring is often a mechanism in search of a mission. In the efforts to integrate academic and vocational education, however, local control—over curriculum, the composition of teachers, the grouping of students, and even the definition of purpose—is absolutely crucial; again, many efforts to integrate have foundered on the shoals of district or state control. The efforts to integrate academic and vocational education provide one answer to the crucial question of the goals for local control: Individual schools need power in order to adopt curricula suited to the interests of students, the occupations that their students aspire to enter, the capacities of teachers, and the composition of the local community. In this sense, the integration of academic and vocational education provides a specificity that restructuring often lacks.

Integrating academic and vocational education is not, of course, the only way of accomplishing the reforms now percolating through American secondary schools. There are many ways of restructuring, or professionalizing teachers, or reforming teaching methods, that have nothing to do with occupational preparation. But even if curriculum integration is not the only path to reform, the incorporation of occupational content still has some clear advantages over other paths—especially those, like restructuring and teacher professionalism, that often leave the ultimate goals of education reform unspecified. Integrating academic and vocational education provides a way of overcoming some deficiencies of the American high school, including those that developed from the original division between academic and vocational subjects and between college-bound students and those bound for work. It provides a way of "contextualizing" instruction, or clarifying the applications of what might otherwise be considered merely academic material. It provides a way of linking what high schools do with what institutions outside the schools do—particularly employers, who can clarify ideas about what the essential point of formal schooling is—and with what postsecondary institutions do, which leads in still other ways to adult lives. Above all, the efforts to integrate academic and vocational education force us all to recognize the varied capacities—general and specific, academic and vocational, manipulative and behavioral, as well as cognitive— that successful adults must have. For these reasons, the effort to integrate academic and vocational education may be the best stimulus for reforming the American high school.

■
NOTES

1. On skills and drills, see Grubb, Kalman, Castellano, Brown, and Bradby (1991) or Grubb and Kalman (1994). Our description of skills and drills, a distillation of the programs we visited and the curricular materials and computer programs we examined, is similar to the teacher-centered instruction described by Cuban (1993) and Knowles (1980); the "bottom up" approach described by advocates of whole language, like Goodman (1986); the "skills development" methods described by Tomlinson (1989); the "conventional wisdom" in elementary classrooms described by Knapp and Turnbull (1990); and the conception of *passive learning* (as distinct from *active learning*) mentioned in many contexts.

2. We have not tried to be comprehensive in this section. Some reforms that appear to concentrate on elementary schools—for example, Henry Levin's Accelerated Schools—have not been included, nor have those like Comer's approach, which stress social services rather than changes in curriculum and teaching.

3. See Prestine and Bowen (1993). We also suspect that Coalition schools will continue to diverge because the Coalition's principles themselves come from contradictory strands of thought about education. The emphasis on "using one's mind well" and on "essential skills" are linked to classical humanism and essentialism, both conservative ideas, while other principles are more Deweyan in spirit.

4. As in the Coalition of Essential Schools, the Paideia principles represent a hybrid from several different traditions, particularly in combining teaching from a core of Great Books with more Deweyan ideas.

5. For information on the variety of OBE, see the special issue of *Educational Leadership 51* (6), March 1994.

PART II

APPROACHES TO INTEGRATION

4

A CONTINUUM OF APPROACHES TO CURRICULUM INTEGRATION

W. NORTON GRUBB

The recommendations to reduce the separation of vocational and academic education, so common over the past century, have never led to much reform. It has never been clear how classroom practices should change, or "what to do on Monday morning." The current interest in integration is quite different, however. Even before federal funding arrived, through the Carl Perkins Act, several states undertook efforts to integrate academic and vocational education, among them California, Ohio, Oregon, and New York; others invested in pilot projects. A consortium of schools in the southeast, led by the Southern Regional Education Board, has pledged its allegiance to principles designed to upgrade the vocational curriculum and improve the basic education of vocational students (see Chapter 2 of Volume II). "Academies" have been started throughout the country, and occupationally oriented magnet schools—in electronics, business, or health, for example—have increased, partly in response to pressure for racial integration. Curriculum development has proceeded as well: A number of publishers now offer materials to incorporate basic skills into vocational courses; and *applied academics* curricula—versions of academic courses like physics, math, and English with more occupationally relevant content—have proliferated.

Not surprisingly, the efforts at integration are extremely varied. In part, this is because there are different views about the purposes of integration—different conceptions about what problems are most important, which students should be served, and which subjects should be integrated. Some schools have chosen to begin their efforts with the English curriculum, others with math or science; some have been most successful with certain vocational programs (electronics, drafting, or machining) while others have tried to include all vocational programs. In addition, existing schools vary enormously: An approach that works for an area vocational school with feeder high schools may be completely unworkable in a comprehensive high school, while one suitable for a magnet high school with a rich array of sophisticated vocational courses will not work in a high school where vocational offerings have been stripped to the minimum. Labor market conditions vary as well, and an agriculture program may make sense in a rural area, where a computer or electronics program would not.

This chapter describes eight approaches to integration based on visits to many schools throughout the country.[1] Subsequent chapters (Chapters 5, 6, 7, and 8) provide additional analysis about the most promising forms of integration. I have chosen to describe general approaches to integration rather than specific schools—approaches that describe the essential practices, the ways in which teachers collaborate (or fail to collaborate), and the institutional structures that facilitate curriculum integration. It is important to think about these approaches flexibly and creatively rather than as rigid prescriptions; each allows many possible variations. For example, curriculum alignment can take place between two teachers, among three, or among all teachers in a magnet school; academies can be developed for a variety of occupational fields, and could include more than four teachers; and the number of clusters or "majors" in a school could vary depending on the size of the school. Since there is considerable variation within each approach, any simple summary—such as that shown in Table 4.1—must be interpreted with care.

In describing a continuum of approaches, the differences among them become clear. Some modify individual courses and leave the basic structure of the high school intact; others can reform the entire high school and every part of the curriculum. Some approaches (especially numbers 1 and 2 in Table 4.1) operate by modifying the vocational curriculum; others (especially number 3) work primarily by changing academic courses, while the most ambitious change both the academic and the vocational curricula. Two approaches (numbers 1 and 3) can be carried out by individual teachers, while the others require collaboration among teachers. In some schools, the academic material incorporated into vocational courses is quite basic or remedial, and the vocational content may be relatively unsophisticated too. In other cases, the most advanced academic subjects have been incorporated into programs that include vocational curricula of relative complexity. Some schools still try to provide job-specific skills in their vocational programs—skills that are useful for employment immediately after high school—while others have come to view vocational education as a more general form of preparation for either employment or postsecondary education.

All of these approaches hold some promise, however, and respond to certain problems that reformers consider crucial. It would be misguided for policymakers to impose a single model for integrating academic and vocational education, or for educators to decide on one approach as the best. Such a tactic could only limit the creativity of teachers and administrators trying to change schools. A single approach also would be doomed to failure in those schools where that particular approach is unsuitable for any number of reasons, including the nature of existing vocational and academic offerings, the interests of students, the attitudes of teachers and administrators, and the resources available.

A final caveat is necessary. These eight approaches describe what teachers (and their students) *might* do, but the extent of change varies from class to class and from school to school. In the first approach, for example, vocational teachers self-consciously include more academic content in their courses; but whether an individual instructor incorporates a great deal of academic content—and correspondingly reduces occupationally specific content—or merely a token amount varies. Similarly, academies, clusters, or magnet schools can facilitate curriculum integration by bringing teachers together and by giving them a common goal; but whether they do, in fact, collaborate, and to what extent, depends on their willingness to work together and to give up the conventional disciplines. In the end, the integration of academic and vocational education—like most school reforms—relies on the interest and ability of teachers to make changes within their classrooms, and no amount of exhortation or institutional change can accomplish what teachers want to resist.

■

MODEL 1:
INCORPORATING MORE ACADEMIC CONTENT IN
VOCATIONAL COURSES

The simplest form of integration is the effort to incorporate more academic material into vocational courses. Sometimes this happens informally, when principals urge their vocational faculty to include more writing or to clarify the mathematics related to a vocational subject. Sometimes vocational teachers uncover basic skill deficiencies and take time to practice the specific mathematics required (e.g., measurement with rulers and protractors in carpentry and metal-working classes, or the algebra underlying Ohm's law in electronics), or to spend time on comprehension exercises drawn from instructional manuals, or to write business letters and resumes in business classes. Many vocational teachers acknowledge the pressure to increase attention to academic exercises, possibly taking time away from vocational content. A common complaint is that incorporating more academic content may compromise the "integrity of the vocational curriculum."

A more formal approach is to rely on curriculum materials designed

(text continues on page 64)

TABLE 4.1. Approaches to Integrating Vocational and Academic Education

Different Approaches	Curriculum Changes	Teacher Changes	Students Targeted	Institutional Changes
1. Incorporating more academic content in vocational courses	Vocational courses include more academic content	Vocational teachers modify courses	Vocational students	None
2. Involving academic teachers in vocational programs to enhance academic content in vocational programs	Vocational programs include more academic content in either vocational courses or in related applied courses	Academic teachers cooperate with vocational teachers	Vocational students	None
3. Making academic courses more vocationally relevant	Academic courses include more vocational content; sometimes new courses (e.g., applied academics) are adopted	Academic teachers (usually) modify courses, or adopt new ones	Potentially all students; in practice, vocational and general track students	None
4. Curricular alignment: horizontal and vertical	Both academic and vocational courses modified and coordinated across courses and/or over time	Academic and vocational teachers cooperate; numbers range from two to many	Potentially all students; actual targets vary	None necessary. Curriculum teams may foster cooperation.
5. Senior projects	Seniors replace electives with a project; earlier courses may change in preparation	None necessary; teachers may develop new courses or modify content to better prepare students	All students	None necessary

6. The academy model	Alignment among academy courses (English, math, science, vocational) *may* take place	Academic and vocational teachers may collaborate on both curriculum and students	Usually potential dropouts; sometimes students interested in specific occupational areas	Schools-within-schools; block rostering; smaller classes; links to employers
7. Occupational high schools and magnet schools	Alignment among all courses may take place, emphasizing the occupational focus	All vocational and academic teachers assigned to an occupational or magnet school within a school; collaboration facilitated	Students interested in specific occupational areas	Creation of a self-contained occupational school or magnet school
8. Occupational clusters, career paths, and majors	Coherent sequences of courses created; alignment may take place among courses within clusters	Teachers belong to occupational clusters rather than (or in addition to) conventional departments; collaboration facilitated	All students	Creation of occupational clusters; enhancement of career counseling; possible cluster activities

to incorporate more basic skills into existing vocational courses. Examples of materials of this kind include: reviews of basic grammar and punctuation, using examples that are occupation-related; writing various kinds of employment-related letters, completing job applications, and filling in income tax forms; developing reading skills (like identifying main ideas, distinguishing fact from opinion) utilizing job-oriented texts like instruction manuals and reference materials; and presenting, in the interest of career education, relatively simple written information about a variety of occupations. Math exercises include: the presentation of simple algebraic formulas (like Ohm's law and Joule's law); making simple arithmetic calculations (e.g., the board feet of lumber required on a project, or the amount of cement a bricklayer might need for a given job); and using measuring devices and reading graphs, charts, and tables of numbers. The applications of science are quite varied, and some are quite far from what any academic teacher would consider to be science. For example, one textbook publisher offers a workbook presenting simple reading passages that describe what people do in their jobs (from astronomers to plumbers), a review of the order of the planets in the solar system, and crossword puzzles using words like "antibody" and "inoculate." Another book, put out by the same publisher, is much more sophisticated, presenting the scientific principles and algebraic formulas appropriate to various machines (turbines, steam engines, band saws, and drill presses) along with an explanation of production processes (injection molding, metal cutting).

Most of these curriculum materials are remedial: the math is simple arithmetic and little of it is more advanced than single-equation algebraic formulas or formulas for the volumes of simple geometric shapes; the literacy exercises stress reading and writing for the purpose of learning and presenting factual information; and the science often doesn't teach anything about scientific principles, methods, or knowledge. These materials use vocational settings and examples to motivate students to learn basic skills that they have missed in their prior schooling, and they sometimes represent examples of contextualized learning (or *functional context training*), but they do not encourage teachers to increase demands on students beyond basic levels. It is also unclear how such materials are used by vocational teachers. Some vocational instructors have reported them to be useless—too time-consuming, not occupationally specific enough, and sometimes inaccurate. For those teachers who are reluctant to shift time away from vocational skills instruction, the mere existence of alternative curriculum materials on the shelf may not provide much incentive to change.

A still more formal approach is to develop model curricula for vocational courses that incorporate academic skills. For example, the state of California has developed model curriculum standards for both academic and vocational courses, involving teachers in developing and testing the initial versions. The frameworks, which are specific to vocational areas (like business, agriculture, and home economics), contain three levels of *competencies:*

1. Core competencies include general employability skills, basic academic capacities, self-management of learning, and career exploration.
2. Cluster competencies cover knowledge and practices pertaining to any entry-level job in an occupational cluster.
3. Job-specific competencies are taught in *capstone* courses at the end of a vocational sequence, to prepare students for placement.

For each competency, there is a list of *proficiencies,* which suggest classroom exercises that teachers could use. The frameworks are not curriculum materials, therefore, but they do indicate which academic abilities ought to be incorporated into specific vocational programs and what exercises might be appropriate in doing so. A similar approach has been taken by the states of Texas and Florida for developing *essential elements* for a variety of academic and vocational courses.

This first approach to integrating academic and vocational education has many obvious advantages. It can be accomplished within the context of existing vocational courses without much disruption or expense, and it does not require the coordination of large groups of teachers (except possibly for the process of developing model curricula). It can also serve as a crucial first step in a longer process of integrating academic and vocational education. However, its ambitions are limited. The academic competencies most frequently stressed are relatively simple. More to the point, this model does nothing to change the essential division between academic and vocational courses, between academic and vocational teachers (since academic teachers need never be involved in this approach), or between academic and vocational students (since only vocational students are affected by these changes). Where enrollments in conventional vocational courses are dwindling, this approach is not especially useful, and it also fails to reform the academic and general tracks. Compared to other approaches, it can remedy only some of the ills resulting from the division between academic and vocational education.

■

MODEL 2:
INVOLVING ACADEMIC TEACHERS IN VOCATIONAL PROGRAMS

A different approach is to involve academic teachers in enhancing academic competencies within vocational programs. A good example is an area vocational school (referred to in this section as Smithville Area Vocational Center) where 2 academic instructors have joined 15 vocational instructors. The academic teachers sometimes teach individual lessons or modules in vocational classrooms, presenting academic materials (or reinforcing existing competencies) relevant to that particular occupational area. They also help vocational instructors develop more "academic" exercises of their own, for example, by collaborating on writing exercises, essay exams, math reviews, and the like. Academic and vocational teachers can collaborate in developing new teaching units; for example, the carpentry teacher and the math teacher were jointly able to develop the algebra underlying rule of thumb calculations, and the printing instructor developed newspaper reading assignments with the help of the English teacher. An academic teacher may pull individual students out of vocational classes for intensive work on subjects where they are having difficulty, serving as an in-house remedial teacher. Finally, the math teacher at Smithville taught one course of Applied Mathematics (the curriculum is described in the following section), allowing students to receive credit toward graduation for a math course that was more related to their vocational programs than the general math course.

The state of Ohio has taken a further, and even more thorough step in this approach by developing the Applied Academics program, which combines academic and vocational teachers (Ohio Department of Education, 1990).[2] In this program, academic instructors teach their subjects applied to specific vocational areas. For example, an applied math instructor will teach one kind of math class to auto body students, another kind, covering different areas of math, to machine shop students, and yet another to students in a computer-assisted drafting (CAD) program. Most academic teachers spend one period a week in each of the vocational laboratories in which they have students in order to become familiar with the vocational content. In some schools, the vocational and the academic instructors team-teach the applied academic subjects. Teachers consistently noted the advantage of the applied academics program in motivating students by providing them with clear reasons for learning, and with new forms of learning—more collaborative, more student-initiated, with constant movement between applications in vocational labs and seat work in adjacent classrooms.

A crucial feature of Ohio's Applied Academics program is that teachers develop their own curriculum materials for each of the classes they teach.[3] As a result, the content of each academic class is closely tailored to occupational requirements, with constant reference to how mathematical operations, communications skills, or scientific approaches will be used both in the vocational classroom and on the job. The cost of having to develop curricula is that teachers have to work harder, and a few teachers noted that it would save time to have materials available "off the shelf"—but almost universally they noted that this would destroy the close connection between academic and vocational subjects, as well as collaboration among teachers.

The real strength of this approach is the collaboration that develops between academic and vocational teachers. Vocational teachers have a resource that is normally unavailable to them, since in most high schools the communication between academic and vocational teachers is poor (for reasons clarified in Volume II, Chapter 3). Similarly, academic teachers who have little knowledge of technologies or of occupational requirements can turn to vocational teachers for examples, which can then be reinforced in both academic and vocational classes. Where there are regular interchanges among faculty, the opportunities for finding common ground and mutual interests increase enormously, as Chapter 4 in Volume II, on the experiences of teachers, clarifies.

Ironically, the greatest drawback of the second approach is a result of its greatest strength. In both the Smithville example and in the state of Ohio, the academic content is driven by the needs of the vocational components. As a result, some vocational programs preparing students for entry-level positions in moderately skilled occupations incorporate only basic academic skills. Although electronics and drafting may require algebra, geometry, and trigonometry, individuals preparing to be secretaries, auto mechanics, and animal care workers need no more than simple arithmetic; and while those students preparing to enter business need sophisticated reading and writing abilities, the relatively simple communications skills required in most entry-level occupations set a ceiling on what it makes sense to teach. Without preparing students for a sequence, or cluster, of occupations requiring higher levels of academic ability, it becomes difficult to provide much instruction in any higher-order competencies.

■

MODEL 3:
MAKING THE ACADEMIC CURRICULUM
MORE VOCATIONALLY RELEVANT

While the previous two approaches modify the vocational curriculum, a different tactic is to modify standard academic courses by incorporating occupational examples and applications. The most widely used applied academics courses include the following:

- *Principles of Technology (PT):* an applied physics course that presents material about various physical principles (force, work, rate, resistance, energy, power, and force transformers) as they relate to four energy systems (mechanical, fluid, electrical, and thermal). It is a lab-based (hands-on) course, with applications both in labs and through textbook material drawn from occupations that use these energy systems.
- *Applied Mathematics:* presents a series of topics drawn from arithmetic,

algebra, geometry, trigonometry, statistics (including frequencies, means, medians, modes, standard deviations), probabilities, and other skills, like problem-solving techniques and estimation. Each of the 22 modules is introduced with a videotape that relates the mathematics within that module to workplaces; examples and problems are drawn from various occupations.

- *Applied Communications:* a course in communications skills, both written and oral, as well as interpersonal relations and some job-search skills; its modules cover topics like "Communicating with Clients and Customers," "Gathering and Using Information in the Workplace," "Evaluating Performance," and "Upgrading, Retraining, and Changing Jobs." Each module has sections that are specific to one of five occupational clusters: health occupations, business and marketing, agriculture, technical/trade/industrial occupations, and home economics.

In addition, an applied course in biology and chemistry is being developed, and some states have developed and approved the use of their own applied math courses. In another example of the development of applied academics courses, Battelle Pacific Northwest Lab has developed a course in Materials Science and Technology, which grew out of the need to train more materials technicians and engineers; it combines the chemistry, physics, and electronics required in the analysis and development of complex materials, along with production techniques like molding and casting. Unlike conventional science labs, where there is always an unambiguously correct answer and therefore no real experimentation, the labs in Materials Science can be truly experimental: students can try out materials whose properties they (and the instructors) don't know, and instructionally useful "failures" can arise. In the process, students need to use the methods of science—hypothesis-formation, searching among alternative solutions, problem solving, analogizing—and to develop the attributes of inquisitiveness and precision. It is particularly instructive to contrast this course, for example, with the Principles of Technology (PT) course: teachers report that PT labs must be precisely set up, or else the answers will turn out incorrectly, confusing students and destroying the lab's educational value.

The use schools make of applied academics courses varies enormously. In one academy, Principles of Technology forms the core course of the school, and is used to organize the teaching of math, English, and science. In some schools, PT is intended to be taken in place of physics or general science by those students enrolled in vocational programs, as a lab science course better related to vocational content. Often, academic teachers will select individual modules from Applied Math or Applied Communication courses in order to teach specific skills that their students need; in such cases, teachers used applied academics courses not as substitutes for

English courses but as complements, with vocational application. In other cases, applied academics courses are used as the basis for subsequent experimentation and synthesis. The state of South Carolina has synthesized the Applied Communications course with literature units (half in British literature and half in American literature), formulating a hybrid course. In teaching Principles of Technology, some teachers have taught necessary math as the course proceeds (rather than requiring a math prerequisite), and others have adopted computer programs to supplement the course. In one Oregon school, Principles of Technology has been adapted for special education students, as a way of bringing into science individuals who would otherwise take no science courses at all. In these cases, the applied academics curricula provide ideas that teachers can then modify, and the final results may look nothing like the standard curricula.

In some schools, Applied Math and Communications courses have been substituted for general math and lower track English courses for students in vocational programs; in these cases, there has been an explicit effort to link the applied academics courses to vocational programs, so that there is some sensible sequence of academic and vocational courses. Sometimes, however, Applied Math and Applied Communications are used "off the shelf," without any modification, simply as remedial courses for either vocational or general track students.[4] In still other schools, the applied academics courses are offered as electives, and large numbers of general track students take them in place of general science, general math (or "consumer math"), and watered-down literature courses. Such a practice may replace general track courses of little content with more substantial courses that relate academic material to future vocations; but it also destroys the link between the applied academics courses and vocational programs.

Applied academics courses have become the most common approach to integration for several reasons. Most teachers appreciate the effort to incorporate vocationally relevant material. Many high school teachers are badly overworked, with most teaching five classes a day of perhaps thirty students, and are therefore forced to look for readily available curriculum materials. A still deeper reason is that individual teachers rarely have training and experience in both academic and vocational subjects, and the resources for collaboration among teachers are relatively scarce—and therefore curriculum materials have become a substitute for teacher collaboration.

Applied academics courses and other efforts that bend the academic curriculum toward greater vocational relevance have real promise, then, particularly in giving academic subjects a more applied context. However, this approach has a limitation analogous to that of the two previous models: it changes only academic courses, and leaves vocational programs untouched. In many cases, this approach has failed to encourage cooperation between academic and vocational teachers, since academic teachers can use curriculum packages "off the shelf" without consulting any other teachers. In addition, applied academics courses have sometimes become remedial programs, or electives without clear purpose, rather than being linked to vocational programs. But integrating academic and vocational education is an activity that could encompass sequences of courses rather than just individual courses—an aspect that other approaches to integration address.

■

MODEL 4:
CURRICULAR ALIGNMENT MODIFYING BOTH
ACADEMIC AND VOCATIONAL COURSES

Still another approach to integrating academic and vocational education has been to change the content of both academic and vocational courses—using more occupationally relevant material in academic courses and more academic content in vocational courses—and to link the two. *Curricular alignment* is the equivalent of what has historically been called the "correlation" of subjects (Tanner & Tanner, 1990), and—as noted in Chapter 3—is similar to efforts to introduce curriculum integration more generally, especially in elementary and middle schools (Fogarty, 1991; Jacobs, 1989; Jenkins & Tanner, 1992). This approach is highly flexible, with many possible variations. It is also potentially low in cost because it stresses coordination of existing teachers and courses rather than additions or complex reconfigurations of high schools.

The extent of coordination and the nature of links among courses can vary substantially, of course. In general, academic and vocational teachers aligning their subjects follow patterns similar to those in other forms of curriculum integration. The most common forms include the following (drawn from Fogarty [1991], Jacobs [1989], and Tanner & Tanner [1990]):

- Parallel approaches, in which two teachers sequence their courses so that similar topics are covered at roughly the same time. Often, for example, academic courses provide the prerequisites for a task in an occupational course, like the math required in an occupational application.
- Thematic or problem-centered approaches, in which an occupational problem or theme becomes the focus of two or more courses. In efforts to integrate academic disciplines, a theme is likely to be an idea or issue, like the role of the individual in society, or the problem of pollution. In efforts to integrate academic and vocational education, an occupationally oriented problem—for example, the design of a car or building, or a business problem, like establishing a new business—is more likely to be used.
- Multidisciplinary units or courses combine material from an academic and a vocational field—like Agricultural Economics or Materials Science.

There are some relatively common combinations of academic and occupational courses, with substantial overlap among subjects: business and English; health occupations, biology, and chemistry; agriculture, biology, and chemistry; drafting and geometry; electronics and algebra. Another common form of alignment involves the math necessary for construction and production-related occupations; for example, in one school an industrial arts teacher and a math teacher have joined forces so that the mathematical topics required in various forms of production—including measurement, area, volume, the algebra associated with electricity and heat transfer, and simple trigonometry—are taught at the same time as they are needed for workshop exercises.

In many cases of integrated instruction, one subject is the lead and the other is used to support it. In schools with an occupational focus (like the Ohio state applied academics programs), the academic subjects are usually subordinated to the occupational subjects so that only the math (or English, or science) considered relevant to that occupational area is included. However, the emphasis of any integrated program could depend on the interests of the teachers and students involved.

In some cases, teachers use integrated instruction to lure students into academic subjects they would not otherwise take. In one example, the drafting teacher reserves one section of Drafting I for students who agree to take geometry, and then uses geometry extensively in the drafting class. In a similar case involving three teachers, six schools have initiated a program sponsored by Northern Illinois University, in which courses in electronics, physics, and math are coordinated; electronics and a complete television studio are the hooks to enroll students who would not ordinarily take science and math. In this example, physics is the lead course and math and electronics support the teaching of physics.

The crucial element of alignment—as in Model 2—is that academic and vocational teachers work together to coordinate their offerings so that courses are consistent and mutually reinforcing rather than disconnected. In this approach, it is difficult to use prepared curricula "off the shelf" since the process of coordinating courses is dependent on the specific topics and the preferences of teachers. Where teachers cooperate extensively, the results are very often thrilling: Teachers find large numbers of unexpected parallels between academic and vocational material; the academic teachers discover (to their surprise) that vocational teachers have a great deal to offer in content, pedagogical methods, and motivation; and vocational teachers discover new ways to reinforce basic skills (Chapter 4 of Volume II describes in greater detail the experience of teachers beginning the process of integration). With the right combination of people, the process can operate quite smoothly; as a teacher in one of the California academies declared, "Alignment is easy; it just takes time."

A different kind of alignment involves a coherent sequence of vocational and academic courses over time—vertical alignment rather than (or in addition to) horizontal alignment across courses at the same time. Indeed, both the Carl Perkins Act and the School-to-Work Opportunities Act require coherent sequences of academic and vocational courses. One variant of this approach has emerged in several southeastern schools. In one example, eighth graders take a state-developed course called "Introduction to Technology," which presents information and lab exercises about new technologies (like lasers, robotics, computer-driven production processes) in four broad industrial clusters: transportation, communications, power, and energy. The course is intended to give students activity-based information about different occupations so that they can make more informed decisions about their high school curricula in ninth grade.[5] Those choosing relatively technical vocational programs take Algebra I in the ninth grade to prepare them for Principles of Technology in the tenth grade (in place of general science). This precedes a vocational program like electronics, machining, or drafting during junior and senior years, when students are likely to take Applied Math and Applied Communication in place of general math and non-college English. The great strength of this approach is that it conceives of integration at the level of a high school *program* rather than at the level of an individual *course*. Other approaches to integration—academies, magnet schools, and clusters or majors—similarly can be used to develop integrated programs rather than courses.

While alignment can be carried out on a small scale, with just two or three teachers, this kind of integration can involve much larger groups of teachers. One pilot site organized seven curriculum teams with 9 to 12 teachers per team from several academic and vocational departments. The teams met weekly to develop integrated curricula, guided by a 5-year plan, thereby providing a formal structure to promote alignment. As we will see, other models of integration—academies, clusters, and magnet schools, described briefly in this chapter as well as in Chapters 5, 6, and 7—are organizational structures that can facilitate (though not guarantee) the regular collaboration of vocational and academic teachers, and thereby encourage integrated programs.

■
MODEL 5:
THE SENIOR PROJECT AS A FORM OF INTEGRATION

An alternative to structuring schools around courses has been the *project method*—organizing the curriculum around student projects that serve as the basis for teaching material from the conventional academic and vocational disciplines.[6] Many teachers—especially vocational teachers—use a series of small-scale projects to develop increasingly sophisticated skills. Electronics, machining, and welding classes, for example, often present students with

projects of increasing complexity that students complete relatively independently; a common project in carpentry or construction programs is to build
a house. However, projects are typically confined to individual courses rather
than encompassing capacities learned in many different classes.

The use of a project undertaken during the senior year is an alternative,
or supplement, to other forms of integration, allowing students to combine
material from different courses and disciplines. In one common approach,
a project consists of a written report, a physical representation of some kind—
requiring the use of vocational shops in most cases—and an oral presentation. Requiring a project to take three different forms forces students to master different competencies and is also consistent with the *whole language*
principle that students should examine various ways of representing ideas.

Initially, a senior project forces the student, rather than instructors, to
integrate material from different courses. However, a project can become a
catalyst for other curricular changes, particularly where teachers realize
that some students lack the skills to carry out a project successfully. In one
school, for example, teachers identified the skills necessary for successful
completion of a project and went back through the curriculum to incorporate these skills—including techniques for research, experimentation, and
problem solving—in the ninth and tenth grades. Another school explicitly
restructured its program to prepare students for the senior project. A freshman course in technology was redesigned to focus on six to seven problems, introducing students to ways of resolving the kinds of problems they
might encounter in their senior projects; the curriculum of individual courses was modified so that students would have some experience in each lab
that they might need for their senior project.

Of course, projects can have an occupational emphasis, though they
need not. Particularly in schools that see themselves as college preparatory,
projects may have a more academic or research-oriented cast to them. The
senior project is therefore not necessarily an approach to integrating academic and vocational education, and its effects on the overall curriculum
depend on whether any curricula changes take place to prepare students
for projects. However, a senior project seems to have real promise as a focus
for students and as an impetus for getting teachers to collaborate. Chapter
8 describes several schools that have adopted vocationally oriented projects.

MODEL 6:
THE ACADEMY MODEL

The Academy model is among the best established approaches to curriculum integration. Academies began in Philadelphia (Snyder & McMullen,
1987), and then spread to California, first with private funds and then with

the help of state revenues. Others operate without special public funding and some have corporate sponsorship: American Express has supported a series of Finance Academies, which focus on preparing students to go into occupations related to financial services (Academy for Educational Development, 1990). Ideas for new kinds of academies keep cropping up: there are academies in the planning stages in law and government, pre-engineering, and tourism, for example.

Academies operate as schools-within-schools. Typically, four teachers collaborate: one in math, one in English, one in science, and one in the vocational subject that is the core of the academy. (Of course, academies could have nonoccupational themes too, like the environment, the problems of cities, or math and science.) Each class of students takes all four subjects from these teachers and the students stay with the same teachers for 2 or 3 years. Other subjects—social studies, history, foreign languages, and other electives—are taken in the "regular" high school, outside the Academy.[7] One essential element of the academy model, then, is that a group of teachers works together, with one group of students, consistently over a period of years. The opportunities for coordinating their courses—that is, for horizontal alignment—are substantial; and because each academy is focused on a cluster of occupations, it becomes relatively easy and natural to integrate vocationally relevant material into academic courses. In addition, because students stay within an academy for 2 or 3 years, creating coherent sequences over time is easier. Teachers also can develop special projects that cut across all four classes. The regular meetings of teachers also help identify particular problems that students are having—for example, with a particular algebraic formulation, with measurement, or with certain types of oral communication—and then the solution can be developed and assigned, either to a specific teacher or to several teachers, for reinforcement.

A second element essential to academies is the relationship established with firms operating in the occupational area of an academy. Thus, the electronics and computer academies located in Silicon Valley have established ties with high-tech firms, a health academy is located near a confluence of hospitals, a technology academy has established good relationships with a high-tech engineering and manufacturing company, and the Finance Academies utilize their connections with American Express. The firms provide mentors to all students, often sending their employees to the schools to talk with students about particular aspects of their operations, give tours of their facilities, and offer summer internships. These initiatives represent other sources of instruction and motivation (cognitive, behavioral, and financial) in addition to that provided by teachers. In general, the links between academies and firms reflect the advantages claimed for other school-business linkages, including youth apprenticeships and the school-to-work partnerships reviewed in Chapter 9 of Volume II.

The academies in California have been designed for at-risk students, defined as those who might otherwise drop out. With this population of students, there is substantial evidence that the academies reduce dropout rates and increase enrollments in postsecondary education (Stern, Dayton, Paik, & Weisberg, 1989).[8] However, the selection of at-risk students is not a necessary aspect of the academy approach, and focusing on this group presents the danger of creating another form of tracking—as clarified in Chapter 5. A different approach to student selection, for example, is a technology academy, which selects students of moderate ability and achievement who want less abstract instruction than that offered by the conventional college preparatory track.

There are still other benefits to academies, apart from fostering integration. The scale of academies is relatively small, in contrast to the chaos and anonymity of large high schools. Partly as a result, students are more likely to form a community—a result crucial to teaching methods that involve cooperative group work. Teachers come to know individual students, their individual strengths and problems, much better than can most high school teachers; it is harder for students to become "lost" in an academy. Entering an academy requires a choice on the student's part, with all the benefits associated with active choice (Chubb & Moe, 1990), including greater interest in the academy's subject and a closer identification with a school that has been voluntarily chosen. At the same time, the need for students to make *informed* choices forces the issue of guidance into the open, and many schools instituting academies have found it necessary to improve their counseling.

■

MODEL 7:
OCCUPATIONAL HIGH SCHOOLS AND MAGNET SCHOOLS

Some city school systems include occupational high schools, which emphasize preparation for clusters of related vocations. These include schools like New York City's Aviation High School, the High School of Fashion Industries, and the Murry Bergtraum High School for Business Careers and Chicago's High School for Agricultural Sciences (all profiled in Mitchell, Russell, & Benson [1989]). A High School for Health Professions is located in Houston. In addition, many districts have opened *magnet schools* as mechanisms of racial desegregation, often with similar orientations to occupational high schools. Many magnet schools have an occupational focus—in electronics, computers, or business, for example. Every student within a magnet is enrolled in a curriculum incorporating courses related to the magnet's focus, though the number of these courses ranges from the relatively trivial—two or three courses within a 4-year sequence, creating a magnet school in name only—to the more substantial.

Occupational high schools and magnet schools are similar to academies in several ways, except that the scale is larger—the academy is school-wide. There are obvious advantages for curriculum integration: since all academic teachers are preparing students within a single, broad occupational area, the incentives to bend academic instruction toward this particular occupation are strong, and the resources to do so—especially the vocational teachers with whom examples and exercises can be developed—are right at hand. Just as the culture of some occupational high schools is distinctive, magnet schools can also develop cultures supporting cooperation among teachers in the development of curriculum. Chapter 7 reviews some of the experiences of occupational high schools and magnet schools, and Chapter 9 describes the experiences of students within magnet schools—in this case, magnets within New York City.

Occupational high schools and magnet schools are also excellent examples of *focus schools* —schools with clear missions, organized to pursue their educational goals and to solve their own problems, innovative as the need arises, and operating with clear social contracts that establish responsibilities for teachers, students, and parents (Hill et al., 1990).[9] An occupational emphasis is not the only way to create a focus school—arts and science magnets, or schools organized around environmental issues, or other problem-centered schools are obvious alternatives. Still, as long as the occupational focus is broad enough to encompass a variety of occupations and a broad spectrum of students, this approach makes a great deal of sense as a device to integrate the curriculum, to connect high school teaching to future life, and to force students to confront what they want to be when they grow up.

■

MODEL 8:
OCCUPATIONAL CLUSTERS, CAREER PATHS, AND MAJORS

Occupational clusters, majors, or *career paths*—discussed more fully in Chapter 6—are an intermediate approach between academies and magnet schools. In some schools, students choose a cluster (representing a cluster of related occupations), or major, commonly at the beginning or end of tenth grade. The cluster then structures the curriculum for the remaining 2 or 3 years of high school. Clusters are therefore somewhat like academies, except that every student elects a cluster or major; in a sense, a school is filled with a series of academies. Clusters have all the potential of academies and magnet schools to create a focus within which integration can take place, and the conception of clusters has been attractive to many groups: the School-to-Work Opportunities Act, for example, requires students to choose "career majors" no later than the beginning of the tenth grade, and several states have adopted similar recommendations.[10]

High schools that have adopted clusters or majors vary substantially in how much of the curriculum is shaped by them. In one well-known technical high school, each student elects one out of about ten majors, which are taught during a double period during eleventh and twelfth grades. Other subjects are taught in conventional classes. Because a typical English or math class includes students from all majors, it is difficult to integrate academic content with occupational applications. At the other extreme, a few schools have replaced conventional discipline-based departments with departments organized along occupational lines. In one example, both academic and vocational instructors are assigned to five departments organized around agriculture, business, trade and industry, public service, and health science. Each department recommends specific course sequences, from the required Career Technology course in the ninth grade—one devoting 9 weeks each to agriculture, business, trade and industry, and health science, as a way of exposing students systematically to the different career clusters—to capstone courses in the junior and senior years requiring job performance, usually held at job sites away from the school. This organization provides focus for each student: Each program has an obvious theme, the recommended course sequence reduces the "milling around" so common in high schools, and regular department meetings can focus on improving programs of study rather than on individual courses independent of one another.

An intermediate approach has been adopted by several other high schools that have retained conventional departments while instituting clusters or majors. In one such case, each student elects a career path at the beginning of tenth grade. Students in a career path are urged, by counselors and brochures describing each career path, to take academic courses related to their paths, as well as a coherent sequence of vocational courses, in addition to the academic courses required for graduation; the career paths function to structure both required courses and electives. Teachers are assigned to career paths as well as to departments, and therefore academic and vocational teachers can plan together the appropriate sequences of academic and vocational courses within each career path. Academic teachers have students from all career paths in their classes—rather than students from one path—and so integrating occupational applications is more difficult. Still, there can be more regular collaboration among teachers in discussing career paths, and greater opportunities for alignment of various kinds.

Academies, occupationally oriented magnet schools, and schools offering clusters or majors vary in their scale, of course, and in the number of courses that are *inside*—taken by all students within a group—rather than *outside,* in the regular courses of the comprehensive high school. But they share certain distinctive features:

- Most schools which have adopted these practices have used broad clusters of related occupations—not the occupation-specific focus of traditional vocational education (automotive repair or secretarial positions, for example) but groupings of related occupations (transportation, or business occupations). The use of broad occupational clusters has several advantages. It provides opportunities for exploring a greater variety of academic topics, avoiding the problem of having moderately skilled jobs dictate the teaching of relatively low-level academic content. It allows students to explore a wider variety of careers, and to understand how occupations are related to one another. And, if properly structured, clusters can reduce the class, racial, and gender segregation common in high schools, as students from very different backgrounds, with varied ambitions, come together in occupational clusters. For example, health clusters can include both would-be doctors and those who aspire to being practical nurses; the industrial technologies and engineering path at one high school includes both future engineers and those who think they might become welders and auto mechanics.
- Academies, magnet schools, and clusters specify related academic and vocational courses for students to take, imposing some coherence on the "shopping mall high school."
- These approaches to integration all provide teachers from different disciplines with a reason for meeting regularly around curriculum issues, increasing opportunities for cooperation between academic and vocational teachers, and for the "alignment" of academic and vocational courses. To be sure, academies, magnet schools, and clusters facilitate such collaboration and cannot ensure it, but they at least provide institutional forms within which collaboration is natural.
- Students must elect academies or clusters, and—at least in cities that have established a variety of magnet schools—must choose among magnets as well. This provides the advantages associated with the choice of a school; but it also requires students to think, early in their high school careers, about their occupational futures. Typically, schools that have adopted academies, clusters, or a magnet theme have been forced to confront how students make choices, and have usually ended up strengthening counseling or developing more active forms of guidance and counseling—as clarified in Chapter 7 of Volume II.
- The use of occupational clusters provides a natural opportunity for linkages with appropriate postsecondary programs in related occupational areas—the subject of Chapter 10 of Volume II on tech-prep programs and other linkages to postsecondary institutions—and with employers in those occupational areas, linkages that are explored more fully in Chapter 5 on academies and in Chapter 9 of Volume II on the roles of employers. These linkages need not seem contrived, as they often are in

the comprehensive high school, since academies, clusters, and magnet programs already have focused the curriculum on occupations of interest to postsecondary institutions and to particular employers.

Above all, academies, magnet schools, and clusters are *systemic* approaches to integrating academic and vocational education—rather than, as in the first four models of curriculum integration, approaches that leave collaboration to the preferences of individual teachers, and that can collapse as teachers lose interest or move on to other things. They are therefore more difficult to put in place, requiring the collaboration of many more teachers—difficulties explored in greater detail in Chapters 2 and 3 of Volume II. But their benefits are also more substantial, since they provide ways of fundamentally restructuring the high school.

CONCEPTIONS OF CURRICULUM INTEGRATION

Given the many ways of integrating academic and vocational education, is it possible to define what integration should be—to know when it is present?[11] Given the variety of purposes behind curriculum integration, no single definition could encompass all current efforts. However, the various approaches all share one or another of these criteria, and the most sophisticated combine several:

- Courses combine content that normally appears in separate academic and vocational courses. Teachers take on the burden of integrating content rather than leaving students to do so, as conventionally occurs when they take a series of independent courses.
- Academic and vocational teachers collaborate in the development of curricula and sometimes in team-teaching. While this does not always happen—Models 1 and 3 can take place without collaboration—the benefits of collaboration are substantial, as teachers themselves attest (this is described more completely in Volume II, Chapter 4).
- Teaching methods change as integrated programs begin to provide a context (or applications, or themes) for academic instruction, and as the more student-centered, project-oriented, cooperative teaching methods prevalent among the best vocational instructors become more widespread. Again, this need not happen—teachers may continue to teach in standard, didactic ways, and "off the shelf" curriculum materials may foster passive learning—but integration efforts at least provide an impetus, embedded in the curriculum itself, to change teaching.
- If programs focus on occupational clusters that are sufficiently broad, they can include students of varying ambitions and backgrounds, pro-

viding a form of class and racial integration not usually present in the highly tracked high school.

• Programs, rather than individual courses, become more coherent. This does not mean that the high school becomes more uniform, as it might if every student followed the conventional college prep curriculum. Instead, the heterogeneity of the shopping mall high school is replaced by a different kind of heterogeneity—where different programs exist for students with different interests, but where each program is internally coherent. Academies, magnet high schools, and schools using clusters or majors all provide institutional structures where integration within programs is encouraged.

In contrast to previous periods, then, there has been considerable experience during the past decade with integrating academic and vocational education. The approaches described in this chapter, and elaborated in subsequent chapters, provide alternatives for high schools of varying sizes, composition, and resources, and for schools with different purposes for curriculum integration, and ambitions ranging from reshaping individual courses to reforming the entire high school.

NOTES

1. The schools initially visited are listed in Grubb, Davis, Lum, Plihal, & Morgaine (1991). Since then, the contributors to this volume have visited many more schools, participated in numerous conferences and workshops, and conducted several studies about the extent of integration for the National Assessment of Vocational Education (e.g., Grubb and Stasz, 1993). Two approaches sometimes considered integration are not included because they result in little or no change. One is the effort to establish new academic requirements before students take vocational programs—the recommendation, for example, of the Committee for Economic Development (1985)—which does nothing to change either the academic or the vocational curriculum, or to integrate courses, teachers, or students. The other is the attempt to get existing vocational courses to count as academic courses for graduation requirements. While such efforts could change the content of vocational courses by incorporating more academic material (as in the first approach), in most cases nothing changes. The approaches presented have all changed educational practice in one form or another, rather than simply relabeling existing practice.

2. This model also exists in other forms, with less substantial changes than in either the state of Ohio or at Smithville. In South Carolina, which requires a basic skills test for graduation, several area vocational schools include academic teachers, principally to provide remedial instruction to students who have previously failed the basic skills test. On the Ohio program, see also the description of the Montgomery County Joint Vocational School in Adelman (1989) and the descriptions in Pritz and Crowe (1987).

3. The Ohio program has little to do with the applied academics courses available from the Center for Occupational Research and Development (CORD) and the Agency for Instructional Technology (AIT), described as part of Model 3. A few teachers in Ohio have borrowed lessons from the CORD and AIT courses, but almost universally, they find these materials not worth using because they are not specific enough to particular occupational areas, are occasionally inaccurate, and fail to motivate students.

4. When applied academics courses are used for remediation, the responses of teachers are sometimes tinged with demeaning attitudes; some reported that they are pleased with applied academics courses because they are better suited to the lower ability levels of vocational (or general track) students, or more appropriate to the "concrete learning styles" they assume these students have.

5. Introduction to Technology can be interpreted as an updating of the traditional shop course, substituting modern technologies for the wood-working and metal-working of the nineteenth century that dominated traditional shop courses—derisively named the "bird house and gun rack" approach by one instructor. In addition, the course contains important elements of career education, systematically illustrating different occupations and their connections to new technologies.

6. On the history of the project method, see Kliebard (1986, Chap. 6). The project method is interesting, partly because its origins drew on both John Dewey, who opposed many aspects of vocational education, and on David Snedden, associated with the movement for job-specific vocational education.

7. While most academies appear to include four teachers, the number could be smaller or larger. This involves the question of which subjects are "inside" the Academy, and therefore more likely to be integrated with other subjects, and which are left "outside."

8. In this evaluation—the only substantial evaluation of any innovation described in this chapter—the control group included students in the general track in the same high schools with grades similar to those of academy students. Unfortunately and unavoidably, this design cannot guard against the possibility that the selection mechanisms of the academies—their choice of the most motivated students among their applicants—explain the positive effects. The Manpower Demonstration Research Corporation is now conducting a random-assignment evaluation of academies.

9. Note, however, that all the public focus schools described by Hill et al. (1990) are occupational high schools, with the exception of one continuation school for especially troublesome students. Parochial schools represent another kind of focus school, with a particular pedagogy and morality.

10. For example, the report of the California High School Task Force, *Second to None,* recommends organizing schools into "clusters" or "program majors" (Agee, 1992). Oregon's program has students choose one of six "program focus areas," and each student's Certificate of Initial Mastery will carry an endorsement for the area chosen.

11. This question recalls the difficulty career education had during the 1970s in defining what it was.

5

THE CAREER ACADEMIES

MARILYN RABY

Career academies are school/business partnerships that offer high school students a rigorous academic/technical curriculum, employability skills, career counseling, work experience, enrichment activities, and mentoring. Career academies' programs are designed to ensure that their graduates are academically and technically proficient, have marketable job skills, and are academically prepared to enroll in postsecondary education.

There are several major career academy programs; best known nationally are the Philadelphia Academies, the National Academy Foundation (NAF), and the California Partnership Academies.[1] The primary focus of this chapter will be the California Partnership Academies program, the development of its integrated curriculum, and problems encountered in the design and implementation of that curriculum. The focus on the Partnership Academies is chosen both because its curriculum encompasses the principal elements of integrated curriculum found in the other major career academies, and because of this author's long-term experience with the program (as director of the first Partnership Academies in California, and of Partnership Academies funded by the U.S. Department of Education as a national demonstration site for dropout prevention through the use of vocational education).

THE CAREER ACADEMY PROGRAM

Academy programs are spreading throughout the United States. In Philadelphia, over 4,000 students are enrolled in academies in 17 high schools. NAF Academies serve over 6,000 students in more than 100 high schools throughout the country. There are presently 45 state-supported California Partnership Academies, in addition to over 45 other academies supported by school districts' general and categorical funds. California academies serve over 10,000 high school students. Career academies modeled on the Partnership Academies are operating in several other states: Hawaii, South Carolina, Tennessee, and Illinois, among others.

CALIFORNIA PARTNERSHIP ACADEMIES

The goal of the California Partnership Academies is to improve the prospects of unmotivated educationally and socioeconomically disadvantaged students by restructuring the learning environment to:

- Provide an integrated curriculum that shows the relevance of academic subjects to work experience
- Give autonomy to teachers to exercise their professional expertise and judgment in curriculum development
- Develop partnerships with businesses to provide mentoring and paid work experience to help students make a smooth transition from school to the workplace.

Curricular innovation in the academies is not a single issue change but a broad attack on student alienation and consequent lack of skills. Although the academy program was originally envisioned as preparing students for employment immediately after high school, most of its graduates have elected to pursue postsecondary education, primarily in community colleges. This option exists because the academy coursework is structured to meet the California State Department of Education's Model Curriculum Standards, and all local and state requirements for graduation from high school.

Academy students are enrolled in a core academic program, consisting of English, mathematics, science and/or social studies, and a technical course in a career field local businesses agree to support. Examples of career fields include electronics, health, business technology, agribusiness, media, environmental science, retailing, graphic arts, and law and government. The content of the core academic courses and the technical course is integrated and taught in a school-within-a-school environment. Academies have a strong career development component that stresses job readiness skills, career planning, job interview techniques, and applying to college. A mentor program that includes firsthand exposure to career information is supplied through the partnership with local businesses. Students enter the program in the tenth grade and those meeting academy standards are rewarded with jobs in local businesses in grades 11 and 12. Students remain with the same teachers for their entire 3 years in the program. The curriculum is demanding and focuses on critical thinking, problem analysis, and practical work simulations. Table 5.1 presents an example of student progression through the program of a health academy.

Although schools have primary responsibility for the development of curriculum in the academies, representatives from business actively participate in its definition. They work with teachers to identify the academic and technical competencies students need for employment in their industry. Teachers integrate the competencies with the academic work and include practical experience in applying the skills taught in the course to career situations. Students receive a foundation in a particular career area in the school's technical courses, while specific job training is provided by the employers during the student's work experience. However, this is not the structured, on-the-job training characteristic of true apprenticeship, which leads to official journeyperson status at its completion.

PHILADELPHIA ACADEMIES

The Philadelphia Academies program began in the late 1960s with an emphasis on dropout prevention. Until 1988, individual academies were managing their own programs to prepare students for jobs that did not specifically require a college degree, such as automobile mechanic, office worker, or electrician. To better manage the continuing expansion of the program, the individual academies were consolidated into a single program, "The

TABLE 5.1. Health Academy Student Progression and Schedule

Grade 10	Grade 11	Summer	Grade 12
Academy Classes			
English II	English III	Work Exp.	English IV
Computer	Health Appl.		Adv. Health
Appl.	Physiology		Chemistry
Biology	Geometry		Work Exp.
Algebra			
World Cultures			
Nonacademy Classes			
P.E.	U.S. History	Summer	Economics/
	Elective	school if	Government
Activities		needed	
Counseling	Counseling		Counseling
Field Trips	Field trips		
Speakers	Speakers		
	Mentors		

Philadelphia High School Academies Inc.," guided and financed by local businesses. The curriculum focus shifted from a vocational curriculum that prepared graduates for the trades to a curriculum of rigorous academics connected to special job-linked skills. This has led to the present enrollment of a broad cross-section of students in nine career fields: automotive repair, environmental technology, and health professions, among others. Teachers receive a stipend for extra duties, which include developing units in their courses that correlate academics to the technical specialty of the academy.

NAF ACADEMIES

A partnership between New York City Public Schools and the American Express Company began the Academy of Finance in 1982. After several years of success, an independent, nonprofit foundation, NAF, was founded to design and support other academies similar to this one throughout the country. The four NAF academies, the Academy of Finance, the Academy of Travel and Tourism, the Academy of Public Service, and the Academy of Manufacturing Services, enroll a heterogeneous group of students based on their interest in these career fields. The NAF Academies differ from the Philadelphia and Partnership Academies in that students entering the program must have a minimum grade-point average and a good attendance record. They take the courses required for graduation in regular high school classes. In addition, each year they take one to three NAF-developed specialized courses—for example, in the Academy of Finance, they choose from courses such as The World of Finance, Banking and Credit, and Mortgage Banking. Academic teachers are encouraged to make explicit connections between their courses and the career courses.

CURRICULUM DEVELOPMENT

In 1981 the Sequoia Union High School District (located on the San Francisco Peninsula just north of Silicon Valley) began the first two California academies, the Peninsula Academies. Their purpose was to provide a learning environment that would increase the graduation rate of the district's at-risk students and meet the needs of the high technology Silicon Valley businesses for better educated and more technically literate entry-level workers. The Peninsula Academies' core academic courses (mathematics, English, and science) and technical course (electronics in one academy and computer technology in the other) were taught in regulation 50-minute periods. For the remainder of the day, students attended other required and elective courses (physical education, foreign language, fine arts, etc.) with the rest of the student body. An enriched curriculum of motivational activities was provided by the business partners, introducing students to the business world and helping them understand why employability skills were required. These activities included field trips, lectures by speakers from business and industry, site tours of participating companies, and student associations with mentors.

Academy teachers were given a common, extra preparation period so that they could work together to develop integrated and relevant instructional units. This flexibility in scheduling allowed time for coordinating the planning and development of their integrated curriculum and for organizing the motivational activities. The school-within-a-school configuration—with its common group of students, block scheduling, and common teacher planning time—was essential. Without these components, the academy staffs would not have been able to move beyond a simple interdisciplinary curriculum to the complex projects described later in this chapter.

Initial attempts at integrating the curriculum were modest attempts at short-term calendar coordination. Academic and technical teachers examined the content in each of their subject areas to find topics where linkages could be made. They worked together to correlate and sequence the core academic courses and the technical course for reinforcement. Applications from the technical course were used to explain math and science concepts, and employability skills were taught in the English and technical classes. For example, if students were using Ohm's law in the electronics class, they were studying Ohm's law in their science class, and similar equations in their math class. In their English class, they wrote business letters and worked on job-related communication skills, such as interviewing and résumé writing.

Results of evaluations of the Peninsula Academies (Reller, 1984) led the California Legislature in 1984 to fund replications of the program at 10 new sites. The funds helped to provide small class sizes, staff training, additional instructional materials, and in many cases the extra common preparation period that made the difference between success and failure in developing the integrated curriculum. The new sites supplied a network of teachers with fresh perspectives about integrating curriculum. A statewide technical assistance team was formed that sponsors yearly conferences to encourage contacts among the academies. Academy teams located near one another began to meet to share ideas. Contacts with colleagues who were struggling with similar problems provided additional insight and information.

In 1987 the state passed legislation to add more sites and to rename the program "The California Partnership Academies." The new sites built further capacity for curriculum experimentation into the program. Networking and increasing staff expertise allowed some academy sites to make significant progress in developing curriculum that incorporated critical thinking skills with the technical knowledge, problem solving, and communication skills associated with the high-performance workplace.

ACADEMIC/TECHNICAL/WORKPLACE CURRICULUM INTEGRATION

Individual academies are at different stages of curriculum development due to a variety of factors (age of the academy, district support, nature of the business partnership). Most academies are currently providing horizontal integration of the core academic courses (English, math, social studies, science) with the career course and with the employability skills (ability to work with others, diligence, knowledge of technology) specified by business. The foundation for work skills is provided by the technical course while the training for specific job skills is provided by the employer. Employability skills are taught by the academies and reinforced by employers.

Academy teachers are finding that integrating curriculum is worth the effort. Many have a wide range of student achievement in their classrooms. This disparity in achievement is often driven by the amount of work students are willing to put into their studies. Since most students, even the academically alienated, find integrated curriculum intrinsically interesting, they are willing to apply the effort required to succeed in the classroom. In addition, students with legitimate academic problems better understand classwork taught in an integrated setting and can participate more fully in the activities of the classroom.

ACADEMIC/TECHNICAL INTEGRATION

Academy curriculum development is progressing from the earlier, limited integration strategies to a close integration of the academic and technical courses. The object is to provide students with critical thinking and problem-solving skills. Throughout the program, teachers emphasize problem analysis and solution: identify the problem, analyze available resources, and work out step-by-step solutions. This process is applied at all levels, from teaching the academic and technical subjects to dealing with job relationships and planning a career. For example, in an academy with a business focus, teachers included problem solving in the English, math, social studies, and business curriculum. They developed instructional units that involved students in solving everyday business problems by pricing merchandise, maintaining inventories, using reports and business letters, figuring and reporting taxes, interpreting simulated situations, dealing with government, and participating in both simulated and real job-seeking activities. In a unit on entrepreneurship, students were asked in mathematics to calculate the costs of a new business; in English to write a paper on venture capitalism; and in social studies to secure applications for business licenses from local governments.

TECHNOLOGY

Academy teachers use computer technology to expand their capacity to create a curriculum that will integrate academics with skills required in companies where technology is pervasive. Students have access to visual and hands-on learning through CD-ROM, television, and computer simulations. English and social studies teachers assign reports to be written on a computer. In math and science, students use computers to simulate experiments, calculate data, and graphically display results. Communications networks provide teachers and students with nationwide access to other professionals for collaborative and distance learning, and to libraries for databases and supplemental instructional materials.

Students relish the control of their own learning that computers afford. Many gain the confidence to try advanced subject areas. Teamwork and cooperative learning are fostered. They find it natural to ask classmates for assistance, or to work together to solve a problem on the computer. Access to technology provides opportunities for creativity, critical thinking, information access, and practicing team skills.

One technology-oriented academy combines computer skills for business with thinking and problem-solving skills to help students advance beyond entry-level jobs. Computer skills include: word processing, keyboarding, constructing databases and spreadsheets, and using electronic mail and multimedia. The teachers designed an innovative curriculum that integrates English, mathematics, history, and computer skills. For example, in grade 11, students study the United States of the 1930s. In their history class, they study the labor issues involved in widespread unemployment and the effects of these issues on different groups (rich, poor, minorities). In English, they read and analyze John Steinbeck's *The Grapes of Wrath* as a work of literature and also for its relevance to the labor issues they are studying in history. In mathematics, they examine data associated with the collapse of the stock market and its effect on business, make databases, and represent their data graphically. Constant use is made of the computer as a teaching and learning tool in all subject areas. Students improve their inquiry skills by using computer on-line services to research databases and libraries.

INTEGRATION OF WORKPLACE SKILLS

Partnerships with businesses are central to the integration of workplace skills with academic and technical coursework. Formation and maintenance of strong school/business partnerships are not easy tasks. Often, neither schools nor businesses know how to collaborate in such efforts, much less take the lead to clearly define the roles for each entity. Academies have managed to form and keep these relationships alive by having all partners focus on their strengths: business develops employability requirements while schools develop a curriculum based on those requirements.

Partnership employers in a broad range of businesses define a similar set of requirements for academy programs. They need competent workers who are computer literate, who can read, write, and calculate, and who are willing to learn and to work diligently. The school's function is to provide students with this foundation by developing a curriculum that provides them with the skills they need to succeed, so that businesses can train them for specific jobs, using either formal or informal on-the-job training. Businesses help define that curriculum and assist students directly by providing mentors, paid work experience, and jobs.

Academic and technical teachers learn from their business partners which basic skills are needed on the job, and then both work together to incorporate them into their instruction. Teachers modify academic courses to introduce career skills as well as to cover the standard course content. They develop employability components that stress problem solving, initiative, cooperation, and use of technology. Representatives from business review the results to ensure that their needs are met. The statewide academies conference held each year also focuses on using industry partners to help in integrating the academic/technical curriculum in a way that teaches students the requirements of their chosen career field. These curriculum requirements include: entry level and advancement skills, community and environmental impacts, resource management, acquisition and use of information, and labor issues.

Students are taught about career paths within companies and try their hands at many tasks with advancement potential, such as customer and sales support, office management, desk-top publishing and project presentations. For example, a student team might simulate making a presentation on a new database management software program to a customer. The team prepares graphic displays and handouts, organizes the room, prepares for questions, and gives the actual presentation. Emphasis is placed on presentation skills, responsibility, and thoroughness of preparation, as well as on computer skills.

A mentor is matched with each student in the eleventh grade. Mentors are business employees who serve as role models. They provide knowledge, experience, and access to the workplace. Mentors act as an instructional resource by helping students develop employability skills. They give students an opportunity to see good work skills in use before they advance to their first job.

From the student's perspective, the most important role for business is to supply meaningful jobs at an adequate wage. From the teacher's perspective, student experiences in the workplace are essential aspects of the academies curriculum. Work experience exposes students to the variety of job opportunities in their career field. It gives meaning to employability skills by introducing students to workplace expectations concerning language, dress, and behavior. Students apply for work experience jobs just as they would for permanent positions. They complete applications, provide résumés, and attend interviews with the prospective employer. They take a portfolio of their best work to present in the job interview. Work experience provides the opportunity for students to see and experience the direct relationship between school and work.

An example of a flourishing partnership is the one between the Oakland Health Academy and local hospitals. One element of their curriculum is an innovative use of a problem-based learning approach to clinical instruction. Students work in teams using a hospital's medical library to diagnose and develop a treatment plan for a simulated patient. The themes of health and medicine are incorporated into the academic subjects. In English classes, students learn medical terminology by reading, writing, and discussing medical ethics and other medical issues. A unit on the history of medicine is included in the history class. A hands-on approach is used in teaching health and medical laboratory techniques in the science class (Jobs for the Future, 1992). The partnership has developed a series of life science mini-units that they share with other health academies.

PROJECT-BASED LEARNING

Academy teachers use student projects as a way to integrate curriculum. Projects combine work from several disciplines to produce a product (a report, videotape, or newsletter) or provide a service to the community. These projects provide powerful learning experiences that are seldom matched by a departmentalized teaching approach. They are less teacher-directed than is most regular classwork, and teach students that there may be more than one answer to any given problem. Teachers stress team decision-making and problem-solving techniques. Projects can begin as early as the first year in an academy and range in duration from several weeks to a year.

Each student team chooses its project and is involved in the development of its interdisciplinary units. Some projects have an entrepreneurial bent. Students must solve practical problems and integrate their academic and technical skills to achieve the project's goals. Team members must define a problem, manage their resources, and work together using a variety of technologies to successfully complete the project. Students learn from and teach one another. They become far more active in their own learning when they are held accountable for contributing to group work or required to help others. Commitment to the work increases when students work with peers, teachers, and the community, and are expected to be responsible problem solvers.

In one project, students in a health academy were faced with the loss of their school nurse because of district budget cutbacks. They formed a Wellness Task Force, and surveyed their school and surrounding community to find pressing health needs. They sought help from their hospital partners to establish a health clinic in their school. Not only did they secure volunteers to restore the nurse's position, they also enlisted the part-time services of a physician. The students became knowledgeable enough to form a Health Affairs Committee, and to publish a newsletter on health issues of interest to their fellow students and to the community. This project involved: survey techniques; studies of epidemiology, substance abuse, and teenage pregnancy; persuasive writing; developing a historical perspective on the needs of the community; and determining social responsibility. For each action, the students planned the work, set schedules, selected needed research, shared information, and acted on their conclusions.

In 1993, through a competitive process, the California State Department of Education selected fourteen academies to participate in a year-long integrated curriculum development venture. The selected academies were divided into three industry groups: telecommunications, banking/finance, and health. Each multischool group was charged with developing integrated curriculum units that culminated in "action-based projects." The projects are designed to link academics with their career fields in ways that allow students to acquire and practice the skills used in high-performance workplaces. At the completion of this project-based curriculum development effort, materials describing the projects and rubrics for their grading will be developed for use by academies and comprehensive high schools that are developing curriculum for career clusters.

Representatives from industry, master teachers from the University of California subject matter projects, and state vocational education consultants work with the project teams. Subject matter experts help the teachers incorporate the academic and technical subjects into the projects in a way that maintains curricular integrity while diminishing the boundaries among disciplines. Teachers visit companies in the banking, telecommunications, and health industries to observe the work of entry-level personnel. These interactions have powerful incentives for all involved. Business representatives help define the curriculum. Subject-matter experts gain valuable experience through direct involvement with teachers who are attempting to integrate curriculum in creative ways. Teachers experience meaningful staff development through communication with peers, industry representatives, and curriculum experts over an extended period.

TECH PREP

A number of academies incorporate their program into the Tech Prep program (Chapter 10 in Volume II describes Tech Prep in detail). Several Tech Prep consortia have been formed that include high school districts, community colleges, and regional occupation programs. The Tech Prep program provides a clear path to community college and a continuation of the career preparation begun in the academy. It furnishes an organizational structure that supports academy programs and leads students to community college certification and/or to an associate degree. Academy teachers work with college staff to develop a competency-based, vertically articulated curriculum between high school and college. The technical curriculum of the academy supplies the required high school technical specialty courses. Staff development on content and instructional strategies is provided by the consortium. Joint advisory committees with business representation advise academy and community college staff on employer needs.

When the college determines that the academy's technical course meets its standard for the articulated college course, it grants advanced placement credit. Earning advanced placement credit encourages students to enroll in college. The outreach and counseling services provided by Tech Prep expedite the process. Promotional materials are distributed and college counselors actively recruit academy students and invite them to visit the campus. Students are given the option of completing college classes for a certificate of mastery or using the required general and elective courses to earn an associate degree. College counselors work closely with students who want to enter California's university system to ensure their admission. At present, academy students are involved in a variety of community college degree or certification programs, including health aide, information specialist, and graphics illustrator.

■
PROBLEMS

Although academies have made significant progress in integrating curriculum, there are problems that have not been completely resolved. These include full acceptance of the curriculum, appropriate staff development, administrative support, and assessment of student performance.

ACCEPTANCE OF INTEGRATED CURRICULUM

Some teachers and administrators question the academic rigor of the integrated curriculum and are concerned that an academy's idea of relevant classwork is not equivalent to the curriculum of the baccalaureate-bound.

They have little faith in a curriculum that is not constrained by standardized tests, textbooks, and traditional course sequences. Others are concerned that the math and science information offered in integrated courses is not covered in sufficient breadth or depth. They doubt their colleagues' ability to find key concepts that organize and structure enough specific information to allow students to be successful in postsecondary education. In addition, some academy teachers may not have sufficient academic background or technical training, or the required credentials, to teach a cross-disciplinary curriculum.

There are several reasons to expect greater acceptance of integrated curricula. The National Science Teachers Association and the National Council for Teachers of Mathematics both have recommended that learning be structured around primary ideas and that learner-relevant curriculum/teaching models be used (Brooks & Brooks, 1993). California has aligned the mathematics and science frameworks with integration concepts and recommended that curricula be designed around real-life experiences. Publishers are responding to the need for integrated materials by producing textbooks and supplemental materials that lend themselves to integration strategies. Discussion has begun in the California Department of Education about the policy issues of aligning integrated curriculum courses to college admissions requirements. Although progress has been slow, the University of California is allowing some integrated courses to meet admission requirements.

STAFF DEVELOPMENT

Many academy teachers lack the expertise required to develop integrated curricula. Academic teachers need training to master procedures to mesh the core subjects with the technical course in a way that will give students a strong set of basic skills in both areas while teaching basic academic competencies. Both academic and technical teachers must be exposed to a variety of resources that provide real-life examples. They need training in classroom management techniques that help build instructional strategies that enhance interdisciplinary teaching, collaboration, and project-based learning. They also need training in the use of technology that can help them design curricula and assess student progress. This all must be accomplished despite the fact that curriculum packages and outside expertise in the integration process are not readily available. These problems are further complicated by the need to adapt the curriculum to a wide range of student abilities and to the requirements of the participating employers.

Teachers require a direct knowledge of the modern workplace. Work internships have been found to be invaluable. Internships broaden the exposure of teachers to the industry environment, increase their ability to counsel students about industry careers, and help them learn methods of applying industry-related skills and experiences in their classrooms. Internships are needed by both academic and technical teachers, so both can understand the elements of curriculum that need to be integrated.

ADMINISTRATIVE SUPPORT

A lack of resources and administrative support can be a serious problem. Successful curriculum integration depends on school and district office administrators who are willing to consider unusual patterns of staffing and scheduling and who show commitment by allocation of resources. Teacher collaboration time and preservice or inservice staff development is needed to design and teach an integrated curriculum. Otherwise, the development of integrated curriculum becomes just another burden for already overworked teachers.

Teachers need to be able to consult with other practitioners and experts as they develop curriculum. Merely providing a common teacher planning period for curriculum development is not adequate, even for a comparatively simple interdisciplinary integration of academic and technical courses. A serious effort requires funding for an additional, common planning period and for a longer work year. Seed money from grants and companies can provide impetus for this work, but local support is needed to sustain the process.

CERTIFICATION AND ASSESSMENT

A widely recognized problem is finding an acceptable method of providing business with an assessment of a high school graduate's competence for a particular job. Many academies solve this problem by awarding their students skills certificates with the high school diploma. The certificate lists the technical competencies earned in the academy program. The level of proficiency is shown along with the type and amount of work experience and any special achievements. For example, in one business technology academy the certificate lists such skills as keyboarding words per minute and the level of proficiency in databases, spreadsheets, desk-top publishing, etc. In some cases the business partners, as well as the technical teachers, certify that the student has mastered a particular skill.

Another approach to solving the assessment problem is Worklinks, a reporting system designed by the Educational Testing Service. The Pasadena Academies have created a Worklinks transcript that contains, among other items, the knowledge skill level for each element in the Certificate of Mastery; a list of specific courses taken and grades for each; average rating for each topic in a work ethics/habits rating scale; and a listing of all work experience, including dates, places, and references (Foothill Associates, 1992).

Some academies are moving beyond certification to a more thoughtful assessment of student achievement. When portfolios were suggested as a way to showcase student work, academy teachers recognized the fit with their integrated curriculum goals. Portfolios have many advantages as a performance-based assessment tool in that they display problem-solving skills and the interdisciplinary set of skills used in creating the portfolio. Compiling the portfolio helps students prepare for postsecondary life by assessing themselves and rethinking the strategies they used to solve the problems presented by the portfolio project. Portfolios give administrators, parents, and employers an image of the content of the academy curriculum, and the instructional strategies used by the program.

Selected academies are participating in a field test of Career Technical Assessment Portfolios (C-TAP), developed by the Far West Laboratory for Educational Research and Development.[2] The portfolios contain a complete career development package that includes a letter of introduction, work applications, college applications, résumés, work samples, writing samples, and evaluation of work skills by employers. Students compile their portfolios in the spring semester of the senior year to display the academic and career technical skills they have mastered. Although teachers assign the portfolio as a project, students select its contents. The audience for the portfolio is the student's prospective employer. Academies with multimedia capacity are developing portfolios that include graphics, audio, and video.

CONCLUSIONS

Career academies are developing models of integrated curriculum that both comprehensive and vocational high schools can emulate as they consider curricular reform. These models address concerns about the fragmentation and lack of context of much present-day curriculum. In academic/technical curriculum integration, academy teachers use applications from technical courses to illustrate academic concepts. Academic subjects are taught in context and interdisciplinary linkages are made. Partnerships with businesses make it possible to further integrate the curriculum to include workplace employability skills. Projects require students to use their academic, technical, and interpersonal skills to successfully complete their tasks, just as they must use them on the job. Teachers integrate technology into the curriculum to provide real-world applications to academic subjects and to prepare students for a future in which the use of technology is widespread. Vertical integration with community colleges through Tech Prep programs creates a coordinated set of courses that culminate in a certificate of mastery of a particular technical skill, or a college degree.

Encouragement of the development and use of integrated curriculum can be seen in recent school reform mandates and federal legislation. California's blueprint for educational reform, *Second to None* (Agee, 1992), recognizes the importance of integrated curriculum for a broad cross-section of students, not just for at-risk students. The 1990 Carl D. Perkins Vocational and Technical Education Act sets vocational education guidelines that stipulate vocational education programs must integrate academic and vocational education through coherent sequences of courses. NAF programs were cited as successful models for integrating SCANS competencies in schools (Secretary's Commission on Achieving Necessary Skills, 1992b). The School to Work Opportunities Act of 1993 cites career academy programs as successful models for states and localities to emulate.

Curriculum integration in career academies shows students connections across disciplines and the importance of workplace skills to their futures. As a result, their attendance, grades, and course completion rates improve. Graduates are successful in job placements and most enroll in postsecondary education. The horizontally integrated academic/technical/workplace curricula, combined with the vertically aligned academy courses and community college articulation, are promising solutions to local and national concerns about the quality and relevance of high school curricular offerings for all students, and the country's need for well-educated, skilled, adaptable workers.

NOTES

1. For further information, contact: Philadelphia High School Academies Inc., 230 Broad Street, 2nd Floor, Philadelphia, PA 19102; National Academy Foundation, 235 Park Avenue South, 7th Floor, New York, NY 10003; California Partnership Academies, California Department of Education, 721 Capitol Mall, Sacramento, CA 95814.

2. For further information, contact: C-TAP project director, Far West Laboratory for Educational Research and Development, 730 Harrison Street, San Francisco, CA 94107-1242.

6

COHERENCE FOR ALL STUDENTS

High Schools with Career Clusters and Majors

W. NORTON GRUBB

In conventional high schools, any coherence in the curriculum is an accidental byproduct of the traditional college-prep curriculum. The dominant pattern of courses is the one that emerged from nineteenth century tradition, reinforced by state graduation requirements—4 years of English, 3 years of math, 2 years of history, with social studies and foreign languages thrown in, and variations from state to state (and among districts within states) depending on local preferences for parent education, or economics, or art, or some other course not part of the standard canon. Aside from its historical sanctification, there is little to hold the conventional curriculum together. In the terms of many observers, the high school has become a "shopping mall," where students choose a series of courses almost at random, with little thought or institutional guidance to how they fit together (Powell et al., 1985).

In contrast, a number of high schools have adopted a very different structure—one in which students choose a career cluster, major, or pathway, usually at the beginning or end of tenth grade. Obviously linked to the choice of a major in college, the high school cluster or major then structures the courses a student takes during the last 2 or 3 years of high school. Thus, students in a health cluster are likely to take courses related to health occupations, as well as biology and chemistry courses that emphasize medical applications, while a pre-engineering major is more likely to emphasize math, physics, and certain computer applications. As an antidote to the formlessness of the shopping mall high school, the adoption of clusters or majors provides a theme, issue, or broad occupational area that can focus both the academic and the vocational content of the high school years.

Clusters or majors have certain obvious advantages. They can accomplish what career academies do, but they reach much larger numbers of students—ideally, every student in a high school. (In practice, there may be a "default," which is the conventional college prep curriculum. The Oregon approach, described below, fosters this kind of division.) Like magnet high schools, they provide a focus or theme for courses and extra-curricular activities, but they are smaller—since a high school is likely to have perhaps three to six clusters—and thereby foster the smaller scale and community ideal more typical of academies. Like both these approaches, they bring academic and vocational teachers together and thereby provide greater opportunities for integration of the curriculum—though, as the descriptions of several schools with clusters will clarify, this does not happen in every case. The development of clusters also provides obvious opportunities for linkages to related businesses and to postsecondary programs, facilitating the kinds of comprehensive programs envisioned in the School-to-Work Opportunities Act.

And a final benefit arises, one not present in most public school systems. Because students must choose among clusters or majors, all the advantages of choice-based systems can develop (Chubb & Moe, 1990). Because students choose a major themselves, they are more likely to end up in a program that fits their interests. Having chosen, they (and their parents) may be more committed to improving the school rather than abandoning it—exercising "voice" rather than "exit." Finally, the process of having to make a choice focuses the attention of both students and the school on decision making itself. Most high schools with clusters and majors have strengthened their guidance and counseling systems in order to prepare students for this choice and, if nothing else, students gain practice in making choices—in weighing alternatives, in considering the different intellectual, social, and personal grounds for choosing one major over another—that normally would not take place until after high school. If learning to make decisions is itself a skill that benefits from activity-based exercise, then the very process of choosing among majors has its own educational benefit.

The conception of adopting clusters or majors has also been popular with state and federal policy initiatives. In California, for example, the High School Task Force recommended adopting "curricular paths" for all students, some based on broadly defined careers and others based on integrated academic disciplines, such as the humanities (Agee, 1992). Oregon's Educational Act for the 21st Century defined six clusters, or *focus areas* for non-college-bound youth, each one governed by its own Certificate of Advanced Mastery: arts and communications; business and management;

health services; human resources; industrial and engineering systems; and natural resources systems. A task force in New York similarly recommended the creation of career pathways for non-college youth, each leading to a Career Pathways Certificate (N.Y. State Job Training Partnership Council, 1992). And the federal School-to-Work Opportunities Act envisions a series of career majors, defined as:

> A coherent sequence of courses or field of study that integrates occupational and academic learning and work-based and school-based learning, and establishes linkages between secondary and postsecondary education; [and] prepares the students for employment in broad occupational clusters or industry sectors.

PROFILES OF SCHOOLS WITH CLUSTERS

As simple and powerful as the idea of clusters or majors is, different schools have adopted this form in very different ways. As the following profiles of four schools illustrate, the crucial elements of a high school adopting clusters or majors can vary substantially. In the process, the potential for integrating academic and vocational education—and indeed, for reshaping the high school in various ways—can vary dramatically.

URBAN TECHNICAL HIGH SCHOOL

Urban Tech,[1] located in a large, urban school district, was established around the turn of the century as a technical high school and its physical facility reflects its origin in the early days of vocational education: it incorporates woodworking shops, metal shops, machine shops with rows of conventional lathes, and an enormous foundry equipped to teach metal molding, a staple from the turn of the century. While it remains a technical high school in name, and in some of its instructional content, it is also one of the selective high schools in the city and therefore attracts an academically well-prepared student body, largely focused on going to college.

During ninth and tenth grades, students take woodshop—a good representative of the "birdhouse and gun rack" approach to shop, with graduated exercises on a variety of machines and techniques—as well as metalshop, mechanical drawing, and drafting. For eleventh and twelfth grades, they elect one of 15 different majors: aerospace engineering; architecture; biomedicine; chemistry; computer science; civil engineering; environmental science; electronic and computer engineering; industrial design; mechanical engineering; media communications; mathematics institute; social science research; a pre-med program called Gateway to Medicine; or a residual category called Technology and the Liberal Arts. These majors occupy a two-period block of time every day, while the other course requirements are taught in the remaining periods. Evidently, the majors in this school include some that are clearly occupational and others that are academic. Inevitably, status rankings among clusters have developed, with academic clusters, and their obvious links to college preparation, having greater status than the more obviously vocational majors.

There appears to be little attention in this school to the problem of how students choose majors. The required ninth and tenth grade courses are not intended to facilitate this choice, and the formal introduction to the various majors takes place over the course of one day, when the heads of each major curriculum section describe the contents of the course for the students. No doubt there is a substantial amount of informal lore circulating among the student body about the desirability of different majors, but the school itself has done little to prepare students for their decision.

Because core academic courses include students from a variety of majors, it is difficult for instructors to integrate occupational applications in their courses. One instructor—in the area of mechanical technology—has initiated discussions about devising a math course specifically for students in this major in order to present certain applications in the math class and cover the uses of math most common to his subject, and this example could obviously be extended to more subjects and to more majors. But the school is not structured to make such integration easy: the tyranny of the master schedule has made it difficult to place all students in this major in the same math course, and nothing in the culture of the institution fosters this kind of collaboration among instructors.

Urban Tech is an interesting example of replacing electives with courses in a specific area, and in that sense it has developed a curriculum that provides students with an area of focus in addition to the conventional high school requirements. However, in other ways the potential for majors to structure the entire high school, and to facilitate integration across high schools, is lacking, because the courses of the majors are as self-contained and as independent of the rest of the curriculum as are the courses of the conventional high school.

BENNIS TECHNICAL HIGH SCHOOL

A variant of this approach has developed in another magnet vocational school, Bennis Technical High School. As in Urban Tech, Bennis students elect one of six occupational "majors" during their junior and senior years: communications technology, electricity/electronics technology, mechanical technology, manufacturing technology, construction technology, and drafting technology. The school also offers a health occupations program that operates as a school-within-a-school. The vocational majors that students select are oriented around clusters of occupations. As the literature on The Bennis Project (a kind of manifesto that justifies the school's organization) describes them: "Vocational-technical curricula [are] structured to move away from a 'crafts' centered approach to a broader-based 'systems' approach."

However, unlike Urban Tech, the election of a major is preceded in grades nine and ten by a two-year sequence of modules that can be roughly described as extended career exploration. During freshman year, students take four 9-week modules: Communications Technology I, Electronics Technology I, Mechanical Technology I, and Manufacturing Technology I, plus introduction to drafting and keyboarding. The modules include labs that teach students about basic principles and production methods and explore other aspects of particular sectors (e.g., the economics of why certain manufacturing sectors are present in some regions but not in others). During sophomore year, students can take modules in Photography, Materials Science, Fabrication I, or Construction Technology, or they can take second-level modules in communications, electronics, mechanical technologies, or manufacturing technologies. By the end of their sophomore year, then, every student has learned about a wide variety of technologies, sectors, and occupations, before they are ready to make their choice of a major.

Within this structure, coordination and integration take several forms. The Bennis Project literature emphasizes the need to combine academic and vocational capabilities.

> [Bennis Tech] is dedicated to producing graduates with a broad, solid base of both academic and vocational/technical skills. This base will enable [Bennis] graduates to be successful in post-high school education and employment and will provide the adaptability necessary to remain successful in a rapidly changing society.

Among the specific examples of integration, one of the most elaborate is the English/Vocational Articulation Program, which links the career exploration courses and English in ninth grade. At the beginning of freshman year, all vocational classes spend time on measurement and measurement instruments, and these skills are reinforced at the same time in math classes.[2] The school has included Principles of Technology I and II.[3] The academic geometry class includes transformational geometry because of its use in drafting and in the machine trades, and a joint course in geometry and drafting has been developed. During the senior year, students can take a course in technical writing, jointly developed by an English teacher and the chair of the drafting department; its intention is "to correlate English class writing experience and vocational cluster class experience." The school is now developing a senior project to be required of all students. In place of a course-specific project in one of a student's vocational courses, or a senior research paper, the senior project combines a research paper, a vocationally oriented project ("a 'hands-on' project to display [the student's] knowledge"), and finally a speech presenting the project—a combination of academic, vocational, and communications skills, like the English/Vocational Articulation Project. Finally, it is common to use vocational examples in math classes, and all academic classes are supposed to emphasize technical literacy and employability skills.

The culture of Bennis Tech, where students have selected themselves into a highly regarded technical high school with competitive admissions, affects what academic teachers do and how academic and vocational teachers interact: Integration is present in several forms because the vocational emphasis of the school is unavoidable.[4] At the same time, Bennis Tech is not fully integrated because students still take their academic subjects with students from a variety of majors. Many of these courses, therefore, still look like conventional, self-contained classrooms, with little integration of occupational content. But this particular school has been more self-conscious than has Urban Tech about developing various projects and modules that explicitly integrate across disciplinary boundaries. Finally, the process of exploring different modules during ninth and tenth grades, in preparation for electing a major, represents a form of career orientation that is more intensive and activity-based than in virtually any other high school.

LANDON HIGH SCHOOL

A different approach to using occupational clusters has been developed in a grade 10-12 comprehensive high school of about 1,500 students. This school can be described as having a matrix structure: In addition to conventional academic and vocational departments, six "career paths" cut across departments—agriculture and natural resources; business and marketing; art and communication; health, home, and recreation; industrial technologies and engineering; and social, human, and governmental services.[5] Each student elects a "career path" at the beginning of tenth grade. Students in a career path are urged, by counselors and brochures describing each career path, to take a set of academic courses related to their paths as well as a coherent sequence of vocational courses, in addition to the academic courses required for high school graduation.[6] Teachers belong to both conventional departments and to clusters, so they are responsible for the programs and activities developed for career paths as well as for the content and standards of their conventional, discipline-based courses.

In this school, the principal developed the career path structure as an antidote to the shopping mall high school. He wanted to see students more aware of the purposes of schooling, better able to see the connections between school experiences and their futures, more self-motivated and better able to define paths through high school that make sense for them, better able to establish goals, to develop plans to meet these goals, and to revise their plans as necessary. Teachers were also disconnected from one another; the vocational faculty was especially estranged because vocational education had become a "dumping ground" and because increased graduation requirements threatened to make vocational education irrelevant. Thus, the career paths are intended both to give a focus to students and to engender cooperation among teachers.

Career paths at Landon are designed to be quite broad. The brochures describing each career path illustrate entry-level, middle-level, and professional-level occupations and typical college majors corresponding to each, clarifying that a career path is an avenue for college-bound students as well as for those who intend to work directly after high school. The brochures also list the academic and vocational courses related to that path, and the very existence of career paths incorporating serious academic and sophisticated vocational courses clarifies to all students—including the college-bound—that occupations require a blend of academic and vocational capacities. Furthermore, the vocational content of each path is substantial: Landon High offers about 60 vocational courses, an extraordinarily large number for a medium-size high school, including many advanced courses, like a third-level course in three-dimensional design and graphics; advanced manufacturing, incorporating numerically controlled milling and lathes; and a comprehensive series in agriculture (as befits a school in the middle of a farming area), with two semesters of agricultural science, animal and crop science, agricultural power, and agricultural fabrication.

The process of selecting career paths has been carefully structured. At the beginning of tenth grade, students take an interest inventory and a personality profile. Then each student sees a counselor individually to choose a career path. Thereafter they can change their career paths at the beginning of each semester, as long as they can convince a counselor that they are doing so for good reasons; thus, choices about career paths have consequences, particularly for course selection and career path activities, but they are far from irreversible. Furthermore, counselors are responsible solely for career counseling, including advising students about career paths. Disciplinary problems have been assigned to other administrators and students' personal problems—having to do with issues revolving around alcohol, drugs, sex, money, parent problems (including abuse and divorce), and suicidal thoughts—that consume the time of many high school counselors are handled by social service organizations with offices on campus. In addition, Landon reduced its student-counselor ratio from the usual 500:1 or 600:1 to about 250:1, so there is a much better chance that counselors can provide substantial amounts of career-related information to individual students, as well as to groups.

The career paths extend to teachers as well: Each teacher is a member not only of a conventional academic or vocational department, but also of a career path. Teachers in particular disciplines are spread among career paths. For example, the ten English teachers are assigned in groups of one and two to each of the six career paths; the eight social studies teachers are assigned so that three are in the social, human, and governmental services path, but each of the other five paths has a social studies teacher; the seven business teachers are spread among six paths so only one path has two business teachers; the five industrial technology teachers are spread among career paths so that only social, human, and governmental services lacks one. Each path also has a counselor, and a lead teacher who serves as convenor. Teachers then meet in their career paths, as well as in their conventional departments, and in these meetings discuss possible career path activities, courses, and ways to orient classes toward the occupations of career paths. The fact that every teacher has a place in the career path structure provides a ready connection to other academic and vocational teachers and a focus on a particular occupation area, facilitating cooperation across courses and the incorporation of vocationally relevant material in academic courses.

Teachers are constantly urged—both by the principal and by at least some other teachers in their career paths—to integrate career-related information and applications in academic courses, and to reinforce academic capacities in vocational courses. There are numerous examples: The English courses focus on certain skills related to job-seeking, like developing personal resumes, and students also write resumes of historical or literary figures as part of the process. The food and nutrition courses and child development courses have increased academic content, and now count as science courses for graduation. The carpentry and welding classes were revised to incorporate more math, and many agriculture courses include large amounts of plant science and soil science. In addition, several new courses have been developed. In meeting the state's requirement for an economics course, for example, students may take a conventional social science-based economics class or courses in business economics, agricultural economics, or home economics—whichever is more appropriate for students in particular career paths. Unlike some other schools with majors, many teachers at Landon are highly aware of the effort to integrate academic and vocational education; one recently arrived agriculture teacher spoke glowingly of the "whole-school" approach to integration, contrasting it with the much more limited and serendipitous efforts in other high schools.

What is noteworthy about the matrix structure of Landon High is that a format exists—the career path meetings of faculty—in which academic and vocational teachers can convene on relatively equal footing to discuss the right balance between academic content and more occupational skills. Not surprisingly, this discussion often generates tension: several vocational instructors (and the principal) mentioned the problem of "maintaining the integrity of the vocational curriculum," the struggle to maintain a vocational purpose in the face of pressures to increase academic content. Academic teachers also resist curriculum integration on the same grounds, often complaining about "watering down" their efforts. This tension is unavoidable, however. The difference is that Landon High, and other schools with an occupational focus, provide a forum in which to discuss the balance, in contrast to the usual American high school where there is no discussion because academic and vocational teachers are isolated.

However, in Landon High academic courses are not limited to students in only one career path; for example, each English course includes students from all career paths.[7] This of course limits the amount of integration that can take place and so—as in Bennis Tech—many classes look like conventional disciplinary courses with few attempts at integration. For instructors who are indifferent to the notion of integration, therefore, the career paths are not especially important: career path meetings are infrequent, there are no requirements to develop the programs within career paths, and several instructors acknowledged that career paths have had little effect on their lives as teachers.

Similarly, the school has not been successful in developing the activities that might make career paths more salient to students, partly because of fiscal limitations. In the original plan, students within each career path were to attend special activities, which would have included visits from professionals in industry, information in the form of profiles of occupations within the career paths, tours of firms and businesses, career-oriented assemblies, visits to postsecondary institutions with related programs of study, and the like. The principal of Landon had developed a justification for these activities that goes beyond the usual purpose of providing students with information about occupational alternatives: He affirmed that these activities would help transfer the task of motivating students—and convincing them about the need to learn both academic and vocational competencies— from teachers to those outside the high school who may have greater persuasive power or moral authority. However, the lack of funding has limited the scope of these activities, and so—as is also the case for many teachers—career paths remain unimportant to many students at Landon.

The inability of Landon High to realize the potential of career paths is itself instructive: In the absence of strong roles for the career paths—for example, substantial career path activities for students and serious use of the materials from the occupations in the curriculum—the conventional disciplinary structure of the high school reasserts itself. Under these conditions, the career paths have become a way of organizing conventional academic courses and an unusually rich set of occupational courses, while providing a process of career-oriented guidance and counseling at the beginning of the tenth grade. But they have not substantially changed the content of most courses, nor modified the disciplinary allegiance of most teachers.

DAUPHIN COUNTY TECHNICAL SCHOOL

A few schools have replaced conventional departments—academic departments like English, math, social studies, and vocational departments like business, agriculture, and industrial arts—with departments organized along occupational lines. One example is Dauphin County Technical School, a comprehensive area vocational school near Harrisburg, Pennsylvania (Adelman, 1989). In response to low academic achievement levels and high dropout rates, caused partly by boredom and frustration with academic courses, administrators restructured the school to establish stronger links between academic courses and vocational classes. The school eliminated conventional departments and organized faculty and students into four occupational clusters: communications and transportation, including the traditional automotive programs and machine trades, as well as graphic arts and commercial art; construction, including the building trades; a service cluster encompassing cosmetology, health, distributive education, horticulture, and food service; and a technical cluster including chemical technology, electronics, data processing, and drafting. Each student takes vocational courses within each cluster, in addition to the usual complement of academic courses required for graduation. Teachers are assigned to clusters; the academic instructors then teach students from specific clusters— for example, tenth grade English to students in the service cluster—giving them greater opportunities to orient the content of their classes to students from a particular cluster. (This is similar to the practice in most Ohio schools adopting the Applied Academics program, described in Chapter 4.)

In addition to adopting departments based on clusters, Dauphin County Technical School has worked to integrate specific academic subjects with vocational coursework. For example, the English sequence has placed greater emphasis on communications skills necessary for the workplace; a central element is a technical paper about a vocational exercise or lab sequence. The integration of math with the vocational curriculum was considered a comparatively easy task, since technical math had been taught prior to the reorganization of Dauphin County Tech, and since business math is well established. In addition, one math teacher has been assigned as a "liaison" to vocational teachers (the same role that academic teachers serve in Smithville Area Vocational School, described in Chapter 4). The science sequence includes Principles of Technology, as well as conventional science courses like earth science, biology, and chemistry. In social studies, the curriculum stresses the historical influences of work and technological advances, as well as employability skills. Tenth graders take a course on the effects of technological changes; eleventh graders take a course called The World of Work, plus a semester of economics; and seniors take psychology and family living. There appears to have been an effort to turn the attention of the school, and the aims of reform, toward one academic area after another, beginning with English, moving to social studies, and then concentrating on sciences. With this progression there is a sense that all academic subjects will eventually be integrated with vocational subjects. The structure of occupational clusters—where each academic class includes students from only one cluster—facilitates such integration among courses.

THE CRUCIAL ELEMENTS OF CLUSTER-BASED HIGH SCHOOLS

Evidently, there are different ways that schools can incorporate clusters, majors, or career paths. The element common to all of them—the election by students of a cluster that structures some or all of their high school programs—has been differently interpreted by various schools, with substantial variations in practice.

DEVISING CLUSTERS

As Urban Technical High School and the Oregon plan illustrate, clusters or majors need not be occupational. A math/science major can coexist with business and health majors, and there can also be problem-focused clusters—an environmental cluster, for example, or one examining the problems of cities.[8] To be sure, where students can choose among both academic clusters and occupational clusters, the status conventionally associated with the college prep track may generate status differences among various majors, with the possibilities for recreating the current divisions between college-bound and non-college-bound students—as is also true in the Oregon plan. Until the time comes when occupational preparation ceases to have the stigma it has inherited from vocational education, the only antidote is the approach of Bennis Tech: the creation of majors, like the health cluster and the manufacturing technology cluster, incorporating enough high-status occupations (doctors and engineers) that a broad range of students are willing to elect them.

Very often, high schools have devised clusters to correspond to related occupations—for example, health occupations. An alternative way to think about clusters is to structure them around occupations within a particular *industry,* on the assumption that individuals are more likely to move among jobs within a particular sector, and need to know the responsibilities and competencies of their coworkers in those sectors (Hoachlander, 1994). Indeed, this often occurs in clusters that are broadly defined, as in clusters including a variety of agricultural occupations—including managerial occupations—or those focused on the building industry, which can include both the traditional building trades as well as occupations related to architecture, planning, and housing policy.

The dominant method of developing clusters, of course, has been to survey the occupational or industrial composition of the local or regional labor market and to emphasize clusters preparing students for local employment. Even in areas where students are more likely to leave the region—in rural areas, for example, or areas with net out-migration—there are advantages to this method: Local economic developments can offer examples for instruction and local employers can provide work experience, mentors, and other complementary activities. But, not surprisingly, only a fraction of students in a major will follow up on that particular career choice. Although there have been no actual surveys of the numbers involved, instructors in cluster programs and in academies estimate that only one quarter to one third of students follow their occupational area after high school. In addition, since many students will leave their home areas, the purpose of clusters should not be job-specific preparation but rather to provide a broad context in which to present a variety of academic and occupational competencies.

At the other end of the spectrum, the practice in some schools of adopting in excess of 20 clusters amounts to a recreation of job-specific vocational programs. A similar result occurs when schools adopt broad clusters, but then allow students to choose specializations within a cluster; for example, one school with a cluster in Applied Engineering and Mechanical Technologies allows specialization in 13 areas: agriculture; auto body repair; automotive technology; carpentry; drafting; electronics; horticulture; industrial engineering technologies; masonry; plumbing/heating, ventilating, and air conditioning; residential wiring; sheet metal; and welding. This practice undermines the role of clusters in providing students with a broad range of occupations to consider, and weakens an important purpose of integrating academic and vocational education: the movement away from the job-specific training that has traditionally dominated vocational education.

THE EXTENT OF FOCUS ON THE MAJOR

The various schools described above vary in the amount of time and attention they devote to the subjects in the major area. In most cases they devote two periods a day to the subject, giving it twice as much time and weight as the other core subjects of the conventional curriculum (like English and math). However, in other cases the lack of specific time devoted to the cluster makes it difficult to assess how much emphasis is placed on the major subject. In Landon High, for example, content related specifically to the pathway is found only in a few elective vocational courses; there are few activities within career pathways, and academic courses include students from all pathways and therefore usually look like conventional courses. This means that, within a 3-year program, students may have only two or three one-semester courses related to their career paths, and need not take even that many. At the other extreme, a school like Dauphin County Tech, where all teaching is done within the cluster, has the potential for considerably more emphasis on the content drawn from the major, since virtually every class can be linked to this subject.

The potential for clusters to restructure the high school depends critically on the extent of focus on the major subject. Those schools without that depth of focus, where students (and teachers) are unsure of what cluster they are in, look like conventional high schools where only a few electives are suggested by the student's major. Only in those schools in which clusters include substantial content in the major area, displacing other electives, is there a substantial departure from the shopping mall high school. This is a problem similar to the one encountered in some magnet schools, where there are only two or three courses in the magnet area available to students during a 3- or 4-year program—a magnet in name only. The effect of magnet schools in improving retention is partly a function of the extent of focus on the magnet's theme (Blank, 1989)—and by extension we might conclude that the effectiveness of basing schools on clusters or majors is probably a function of the extent to which the subject of each cluster permeates a student's high school program.

PREPARING STUDENTS FOR CHOICES

The schools described in the previous section vary dramatically in the time and energy devoted to preparing students to choose a major or pathway. At one end of the spectrum, Bennis Tech devotes the equivalent of one course during 2 years to such preparation. The sequence of introductory 9-week modules allows students to experience the techniques and procedures of various occupational areas, and the program there is probably as good an example of activity-based career exploration as exists in the country—a strong alternative to conventional career guidance, which in most high schools consists only of passive information transfer. At Landon High, the methods of preparing students to elect their career pathways take much less time—one month at the beginning of tenth grade—but there are at least some activities specifically focused on the problem of choice. At the other end of the spectrum, Urban Tech does virtually nothing to prepare its students: the ninth and tenth grade courses in woodshop, metals, and drafting are holdovers from a distant past and have very little to do with most of the majors offered in the school.

The existence of clusters within a school provides an opportunity for the exercise of choice and for the kind of career-oriented counseling missing in the conventional high school, where the dominant issues about the future relate to going to college. The kind of activity-based career guidance, embedded in the fabric of the curriculum and shared among teachers and counselors (described in Chapter 7 of Volume II), is exemplified by the program preparing students for the choice of a cluster in Bennis Tech and in Landon High. While these require substantial resources, they are simpler to organize in a school incorporating clusters, while in the conventional academic high school, such efforts look contrived and must be established independently of the curriculum.

THE EXTENT OF CURRICULUM INTEGRATION

The schools profiled above vary in obvious ways in the extent to which academic and vocational content is integrated. On the one hand, schools like Urban Tech have a structure in which integration of content between the two-period major and conventional academic subjects is not intended, and only the initiative of individual instructors—often thwarted by the rigidities of the master schedule—can foster integration across subject lines. Indeed, in every school where conventional academic courses are outside the boundary of the cluster or major, and in which academic instructors find students from every cluster in their classes, the integration of occupational content in conventional academic classes is difficult, and the responsibility for integration tends to reside with the vocational instructors in the areas of the majors. Only where academic courses are taught within clusters, as they are in Dauphin County Technical School—that is, where they are *inside* the cluster, as math, English, and science tend to be in most academies—is integration across subjects easy to accomplish.

To be sure, even where instructors fail to integrate academic and vocational education, students in clusters or majors may themselves integrate content because they can—if they are active and curious students—make the links between the content in academic courses and its application in occupational areas. In addition, students can still pursue a "two track" strategy of preparing either for employment after high school or for postsecondary education, or for that combination of employment and education that has become typical of postsecondary students. (On the tendency of students to pursue a two track strategy in magnet schools, see Chapters 7 and 9.) However, these forms of integration rely on students, rather than on structuring integration in the curriculum and on cooperation among teachers.

LINKS TO BUSINESS AND POSTSECONDARY INSTITUTIONS

Virtually every high school that has adopted clusters or majors has established links with local colleges, often community colleges. Very often, these take the form of articulation agreements providing credit to students for courses taken during high school, but courses taken at the college are often included as well. Once a high school has developed an occupational focus, such linkages with corresponding programs at the postsecondary level become natural and harness the interest of community colleges in recruiting well prepared students—in other cases, however, tech prep programs linking high schools and community colleges have found it difficult to sell the program to colleges.

Clusters and majors also have the same potential for forming links with businesses, since the connection between an occupationally oriented program and related employers seems natural rather than opportunistic or contrived. Here, however, success has been more mixed, since the resources schools need to develop links to employers—to recruit them, to establish work experience programs or summer jobs, to continue monitoring their quality, to persuade business representatives to serve as mentors—often do not exist. (On the various kinds of activities necessary to establish high-quality, work-based learning, see Chapter 9 of Volume II.) This is, of course, part of a larger problem, in which resources for ancillary and related services—services other than classroom instruction—have always been scarce in American schools; one possible solution is utilizing the resources for work-based programs available through school-to-work programs. But whatever the solution to the problem of resources, restructuring schools with occupationally oriented clusters and majors provides a natural connection to work-based learning—in contrast to the conventional academic high school, in which such connections are inevitably contrived.

■

CONCLUSIONS: RESTRUCTURING HIGH SCHOOLS VIA CLUSTERS AND MAJORS

In many ways, high schools incorporating clusters or majors are intermediate in scale between career academies and magnet schools—reaching more students than do academies but smaller in scope than are occupational magnet schools. They have many of the advantages of academies and magnets. With the adoption of clusters or majors, high schools begin to look quite different: communities of teachers are created around clusters rather than (or in addition to) disciplines; communities of students are created; and the amorphous purpose of the shopping mall high schools is replaced by a focus (Hill et al., 1990).

As vehicles for curriculum integration, schools incorporating clusters or majors have substantial promise. Of course, they integrate academic and vocational content, since students take coursework in both academic and vocational subjects. However, like academies and magnet schools, integration in the deeper sense—in the form where teachers coordinate the content in two or more courses, forging the linkages that students would otherwise have to make for themselves—may or may not happen, depending on the particular form that clusters take. That is, academies, clusters, and magnet schools can *encourage* integration in this sense, but they cannot *guarantee* that it takes place.

Within these kinds of restructured high schools, heterogeneity—accommodating the curriculum to student differences—takes very different forms. In the conventional high school, students differ in the electives they take, of course, and the core academic courses vary as well, despite the presumption of uniformity because of the variation in the horizontal curriculum (Powell et al., 1985): that is, an upper track English course bears little relationship to a lower track course, where film is likely to replace written text and opinion-mongering displaces careful analysis. These kinds of accommodations to student differences—defined variously as student ability or student motivation—have operated to empty many lower track courses of their content. In contrast, a school defined by clusters (either occupational or nonoccupational) establishes differences based on student interests— interests defined over a sequence of courses, rather than by independent electives. In this sense, such schools are student-centered in a way that conventional high schools are not, allowing some exercise of preference—and providing, to varying degree, the preparation to make that preference informed—that is more systematic than the usual selection of electives.

Finally, with a focus on clusters or majors, the high school can be fundamentally restructured—not just for a few students and teachers, as in academies, but for *all* students and teachers. The selection of courses, the communities of students, the interactions among teachers, the possibilities for interdisciplinary work, the links to external organizations like businesses and community groups—all these elements of schools necessarily change, the more so as clusters are given greater weight compared to the usual discipline-based courses and organization of the high school. Because of these far-reaching possibilities, the focus on clusters or majors provides one of the most powerful tools for reforming the high school in substantial ways, rather than merely reshaping part of the vocational curriculum for a few students.

NOTES

1. The schools profiled in this section are described by pseudonyms, except for Dauphin County Technical School.

2. Many vocational instructors have reported that students have difficulty with all kinds of measurement. We interpret this to be a problem with representing concrete objects in relatively abstract representational systems, similar to the problems we have seen with reading blueprints, electrical diagrams, and refrigerant diagrams.

3. One section of Applied Math is taught, but as a remedial course. Because of the freshman English/Vocational Articulation Project and the senior technical writing course, teachers felt that Applied Communications would be redundant.

4. The vocational emphasis at Bennis Tech is not an emphasis on a terminal education. In the 1988 graduating class, 68% planned to go on to postsecondary education, including 47% who planned to go on to 4-year colleges. Both of these figures are above the national average. The links between Bennis Tech and the local community college are especially strong.

5. These 6 were created from about 20 career clusters developed by a higher education organization in that region, which has put together a manual about career areas in order to facilitate articulation between community colleges and 4-year colleges. The career paths therefore facilitate articulation with occupational programs in postsecondary education.

6. Several vocational courses, like foods and nutrition and child development, have been rewritten to count toward the science requirement for graduation, facilitating the problem of accumulating enough graduation credits while still completing a meaningful number of courses in a career path.

7. Such an approach—with separate academic courses for each career path—requires sufficient numbers of students in each career path and is therefore difficult to achieve in a comparatively small high school like Landon.

8. The CityWorks programs at Rindge School of Technical Arts in Cambridge, Massachusetts, is a partial example of a school with a focus on urban problems. Freshmen and sophomores spend five and three periods, respectively, in programs of integrated studies investigating the industries, neighborhoods, systems, and resources that make up an urban community, using Cambridge as a "textbook."

7

Urban Career Magnet High Schools

RUTH H. KATZ
LOLA JEFFRIES JACKSON
KATHY REEVES
CHARLES S. BENSON

Effective *magnet high schools,* sometimes known as *career oriented high schools* or *occupational theme high schools,* help students learn and succeed by emphasizing specialized interests and skills and focusing courses around a career or thematic area. Magnet schools generally have the dual mission of preparing students for college and for specific occupational fields. These schools therefore are not narrowly vocational, nor do they focus exclusively on the college prep curriculum; they provide the classical curriculum, along with an industry-wide perspective on occupations. Career magnets also: offer highly specialized, occupationally specific, up-to-date courses that can be more rigorous than the high school norm; employ industry-knowledgeable faculty and advisors; and augment school-based learning with a range of industry-related outreach activities. Students in successful magnet programs have a clearer understanding of the world of work and its many components. They are skilled at working in teams and comfortable interacting with a wide range of individuals. Students from magnet schools, to a greater extent than many of their comprehensive school peers, are able to connect high school education to future aspirations, and to understand *why* learning is important.

In many respects, magnet schools foster an environment in which the integration of academic and vocational studies can occur. The focus or theme of the school provides a base for blended curricula, and the resources (equipment, knowledge of a subject or career area, industry advisory boards) to aid in integration are more plentiful at magnet schools than at comprehensive schools. In addition, the interest level in developing and implementing an integrated course of study can be high among faculty: The students they serve have selected to attend the magnet school because of the theme area, and making the most of that theme would seem a natural means of engaging students in learning.

In large, urban school districts, magnet schools have grown in popularity over the past 20 years and now enroll an average of 20% of high school students in these districts (Blank, 1989). Many school districts have seen magnet schools as an effective tool for facilitating voluntary desegregation, and have thus encouraged their development. In examining urban career magnet schools, then, it is important to examine the *urban* along with the *magnet*. Major metropolitan school districts face a host of challenges, generally serving large numbers of disadvantaged students, low-income families, and a multiethnic population. They are frustrated by diminishing resources and plagued by high drop-out rates, low daily attendance, and in-school violence. That urban magnet schools are successful despite the context within which they operate attests even more strongly to what they do right—the sense of purpose to education they provide for their students. The pervasive character of the occupational focus in these schools enables students to create a context for theoretical constructs on their own, both individually and in their cooperative learning groups. This understanding of why they are learning helps students remain engaged in what they are learning. Even where the integration of academic and vocational education, as typically defined in the literature, is absent from these programs, another systemic integration occurs nonetheless. We describe this as *mission integration.*

Career magnets offer educational experiences similar to the generic practices anticipated to be expanded under the federal School to Work Opportunities Act of 1994. Existing examples of these school-to-work programs have been evaluated by the Manpower Demonstration Research Corporation (MDRC). MDRC (Pauly, Kopp, & Haimson, 1994) reported that school-to-work programs appear to provide students with higher qualities of the educational experience. For example, the programs are said to induce students to take more math, science, and technical subjects than do their peers in conventional school and college settings. These programs serve a diverse student population, ranging from the academically motivated to the disadvantaged and low-achieving. Teachers reported that many disadvantaged and low-achieving students learned more successfully in school-to-work programs than they had previously (Pauly, Kopp, & Haimson, 1994).

In 1989, researchers from the National Center for Research in Vocational Education (NCRVE) visited exemplary urban, career-oriented high schools in several large cities and produced a report documenting the factors that made the schools successful (Mitchell et al., 1989). At the time of that report, NCRVE had not yet examined the integration of academic and vocational studies in depth. The current direction of research on integration by the authors of this chapter suggests that integrated programs have pedagogical strengths not found in didactic and intellectually isolated programs of instruction. Because we believed career magnets might be natural settings for integration, we felt it was important to revisit some of these schools. Thus, the main focus of this chapter is an examination of the nature of integration found in three of the New York City career magnet schools: Aviation High School, the High School of Fashion Industries, and the Manhattan Center High School for Science and Mathematics. This chapter also profiles a specialized electronics tech prep program at George Westinghouse Vocational Technical High School, a school not included in the 1989 report.

In this chapter we do not offer rigorous quantitative evaluations of student outcomes, comparing results for students in New York City's magnet schools with results for New York City's zoned (or comprehensive) secondary schools. This has been done in detail in other studies conducted by NCRVE, and the results are generally positive (Crain, Heebner, Si, Jordan, & Kiefer, 1992). However, all of the programs we profile share certain general measures of success. Attendance is high, dropout is low, and discipline problems are rarer than in New York's comprehensive schools. Based on numbers of students applying to the schools, all of these programs are becoming more and more popular with students and parents. All of them are attracting a large number of students whose sisters or brothers attended the school in the past. Based on our observations, we believe the special focus of each of these schools, and the strong programs each has created around that focus, are largely responsible for their successes.

The survival of these specialized programs constitutes the second focus of this chapter. Career magnet schools are different from most urban high schools, and they can be classified as innovations. The life span of most educational innovations is notoriously short. Worse than that, the career magnets are caught foursquare between two strong opposing forces: the increased mandates of the State of New York Board of Regents and the budget cuts in the New York City Public Schools. How the career magnets are coping with these opposing forces of mandates on one side and budget cuts on the other is a central focus of this chapter. Embedded in this focus is a general concern about the future prospects of this group of exemplary institutions.

CAREER MAGNET PROFILES

High schools in New York City are classified as Academic/Comprehensive Schools, Vocational Schools, or Alternative Schools. Academic/Comprehensive Schools are divided into Zoned Schools (which hold seats for all students based on where they live), Specialized High Schools (which select students on the basis of examination scores), and Educational Options Schools (which provide instruction in specific career areas and accept students on the basis of a range of selection criteria). Prior to entering high school in the ninth or tenth grade, students citywide are required to fill out an application form listing their choices of school (whether it is their neighborhood Zoned School or any other school in the system) in order of preference. Thus, it is just as easy for students to apply to a Specialized School as to stay at their home school. The schools we profile all engage in a range of recruitment activities aimed at junior high students. Admission procedures vary from school to school in this study, but none accepts students on the basis of academic test scores.

It is important to note that the programs we describe, while sharing commonalties, are not all of one design. The definition of magnet programs is broad, and encompasses a range of models, from that of a program within a school (not dissimilar to the academy model) to that of an entire school, varying from a wide to a narrow thematic focus. Three of the schools we profile (Aviation High School, the High School of Fashion Industries, and the Manhattan Center High School for Science and Mathematics) are classified as Educational Options Schools by the New York City Unified School District. Both the High School of Fashion Industries and Aviation High School are whole schools organized around and dominated by an occupational focus area. The focus of study at the Manhattan Center High School for Science and Mathematics is far broader than the occupational themes of the other magnet programs. All students in this school pursue a college preparatory course of study with emphasis on math, science, and technology. While more traditionally academic than the other schools described here, Manhattan Center's program also provides a focus, orients electives, and integrates curriculum to provide a context for teaching and learning for its students. George Westinghouse Vocational Technical High School is classified by the city as a Vocational School, and offers multiple occupational programs in a more traditional vocational school setting. However, its innovative electronics program shares many commonalities—among them a career-area focus and the implementation of an integrated course of study—with the other programs we profile, and fits the characteristics of a magnet program within a school. Each of these approaches is successful because each is able to provide curriculum and an environment that helps students aspire to higher goals. The schools create for students a sense of belonging and an understanding of the purpose of education.

AVIATION HIGH SCHOOL

At Aviation High School, students can specialize in aviation mechanics and engineering and graduate with a Federal Aviation Administration (FAA) license in airframe maintenance, in power plant maintenance, and/or a Federal Communications Commission (FCC) license in Avionics—in addition to their high school diploma. Unlike Regents examination measures, which impose academic standards, these licenses are external measures that are occupational and related to industry skills standards. Aviation High School prepares students for careers in aviation and related technical areas, as well as for college. It boasts a bustling hanger full of small planes and a range of highly specialized shops, including a propeller shop and a jet engine shop. An electronics course focuses on pre-avionics and a history class includes the history of flight. The school does not teach students to fly planes, although many are currently learning to do so on their own, and others plan to learn to fly in the future.

Aviation High is a secondary school in which approximately half of the curriculum is regulated by industry skills standards (FAA and FCC). The other half is regulated by the college prep program. This leaves little room for electives, but there are still a few, such as a course in law. Not having a wide choice of electives may be a loss, but in our view the benefits of focusing on mastery of academic- and aviation-related competencies far outweigh the costs for the great majority of students. Aviation High treats student time as if it has value. Whereas a large number of community colleges offer FAA licenses in airframe and power plant maintenance after 14 years of formal education, Aviation High qualifies its graduates for the license in the twelfth year. At the same time, completing the college prep sequence offers students options over the whole field of occupations based on the baccalaureate. We note that the use of industry skills standards in both the design and evaluation of educational programs is attracting attention across the country. Aviation High is a model with which to examine the process of relating program content to industry skills standards.

A longer than usual school day is necessary to incorporate Regents as well as major requirements. This results in a high attrition rate among students in their first year. Those willing to persevere know that they are gaining a great deal from their specialized high school education. The licenses they can obtain through their high school work are costly to acquire outside school. The skills they develop within their course of study prepare them for entry-level jobs that pay a great deal more than jobs in the clerical or service sector. However, the current reality in the aviation industry, and in New York State in particular, is that these jobs are more and more difficult to obtain. There are currently no summer work programs or internships in aviation-related jobs available to students, and—with the exception of special opportunities available for females in these traditionally male fields—jobs for new high school graduates are few and far between.

The student population at Aviation High is 58.1% Hispanic, 15.7% African American, 13.8% white, and 11.9% Asian. About 5% of the student body is female—a percentage that has remained constant over the past 5 years. Although female students are outnumbered by their male counterparts, they are active participants in school activities. They hold leadership positions in school clubs and teams and they are strong advocates for the school. In the 1993-94 school year, a recent female Aviation High graduate joined the staff as a Substitute Vocational Assistant (SVA), and a second female SVA will join the staff in 1994-95. SVAs serve as teaching assistants while attending college, and are certified as vocational teachers at the end of 5 years in that position.

Aviation High School has an active alumni association, as well as an advisory commission, which help the school and its students in myriad ways. They provide career counseling and host special career days. They also offer job shadowing opportunities to Aviation staff to help them stay up-to-date with changes in the industry. The advisory commission has played a key role in compensating for school district cuts in staff development resources, most recently hosting a staff development day at Tower Air. Nearly one third of the teachers at Aviation are also graduates of the school, a fact that administrators, teachers, and students convey with evident pride. Understandably, students feel a great deal of connection to these teachers, and several, in discussing their own future plans, stated a desire to return to Aviation High as teachers—either immediately or following a career in the aviation industry.

The active involvement of industry advisors, alumni, and teachers who were once students enhances the students' sense of connectedness to the school, and their ability to link what they are learning in school with the world of work. Students appear motivated to learn at this school—and not just in aviation-specific classes. The principal feels that her students understand the importance of being well educated about their career plans, as well as their need to keep a range of future options open.

THE HIGH SCHOOL OF FASHION INDUSTRIES

The High School of Fashion Industries prepares students for careers in fashion design, costume design, fashion art (including jewelry design, fashion graphics and illustration, and textile and interior design), and fashion business (fashion merchandising and business and visual merchandising and display). In addition, the school offers advanced placement and Regents-level academic courses, as well as a full range of English as Second Language (ESL) classes. Although many Fashion High graduates continue their education at the Fashion Institute of Technology (FIT), Parsons, and similar fashion and art schools, others go on to more traditional 4-year colleges or to non-fashion-related careers. Currently, 89% of Fashion High students continue their education in 2- or 4-year postsecondary programs. This number is steadily increasing. Jobs in the fashion industry are not as plentiful as they once were, and students can no longer expect to enter the fashion trade immediately after graduation from high school. Accordingly, administrators and teachers stress the importance of preparing students for a range of career options, as well as the importance of higher education.

Fashion High is located in New York's garment district, in close proximity to all aspects of the industry with which the students are involved. Visits to designers, theaters, stores and store window displays are common, as are visits to the school by the professionals involved in all of these enterprises. The school has excellent connections with designers and retailers in the fashion trade, many of whom play active roles as advisors and mentors to Fashion High students. The Liz Claiborne Foundation has adopted the school, providing scholarship money, materials, and sponsorship of special courses (such as a course entitled The Roots of American Design). Each year a large number of fashion industry professionals participate in a career day exclusively for Fashion High students, held at the school. In the past a local jewelry company adopted the jewelry-making class, and sponsored a design competition. Winners received college scholarships and savings bonds. The industry contributes materials and equipment to support the school's nationally recognized year-end fashion show, which highlights student designs and creations modeled by Fashion High students.

In the spring of 1989, Fashion High began an adopt-a-student program with the goals of encouraging at-risk students to stay in school and of strengthening business, academic, and social skills to help them succeed after graduation. Currently, nearly 60 students are matched with more than 40 mentors from fashion and related industries. Students are matched with mentors during the ninth or tenth grade in a partnership that lasts through graduation, and sometimes beyond. Mentors maintain weekly contact with students and meet with them in a structured work environment at least once every six weeks. The program also encourages mentors to include their adopted students in social and cultural activities.

Of the students at Fashion High, 89% are female. The school is approximately 51% Hispanic, 35% African American, 10% Asian, and 4% White; 15% of the students are considered limited-English-proficient. The school's entering students tend to be weaker in reading and math skills than the city average. However, by the end of their junior year, 90% of the students meet or exceed the city average in these subject areas. The students we met had a great deal of self-confidence and a strong sense of purpose.

Teachers and administrators at Fashion High emphasize the commitment and professionalism they demand of their students. Many teachers have worked in the fashion industry and require the same high standards that the students would experience in the workplace. In the shops we observed, students worked in groups or independently, all with a great

sense of purpose. Although each student's fashion creations are highly individualized, a good deal of classwork—in both occupational and academic
classes—takes place in cooperative work settings. Students say they learn
to appreciate and make the most of each individual's special talents through
their work in such groups. Through the groups, barriers of race and appearance are also broken down and replaced by recognition of shared interest.

Fashion High has not implemented a formal program integrating academic and vocational education. However, we observed many innovative
examples of integration within individual classrooms at Fashion High. In
a class on window display, a teacher shared with us a photo album documenting a project undertaken the previous winter. Students read Dickens'
"A Christmas Carol," made presentations and reports, and came to agreement about the six most pivotal scenes in the story. They designed window
displays to convey the scenes in the story, created the displays from their
designs, and installed the displays in the school windows.

THE MANHATTAN CENTER HIGH SCHOOL FOR SCIENCE AND MATHEMATICS

The importance of education is clearly a motivating factor for students at The
Manhattan Center High School for Science and Mathematics. Manhattan
Center High School focuses on rigorous academics and on preparing its students for 4-year colleges. The school, which is located in East Harlem, offers
many advanced placement and enrichment courses and special programs
and opportunities that enable the vast majority of its students—many of
whom are from Harlem—to gain admission to 4-year colleges.

The population of the Manhattan Center High School is roughly 50%
African American, 49% Hispanic, and 1% other. There are equal numbers
of male and female students and staff are eager to point to the high representation of females in upper level math and science classes. The school is
part of a national network of schools receiving generous support from the
General Electric Foundation. This, in combination with an aggressive (and
highly successful) fund- and resource-raising campaign organized by the
principal, has helped to compensate for the continuing cutbacks in school
district funds, and enabled students at the school to participate in a wide
range of special programs and opportunities. One of the newest projects is
a collaboration with Mount Sinai Medical Center, in which students, after
completing biology and medical lab science classes during their sophomore year, and a special after-school molecular biology course during their
junior year, participate in a summer of medical research at Mount Sinai,
paired with second-year medical student mentors. One goal of this program is for Manhattan Center students, after completing college, to return
to Mount Sinai as medical students.

In another innovative program, Project MUST (an acronym for "mentoring urban students for teaching tomorrow's community leaders"), doctoral candidates at New York University work twice a week with 25 Manhattan Center juniors teaching communication and leadership skills. In turn, each junior serves as a mentor to three junior high students, meets with them twice a week after school, and teaches lessons he or she has organized and developed. The juniors earn college credit and learn a great deal about teaching and responsibility through their participation in this program.

Special endeavors, such as a greenhouse project based in Central Park and the use of computers across the curriculum, integrate theory and practice. Other courses, such as electronics, photography, and environmental studies, also combine academic learning with hands-on applications. Although the school is not involved in any formal academic-vocational integration, a focus and context for learning, very similar to that which is found in the other schools we profile, exists at Manhattan Center as well. Manhattan Center emphasizes high-level academics and preparing students for 4-year college. By focusing on math and science career opportunities, it enables its students to connect classroom learning to future goals in a concrete way. The school stresses a rigorous academic curriculum that is supplemented by many innovative approaches, such as extensive student research projects in conjunction with professional practitioners in their work sites and the inclusion of many advanced science and math courses, several of which are conducted in college classrooms. Attendance, graduation, and college acceptance rates (all above 90%) indicate that this multifaceted and focused approach to preparing students for careers in math and science is successful.

GEORGE WESTINGHOUSE VOCATIONAL TECHNICAL HIGH SCHOOL

Science and math are also key to the courses of study (such as electronics, optometry, and communications) students may select at George Westinghouse Vocational Technical High School, but as the school's name suggests, students who apply and are selected to attend this school are drawn to its vocational and technical careers focus. Located in Brooklyn, Westinghouse is not classified by the city as a magnet school and, in some respects, is very different from the other schools profiled in this chapter. However, we include it here because it has developed a strong tech prep program with neighboring New York City Technical College (NYCTC), and the cadre of students we observed in the tech prep electronics program share many attributes with their counterparts enrolled in magnet school programs.

The student population at Westinghouse is 76% African American, 21% Hispanic, 2% Asian, and 1% other. Although the student body is currently 75% male, an ambitious program to increase the number of female students in the school and to improve their performance in areas such as science and electronics has recently been launched. Unlike the other schools profiled here, which draw students from all boroughs of the city, 85% of Westinghouse students live in Brooklyn. Although the student population is actually smaller than in most of the other schools we visited, the school *felt* bigger, and more alienating. Unlike the three Educational Options schools we visited, where security guards are present but unobtrusive, at Westinghouse guards with metal detectors monitor the entrances to the school. This school is more typical of the New York City public schools as a whole, where the incidence of crime and violence is high ("Violence in the Schools: A Search for Safety," 1993). Classrooms are orderly, but in the hallways we saw few of the social interchanges between adults and students that were a common occurrence at the other schools we visited.

Given the tough obstacles faced by the school, its progress in the development of an integrated electronics curriculum, articulated with NYCTC, is all the more impressive. Westinghouse and NYCTC began a tech prep partnership in 1991 and were selected to participate in NCRVE's Urban Schools Network (30 sites nationwide actively developing programs of integration and tech prep through a team-based approach to school reform) in 1992.

The tech prep students, who begin their specialized course of study in the eleventh grade, are block-scheduled so that they can easily move as a cohort from class to class. Similar to the academy model of integration, this approach is a common one in magnet programs within schools. Teachers released from some of their traditional assignments are able to observe one another and to engage in team teaching across vocational and academic subjects. Many of the tech prep students are involved in Total Quality Management (TQM) and leadership classes, in summer work experience, and in coop work experience programs. There is a special focus to their school work and clear connections to postsecondary and career opportunities. High school tech prep students attend classes on the nearby New York City Technical College campus, and educators from each institution are familiar with one another's classes, curricula, and students.

Like academies and other magnet schools, Westinghouse's electronics program provides opportunities for teachers to collaborate and to integrate curricula. Over the past school year, a math teacher has worked with the technology, drafting, and electronics teachers to develop specialized applied math materials to be used in the occupational classes. Students in a communications class work cooperatively, combining academics and technical skills, to create and develop video productions. A new ham radio and weather station has been installed in the school, and will be connected with communications and English classes. And the development of a model city project—incorporating English, social studies, economics, and physics—will involve all electronics students schoolwide. At the time of our visit to Westinghouse, students were creating CADD designs for a model city, and student planning teams were in the process of writing formal proposals to present to a hypothetical planning board. Later, scale models will be created and technology students will design and develop transportation and communications networks for the city. Business and industry advisors will participate in the project, which communications students will videotape from start to finish.

Discipline problems are fewer and motivation is higher among those students at Westinghouse who are involved in the tech prep electronics program. The program provides students with a focus and teaching and learning techniques emphasize cooperation. These elements, combined with outreach activities and connections to the technical college and business world, are similar to what we saw at the other magnet schools. Westinghouse's tech prep students share a special "home" within their school, a focused course of study, connections to the world beyond high school, and a staff working together to make innovative projects succeed.

CONNECTIONS TO SUCCESS

Are these schools successful because they admit superior students? Or do they manage to be successful with students who are typical of New York City's school population? Only three of the city's high schools (none of which is profiled here) are still allowed to screen applicants through traditional testing. Westinghouse High School fills 50% of its incoming classes through a citywide lottery, conducted by Educational Testing Service. Fashion High students are accepted on the basis of an art exam, and Aviation and the Manhattan Center admit on the basis of course marks and attendance records. All these schools perceive their average student as at or below national grade level at the point of admission. We conclude that the career magnets for the most part serve the broad middle level of New York City's secondary school cohorts: The schools do not enroll many of the very brightest students, nor many of the very lowest performers, but pretty much everybody else. At the very least, one can say that the schools' rate of success is not guaranteed by the caliber of students they admit.

The schools profiled in this chapter are very different from one another, yet they share many common characteristics. Although the neighborhoods that house them are formidable in many ways, once inside the school building there is a feeling of safety, warmth, and orderliness. Resources are few, and bulletin boards and other displays are worn and faded. Desks and blackboards are old and in dire need of replacement. However, the school classrooms and hallways are clean, devoid of trash, and without graffiti. Students are full of purpose and the schools buzz with a positive energy.

We found a great sense of community or "family" in each of these schools. At both Aviation High and Fashion High, when students were asked to describe their school their first response was "It's like a family here." Teachers or administrators walking through the hallways between classes greet and are greeted by students, many of whom they know by name. Navigating the crowded hallways of Aviation High School, the principal frequently paused to commend a student on a recent success—in academics, sports, or extracurricular activities—and to introduce students to visitors. Each student was recognized for his or her accomplishments and made to feel special. In all of the schools, these hallway encounters seemed to be much more than perfunctory; students were anxious to share news with adults and adults were genuinely interested in what the students had to say.

Students clearly feel a connection with fellow students, with staff, and with the essence of the school itself. Students are drawn to one another because of shared interests. Cooperative work teams and the need for teamwork in occupational classes reinforces these connections. Many students, commenting on what they liked about their school, mentioned working and becoming friends with people they never would have approached in their home neighborhoods or middle schools. In some instances, initial connections were made by a teacher's assignment to work groups but, in the course of working together, natural connections developed. Students seemed amazed at how their racial, ethnic, and gender stereotypes diminished in this environment. Both girls at Aviation High School and boys at Fashion High were accepted as peers because of their talents and interest in their work. Students told us that racial tension was rare because here "who you are" is defined by "what you do." This response reinforced reports on school safety that rank Aviation and Fashion among the safest schools citywide ("Violence and the Schools," 1993).

Cooperative learning was prevalent in the schools we visited and was not confined to vocational classes. In an English class at Fashion High, students worked in groups on a project entitled "Tech Prep Meets Macbeth." One assignment required each group to assume the role of a small repertory theater company that had received a grant from the New York State Council on the Arts to mount a production of the play. Their future viability would depend on their ability to stage a production that would attract large audiences, including audiences of students and wealthy donors. Students were provided with details, such as the dimensions of the stage, lobby, and concession area, as well as information on ticket price restrictions, and were assigned the task of developing marketing plans, special events, creative casting and other strategies to achieve their goals. Their ideas (including an exhibit of historical costumes, a reception featuring roving witches, and excerpts from modern-language versions of the play) all evidenced an understanding of the plot, characters, and details of the play.

At Aviation High, the teacher in a law class divided her students into six groups, each group making a presentation to the "judge" and each presentation being graded, with justification for the assigned mark, by the other five. In the Westinghouse school television studio, students worked in teams, as they did on all aspects of their model city program (described in the previous section). Students in several of the schools we visited said that cooperative work projects were common in their academic classes and that this was markedly different from their elementary and middle school experiences. Perhaps the prevalence of cooperative learning projects in these schools is in part due to the success of such projects in occupational labs (such as the jet engine lab at Aviation High), where cooperative efforts are a necessity. Students enjoyed working in teams and said they learned to value each team member's special skills and contributions. Friendly competition between groups motivated many of the students. In the groups we observed, students were actively engaged in their assignments.

In each of the three schools with a specific career focus (Aviation, Fashion, and the Electronics program at Westinghouse) we met students who did not plan to pursue careers in these occupational areas. Students in the programs we visited professed interest in law, criminal justice, psychology, and liberal arts. None of these students seemed sorry they had participated in the focus program, however. They felt positively about the teachers, administrators, alumni, and mentors who had assisted them in their high school years. Many students told us that the specialized education they had received would provide them with skills they could "fall back on" as they worked their way through college. The level of self-confidence in the students with whom we spoke was impressive. The students felt they had merit because of the skills they had acquired, the special role they played in the group work they did in school, and because the adults in the school and the adult advisors to the school made them feel special. Teachers, administrators, and students in all of these programs mentioned the special bond that develops between teachers and students in the specialized area, where the program structure enables them to spend several years working together and fosters the building of relationships.

All of the programs we profile are supported by advisory committees and business and industry programs. Each of them makes use of community resources and person-power, and does not rely solely on grants or financial support. Programs to connect students to higher education, to jobs, and to job readiness are in place. Resources to help at-risk students are well established. To compensate for a dearth of parental and family involvement (a common concern of urban schools) these schools have developed "family" ties with community partners, as well as a sense of family within the walls of the schools.

In all of the schools we visited we met energetic and caring teachers and administrators who compensated for budget and resource cutbacks by giving more and more of themselves. Students told us that teachers helped with schoolwork before and after school. At Fashion High, a computer design classroom was open to students whenever classes were not in session, and the room was always full of students at work. Westinghouse teachers visited New York City Technical College classrooms and labs after the high school day had ended, to learn more about college requirements and facilitate the transition to college for their students. Teachers at Aviation High, where there was a shortage of funds to enable teachers to retrain on new technology, made up for this loss by spending their evening hours and free time to "get up to speed." Teachers at Manhattan Center sometimes stayed at school until 9 p.m., and some held extra tutoring sessions in their homes. In every program, teachers and administrators had taken on formal or informal roles as grant writers. That these schools can still be considered exemplary, despite budget cuts and diminishing resources, is due in large part to faculty who are willing and able to go the extra mile for their students and their programs.

INTEGRATION IN THE CAREER MAGNETS: IMPLEMENTATION PROBLEMS

Magnet schools offer the perfect setting in which the integration of academic and vocational education can occur, yet in the schools we visited in New York City, and from what we have learned of magnet schools elsewhere, integrated courses are the exception and not the rule. Where we found coursewide integration taking place, it was due to the efforts of a teacher or small cadre of teachers and not because of any comprehensive strategy or philosophy of the school. There are many reasons for the lack of more wide-scale implementation. In New York City, as in too many school districts around the country, a key barrier to the development and implementation of courses integrating academic and vocational education is a combination of diminishing resources and increasing academic graduation requirements.

More and more stringent budget cuts in the New York City schools have been a fact of life over the past decade, and a 13% cut has been sustained over the past 3 years. The impact of these cuts on programs, personnel, and students has been far-reaching. Special programs, such as after-school tutorials and enrichment classes, have disappeared. In one of the schools we visited, juniors and seniors leave school early because there are no elective classes available to them. In every school, teacher and counselor positions have been eliminated and staff development has been reduced to one day per semester. Equipment is badly in need of modernization and resources are sparse. In most cases the resources—for example, staff development time, curriculum development time, time for common planning, curriculum materials, and so forth—necessary for the development of integrated courses and curricula are simply not available. In addition, teachers are stretched thin—teaching more students with fewer free periods in a day, and in many instances making up for lost services by providing informal assistance to students before school, after school, and during lunch hours. In such an environment, maintenance, not innovation, is the operational mode.

Coupled with these resource cuts have been changes in graduation requirements imposed by New York State and New York City. In 1984 the New York Board of Regents formally adopted the Regents Action Plan to improve elementary and secondary education results in New York (The University of the State of New York, 1989). This plan laid the groundwork for a series of comprehensive changes in the education requirements for all students in New York State. Current Regents Requirements for high school graduation are: English—4 units; Social Studies—4 units; Math—3 units; Science—2 units; Introduction to Humanities (including second language)—2 units; Health and Physical Education—1/2 unit. Each unit equals two terms of work. To obtain a high school diploma, a student must accumulate at least 20 units of credit. All students must also take the required Regents competency tests and achieve a minimum passing score of 65% in reading, writing, mathematics, science, global history, and U.S. history.

Diplomas may be granted with a Regents endorsement to students who meet all the above requirements and who also complete 3 units of a second language (this requirement is waived for students with occupational education majors) and who pass the New York State Regents exams in English, Global Studies, American History and Government, Second Language, Math (two Regents exams), Science (two Regents exams), and subjects selected in areas of concentration (New York City Public Schools, 1993–94). Meeting sequence requirements for Regents endorsement may necessitate students completing more than 20 units. Requirements for art, music, and occupational education vary depending on the subject area, but the minimum requirement is 3 units. For occupational education students, the minimum may be 5 units and require additional "hands on" experience in a vocational shop or supervised clinic. Students with occupational majors are required to pass a proficiency exam.

New York City schools have added additional requirements for students entering the ninth grade in September 1994. They will be required to take 2 units of science (one of which is a laboratory course). Students entering ninth grade in 1995 will be required to take 3 units of science, two of which are laboratory courses (New York City Public Schools, 1992–93). This additional requirement could have a devastating effect on students choosing occupational education.

In order to prepare students for the Regents Exams, courses must cover very specific topics in very specific detail. This leaves teachers little leeway for developing innovative ways of presenting material. Combined with budget cuts (which have in some cases reduced a 9-period day to a 7-period day) the increased requirements also greatly reduce the number of occupational or integrated classes a student may take—the very courses that set the magnet schools apart. At Fashion High, students who 5 years ago would have taken 22 credits in their vocational major now graduate with 14 of these credits. Labs and shops for first-year students have been reduced by half. Students at Aviation High School attend summer school, put in longer than normal school days, and often return to the school for a fifth year in order to obtain their licenses and meet the city's graduation requirements.

Magnet schools attempt to balance academic and vocational content, but there is precious little room within this system and the schedule it imposes for courses that integrate academic and vocational studies. Ironically, academic teachers in several schools find that cutbacks in specialty courses affect the students in the academic classrooms as well. In several schools, teachers mentioned that math skills such as measuring, which students once learned in context in their lab classes, now require significantly more learning time in math classrooms. The stringent Global Studies curriculum has forced the elimination of Fashion High's focus on historical dress within a social studies class.

On the whole, students appear to be succeeding in the magnet programs despite the changes and cutbacks—at least for now. Compared with students in other high schools, students in magnet schools appear to have a clearer sense of purpose about school and a belief that they *need* to learn in order to succeed in future careers (Heebner, Crain, Kiefer, & Si, 1992). Students in a plant biology class at Aviation High, and others studying *Beowulf* in English, were engaged and focused. In addition, these students were willing to put in long days (or, in the case of Aviation students, a fifth year of study, in order to attain an additional license) in order to augment the district's required classes with the specialty courses they need for their career major. But continued cutbacks, and continued replacement of specialty classes with standardized district requirements, cannot help but make these specialized schools less special, and thus diminish their impact.

Almost all of the schools we visited supplement their curriculum with the help of special grants, private funding, and courses offered after school. All of the arts courses offered at the Manhattan Center are funded through private sources, as is Fashion High's Roots of American Design course. Aviation High funds its after-school tutorial program with the help of special grant money from the Superintendent, and many special activities for Westinghouse students are supported by New York City Technical College. Administrators and teachers have been innovative in making up for cutbacks in staff and in staff development monies. Many of the schools rely on their advisory boards for help with industry-specific staff development. Aviation High's

Advisory Commission sponsored a staff training day at Tower Air. The principal at Fashion High has eliminated monthly, all-staff meetings and replaced them with a series of seminars for all interested faculty focusing on teacher-initiated, staff development topics. At The Manhattan Center, the principal makes use of grants and special funds to enable teachers to attend summer workshops and receive specialized training. The support of business and industry, and the creative solutions found by teachers and administrators, are both to be commended. But these activities should augment a strong, district-supported program, *not* compensate for what is lacking in such a program.

We would be remiss to suggest that if funding and policy allowed, integration would magically become systemic at these magnet schools. Other factors have and would continue to impede such efforts. Faculty resistance to change was evident to some degree in all of these schools (although if the system encouraged innovation, one has the sense that these barriers could be more easily overcome). In some instances, integration took place in vocational courses, but academic teachers insisted they keep their courses "pure." Administrators at one school told us they didn't believe in "experimental" courses, and an academic teacher at another school told us she would quit before she would alter the content and delivery of her classes. This same teacher had worked with shop teachers to infuse English into their classes, however, and was willing to continue this effort.

A final impediment to integration is the low level of academic skills of incoming students and the need for remediation. For example, in a ninth grade math class at Aviation High, students put their homework problems on the board and showed clear mastery of the rules for reducing complicated ratios of exponents. The day's lesson was on solving equations with decimals. Again, the students had the rules for solving equations down pat. Yet, the class as a whole had difficulty with simple computation: adding, subtracting, and so forth. The fact that the students could deal with the logic of algebra but could not compute was confirmed in a subsequent conversation with the instructor. In effect, he said he was expected to teach Algebra I *and* to repair the deficiencies in their earlier mathematical training, all in the ninth grade. In every school we visited, teachers mentioned the lack of academic preparedness of incoming students. In three of the four schools we visited, teachers gave specific examples of ninth grade students who had to be taught how to read a ruler! Clearly, high-end integration cannot occur when students are unprepared to tackle the subjects such integration is designed to unite.

Perhaps there is less need for formal programs integrating academic and vocational education in magnet schools because a kind of natural integration already occurs within them. The focus of the magnet school provides a unifying theme for all the work in which students are engaged, and a context in which students, singly or in groups, can make their own translations of theory into application. In this environment, students more read-ily make connections among subjects, as they more readily make interest-based connections with one another. They understand instinctively the applications of theoretical constructs in the world of work. In these respects, even without relying on the formal coursework (on the academic side) to integrate academic and vocational education, the magnet schools we vis-ited do achieve integration's goals. We call this mission integration, that is, integration fostered simply because the school's mission provides links between theory and context. By way of contrast, in a school with no occu-pational focus—a general comprehensive school, perhaps—students may need *written course integration* to gain the depth of understanding that con-textualized teaching/learning offers.

AREAS OF CONCERN

We must now sound a few notes of caution about magnet school programs in general. First, the term magnet school has been overused, and merely labeling a school *the math magnet* or *the communications high school* will not magically cause a special program to emerge. Nor will schools that add a specialized course or two to a traditional 4-year curriculum be transformed into successful magnet programs. The schools and educational approach-es we have discussed here are the product of a great deal of hard work by the planners who created them and by the educators who ensure that their integrity and focus are maintained. The schools provide students with high-ly specialized, occupationally specific courses not found in any other school in the district, as well as with support structures (career and college coun-seling, internship and job opportunities, and mentoring programs) specif-ically connected to that occupational area. They do not limit students' options to a specific area of study, but do provide a sound educational back-ground for students who plan to continue their education, and/or to pur-sue a range of careers, by teaching students how to learn, how to work, and how to connect the two.

Specialized magnet schools also are more expensive to run than are comprehensive high schools. They require specialized equipment and spe-cialized labs in which to house the equipment. New technology renders old equipment quickly obsolete, and yesterday's equipment cannot be effec-tive in training today's students for tomorrow's jobs. Likewise, teachers need regular retraining in their specialized fields. In addition, the increased New York State Regents examinations and New York City graduation requirements, combined with the need for students to be occupationally skilled for the global economy, have led administrators, teachers, and stu-dents in magnet school programs to call for flexibility in the current school day. To accommodate education and reform initiatives, the school day may need to be lengthened. We believe, for example, that schools such as the ones we profile should be open during evening hours and on weekends, and that teachers should be provided with extra time to work together on joint curriculum, and should be paid for their efforts.

When school district cutbacks reduce the amount of money allocated to specialty schools, and when district policies force the reduction of courses that make these schools special, the effectiveness of the schools will diminish. To a large extent, the extra efforts of teachers, administrators, business partners, and advisory boards have kept this from happening thus far in the schools we have profiled. But such Herculean efforts cannot continue indefinitely, nor should the teachers, administrators, and advisors be expected to devote so much of their energy to such endeavors.

Another concern is the negative perception in our society of an occupational focus at the high school level—something that many feel goes against the grain of American culture. As a recent policy statement notes:

> Skepticism regarding the value of job-specific training at the high school level should not be ignored, given the slim evidence that participants benefit in any significant way....The career interests of youths ... are exceedingly volatile, and occupational mobility rates in the United States are extremely high. The "practical" notion of training students for a trade is often shortsighted in the context of an individual's entire working life. (Levitan & Gallo, 1993)

This statement represents a common position. In response, we note that, first of all, the occupational training offered in career magnets is not necessarily narrowly job-specific. In terms of the definitions used in the 1990 Amendments to the Carl D. Perkins Act, students learn "all aspects of the industry they are preparing to enter." Secondly, some students do find the occupational focus of a career magnet so distasteful that they seek transfer to another high school. This is readily permitted, and since these students have been studying a full range of academic subjects, the change of school does not alter their plans for graduation.

Thirdly, and most important, many students appear to appreciate and value an occupational focus, even when they know they will eventually look for different fields to enter. Being multiskilled is a useful objective. (Aviation High's graduates include medical doctors and lawyers; both sets of professionals report uses for the knowledge embodied in their FAA licenses.) Having an employable skill at the time of high school graduation can help pay for college or for other training. Just as learning one foreign language provides skill and confidence to better learn a second and a third, mastering one occupation appears to ease the way toward mastering others.

Our final concern is that broad policies that attempt to mandate what and how all students must learn are sometimes implemented at the expense of innovative programs with proven track records of success. Administrators and teachers with whom we spoke were angered and saddened by the City University of New York's College Prep Initiative, which is driving the academic college entrance requirements for all students in the New York Public Schools. The rigidity of these entrance requirements precludes innovative programming and all but ignores vocational studies. In the experience of the educators with whom we spoke, new initiatives always seem to come at the expense of vocational courses. Efforts at innovations such as integration are stifled by lack of resources, lack of common planning time, and increasing restrictions on what must be included in the curriculum. Given what we know about different learning styles, and given the successes (high student retention, high daily attendance, high graduation rates, low rates of violence, and few discipline problems) of these career-oriented programs, we feel such programs should be encouraged to do the job they do, and not be forced to fit into another—and possibly less effective—mold.

CONCLUSION

Magnet schools cost more than do comprehensive schools. But they seem to be more effective as well, producing higher than average numbers of graduates who are self-assured and productive citizens. Effective magnet schools provide a very special educational experience. They provide students with a focus, and with a sense of connection—to a larger community and to their own futures. They create an atmosphere that encourages students to explore their talents, interests, and abilities, teaches them how to work with and appreciate others, encourages them to take risks, and enables them to grow in self-confidence as they grow in intellectual ability. The schools we visited are not perfect, nor are they even the best that they could be. But in a time when we hear so much and so often about what is wrong with urban education, very much of what these schools are doing is very right.

A NOTE OF ACKNOWLEDGMENT

The authors wish to thank the administrators, teachers, and students at the high schools we profiled, the New York City Schools Office of Occupational Education, the New York City Schools Division of Strategic Planning/Research and Development, and the New York State Education Department, Division of Occupational Education, for their invaluable assistance in the preparation of this chapter.

8

SENIOR PROJECTS

Flexible Opportunities for Integration

MAYO TSUZUKI

The senior project provides a process for accomplishing three objectives of integrating academic and vocational education without being dependent on other major reforms, making it attractive to many schools. First, it can be required of and benefit *all* students, thereby addressing tracking issues. Second, it can develop the independent thinking, research, problem-solving and presentation skills that students need to pursue postsecondary education as well as high-skill job opportunities. Third, it changes the nature of learning and teaching relationships to increase student involvement and motivation and build bonds across curriculum areas both within schools and between the schools and their communities.

A key characteristic of senior projects in schools that have adopted them is flexibility within a structured framework. Typically, students are given a great deal of latitude to select topics, but all projects must have several required components. These components vary depending on the desired student outcomes of the project but emphasize the development of several kinds of communication and presentation skills. For example, projects often require a research paper, a physical product or demonstration, and an oral presentation. Other forms of projects may require a work experience component instead of, or in addition to, these. The project encourages students to develop and pursue their own interests in self-directed exploration, but one or two core subjects, which may be either academic or vocational-technical in nature, generally provide a conceptual anchor.

Self-directed exploration is intended to ensure the integration of knowledge and skills gained in different contexts. Typically, these contexts are a vocational or technical class and an academic class, but senior projects can also involve an academic subject combined with a job site internship, or a combination of all three—vocational-technical, academic, and work experience. Throughout the project, many adults—including teachers, workplace supervisors, and community members—are also integrated into the student's exploration-research experience, playing many roles, such as advisor, resource manager, coach, and evaluator.

This chapter will explore the senior project as an effective vehicle for integrating vocational-technical and academic education. It will also examine the difficulties involved in instituting senior projects. Since it can be such an individualized experience for students, and since it encourages learning and experimenting in nontraditional forms, it can become an administrative nightmare if school leadership is not fully committed to the idea. In order to thoroughly consider the issues, the experiences of three schools that successfully introduced the senior project as a graduation requirement will be presented. These include a vocational-technical high school, a comprehensive high school, and a high school that specializes in math, science, and technology education.

WHY THE SENIOR PROJECT?
GETTING COMMITMENT AND LEADERSHIP

The project approach to learning and its emphasis on integrating abstract concepts with real-life applications is not a new idea by any means. In his discussion, Kliebard (1986) traces the origins of the project method to 1908, when a Massachusetts agricultural school teacher combined home farm work experience with classroom learning to improve the effectiveness of the vocational agricultural curriculum. In the decades that followed, the project approach expanded beyond agricultural education to include the academic curriculum, in particular the science curriculum. Although it was hailed in some circles as a powerful, child-centered reform, constant and heated philosophical debates narrowed the discussion to an argument about the usefulness or inherent need for traditional subject divisions in the curriculum. The project method's emphasis on crossing these traditional lines is its strength, but this emphasis also kept it from ever achieving a permanent place in the public school curriculum.

Today, traditional education in most American comprehensive secondary schools has meant that students, teachers, and knowledge are strictly divided according to academic or vocational subjects, resulting in the feeling that there are two schools in one. One school produces students who go on to a 4-year university education and the other school produces students who, without the prerequisites to do so, are often unprepared for any other postsecondary future. In these schools, the senior project, and the way in which it integrates abstract with applied concepts, skills, learning, and knowledge, provides a desirable alternative. The multiple components of the project—a research paper, a physical product, and a presentation—provide a mechanism for the integration of academic and vocational teachers and concepts. In the case of projects that include work experience, the workplace supervisor assumes the role of the vocational teacher, overseeing another type of context in which the student applies abstract concepts in the real world.

In situations where the academic, vocational, and/or workplace contexts might have otherwise operated in isolation, the senior project illustrates that this is the least effective use of time, energy, and resources. The academic teacher cannot provide meaningful assistance on the research paper component of the project without any familiarity with the physical product or communication with the workplace supervisor. The vocational teacher cannot oversee the student's work on the physical product component (and supervisor cannot evaluate the student's performance in the workplace) in the absence of discussions with the academic teacher regarding the scope of the student's topic and the direction of the student's research.

From the student's perspective, work in either the vocational or academic classroom or workplace cannot proceed in a disconnected fashion. Where previously students may have been unable to perceive the links between the learning they do with academic and vocational teachers, students in senior projects select a topic in conjuction with at least two teacher-advisors, usually one academic and one vocational. Although only one teacher may serve formally as the Project Advisor, all adults involved, including workplace supervisors, must be committed to helping the student succeed in all components of the project. This requires advising the student and managing his or her progress toward project completion through a series of meetings that involve teachers and advisors with the student.

Thus, everyone must acknowledge the interdependence of the project's components. The research and writing component will affect the physical product or workplace experience because the abstract ideas identified in the paper must direct the physical demonstration of them. Challenges in the physical product development or in workplace applications will create new questions to be researched and answered in the written component, since the student must demonstrate new knowledge gained in both written and physical forms. In the final presentation and evaluation, the student receives graduation grades from all teacher-advisors involved, so these adults must discuss and agree on the evaluation criteria and the grading system to be used.

Given the kind of collaboration the senior project requires, those who serve as teacher-advisors must commit substantial amounts of time to the process of helping advisees through the project, attending and evaluating final presentations, and coordinating time and viewpoints with other teacher-advisors and the student. Teachers must also feel that they have the commitment of school leadership in order to make decisions about the flexibility of their time, the criteria they use to approve project topics, and the criteria they use to evaluate final presentations.

One of the first challenges schools face in instituting the senior project, therefore, is gaining consensus on the objectives of the senior project and how it fits into the school's overall educational philosophy and direction. In many secondary institutions, particularly large comprehensive high schools that try to meet the needs of heterogeneous student populations, there may not be a single view of the school's educational purpose shared by the teachers within one department, let alone among vocational and academic teachers. Teachers often define their roles in vastly different ways (as Chapter 3 of Volume II clarifies). Some teachers see themselves as subject experts and expect all of their students to be college-bound. For these teachers, the senior project may be viewed as an in-depth research experience that provides excellent opportunities for independent research and experimentation. Other teachers define their role as mentor or coach. Vocational teachers in particular recognize that their students may not be interested in 4-year colleges but can seek a 2-year associate degree in a specific career field. For these teachers, the senior project can be viewed as an important step in students' career exploration, allowing students with a variety of different learning styles to benefit from more individualized attention. The beauty of the senior project is its ability to meet many different conceptions of self-directed and integrated learning. However, in any one school, the objectives of the senior project must be explicitly defined and agreed to by both faculty and leadership because disagreements can effectively derail any reform efforts before students have the opportunity to experience their benefits.

Teachers and administration at Thomas Jefferson High School for Science and Technology (TJHSST) in Virginia had no difficulty reaching consensus on the school's philosophy and, therefore, on the objectives of the senior project. Founded in 1985, TJHSST was created through a partnership of business and education to improve science, mathematics, and technology education. It is a public school and all students in the district are eligible to apply, but students are selected on the basis of demonstrated aptitude and interest in the biological, physical, mathematical, and computer sciences and on the basis of their intention to pursue college preparation in the sciences, engineering, or related fields. Teachers and staff are committed to two goals: providing a college preparatory curriculum to educate future scientific leaders and encouraging cooperation among the school, scientific, and business communities. The senior project at TJHSST is designed to be consistent with both of these. It emphasizes independent research and makes extensive use of the school's business partners to place students in research internships where classroom theories and concepts are tested in real-life conditions.

At Paul M. Hodgson Vocational-Technical High School in Delaware, the principal saw a compatibility between the senior project and the direction in which he sought to move the school. He initiated a series of open discussions with faculty to build a consensus about the school's philosophy. Out of these discussions, both faculty and principal agreed on two long-term educational objectives. The first of these was inspired by the goals set by the Southern Regional Education Board (SREB) for higher expectations of vocational students in the academic areas of math, science, and communication. The second objective was to award high school diplomas based entirely on student exhibitions of skills, an idea championed by Theodore Sizer and the Coalition of Essential Schools. The senior project, with its emphasis on higher level research, problem solving, and presentation skills, was identified as a way to support both of these objectives. In addition, the senior project was consistent with two preexisting school practices. First, there was already a tradition of skill mastery by demonstration in the vocational-technical shop classes (Godowsky, Scarbrough, & Steinwedel, 1992). Second, the English department already required seniors to do a research paper that integrated vocational and academic learning (Ancess & Darling-Hammond, in press).

It is important to consider the factors that can make the process of achieving consensus either easier or more difficult. Both TJHSST and Hodgson have the advantage of a student population that is already well defined by the curricular emphasis. Therefore, the purpose of integrating learning contexts and teacher-advisors is more widely accepted and supported. In both cases, school leadership was strongly committed to using the senior project to make the school's goals of vocational and academic integration and exhibition of skill mastery explicit. In addition, a core of consensus in the faculty ensured commitment to implementing the substantial changes in student learning and teacher interaction the senior project involves.

In comprehensive high schools with vocational programs, by contrast, both faculty and students are often sharply divided according to the curriculum. Students on a 4-year university track may never enter a vocational-technical classroom. Similarly, vocational and academic teachers may feel they never have the need or opportunity to discuss ways to integrate their subject content, let alone coordinate time to meet with one another and with individual students. In such segregated environments, it is essential that faculty and school leadership invest the time to come to an agreement on the importance of vocational and academic integration, and on the way in which the senior project reflects this importance.

In 1986, teachers at Oregon's South Medford High School agreed with the local school board that a high school diploma should represent more than a student's ability to be present for 4 years of a disconnected, insufficient curriculum. A group of teachers was given the task to develop the curriculum for a new high school. This group identified two problems of the traditional high school and curriculum—the difficulty of keeping seniors involved and motivated in their last year of public school education and the lack of a requirement that all graduates demonstrate mastery of specific skills that merit a high school diploma and represent 12 years of education. The senior project was determined to be a mechanism for requiring seniors to effectively address both problems. Thus, consensus was achieved at two levels—between the faculty and the board and among the faculty itself (Chadwell, 1991).

While it may be easy for a school to achieve consensus on the idea that the current curriculum or school structure is not providing students with an adequate preparation for postsecondary lives, it is essential that discussion of reform eventually move to a level of specific, desired student outcomes, and of the role that senior projects can play in achieving them. Guiding questions that should be considered in these preliminary discussions include:

1. Which students should benefit from the senior project?
2. What skills do we want the senior project experience to develop?
3. What senior project components will demonstrate that the student has mastered these skills?

These are not simple discussions that can be addressed in one or two meetings; they are questions that go to the heart of a school's educational mission and the methods that can be identified to implement that mission. Leaders of these discussions should try to keep participants focused on the needs of the students. In doing so, participants may discover that some students are very well served by the school's present curricular structure. Identifying the strengths of the school's programs (e.g. Hodgson's tradition of exhibitions in its shop classes and the English department's requirement of a research paper that integrates vocational and academic learning) may be a fruitful starting point for beginning to look at how to address the areas that need improvement.

Once these issues have been discussed in a way that engenders school-wide understanding of and ownership in the concept of the senior project, the real work of planning and implementing the idea can begin.

■
DEFINING AND BEGINNING THE SENIOR PROJECT PROCESS

Because of the dramatic ways in which the senior project changes the nature of interactions among the school population, it must be emphasized that teachers alone cannot make the changes happen. It is critical that school leadership demonstrate its commitment to the goals of vocational and academic integration, and to the method of the senior project, by giving teachers the power to define the senior project so that the agreed upon student outcomes can be achieved.

PLANNING

One of the first decisions to be made is what exactly the senior project will make students do. One defining characteristic of the senior project is that it substitutes for the traditional curriculum a qualitatively different kind of learning. But whether this experience comes in the form of learning at a job site, apprenticeship style, or as an independent investigation of a theoretical concept involving the production of a physical demonstration, is dependent on the way a school defines the specific objectives of the senior project itself. Teachers who have defined the purposes of integrating vocational and academic education, and who know the students who are expected to benefit from this integration, are those best able to define the specific ways in which the senior project will reflect these purposes for these students. However, the teachers must have the power to establish links and to collaborate with local employers if workplace learning is a priority, or to arrange shared planning periods with other teachers if the senior projects will consist of self-directed exploration.

Second, the manner in which students will receive credit for completing the senior project must be determined. This issue requires schools to determine whether, and how, to make the senior project a graduation requirement. Since the traditional curriculum is usually designed to meet district and state curriculum guidelines and requirements, the school must be able to justify the equivalence or superiority of the senior project's content. Most schools get around this by incorporating the various components of the senior project into already existing classes. The research paper is required in the senior English or Social Studies class, the physical product in a vocational or technical class. Oral presentations can meet requirements in both academic and vocational-technical classes. Workplace or internship experience can be treated as part of the student's work in either a social science or civics class requirement.

A second aspect of senior projects that needs definition is the way in which students' work will be assessed. This turns out to be a thorny issue for several reasons. Traditionally, individual teachers have had almost absolute control over their grading criteria and assessment methods. With the collaboration required by senior projects, teachers and/or job-site supervisors must develop a process for sharing and making explicit student assessment criteria. Issues to be considered in this context include:

- *The number and kind of assessments to be made prior to the final presentation or assessment:* To ensure progress toward the final product, paper, or presentation, teachers and/or supervisors need to have regular meetings with the student and to be able to provide feedback on work completed. Appropriate assessment points might include the end of each of several rotations at a job site, or an outline or rough drafts of the research paper, or a drawing or small part of the physical product or demonstration. Students may need redirection of their research efforts, or specific help in technical writing or on a component of the physical product development.
- *The portion of the vocational or academic class grade to be given to the senior project or any one aspect thereof:* Some teachers may feel that the work required by the senior project should comprise only a part and not the entirety of students' final grades in their class. This may be a way of accommodating senior projects of varying depth or scope, but specific teacher expectations must be made clear to the student, as well as to other project advisors involved at the start of the process.
- *The manner in which incomplete projects will be handled:* Although a process that includes many "checkpoints" may help avoid the problem of students who are not completing the work, this problem is still important to consider. For example, a student may complete the job-site experience portion but may not complete a written report or research paper; or a student may write a paper but refuse to make an oral presentation. Not all schools make the senior project a graduation requirement, but in cases where it is defined this way, what level of incomplete work should be considered grounds for refusing a student the sufficient number of credits to receive a high school diploma?

At South Medford, the senior project requires a research paper in the English class, a physical product in a vocational or technical class, and an oral presentation before a board of adults including teachers, administrators, and community members. Teachers find that three or four students each year do not complete all three of the senior project components. Some of these students complete the diploma requirements at the community college or by taking the equivalency examination. Others, however, return to the school in succeeding years to complete the project and obtain the necessary credits (Chadwell, 1991).

Inherent in each of the above issues is the need to allow teachers (and other project supervisors) the time to meet *with each other and with the student* to discuss the student's progress, work completed, or problems. Student advising and assessment throughout the senior project process must be collaborative in order to be fair.

GETTING FEEDBACK AND ENOUGH SUPPORT TO IMPLEMENT THE PLAN

While it is clear that one person alone, whether it be the principal or a teacher, cannot make the planning decisions we have been discussing, it is also clear that attempts to involve all faculty and staff in the planning process would be unwieldy. Typically, there is a core of four to six committed teachers who are empowered with the time and training to act as the planning committee, and a method exists for allowing others the opportunity to express feedback and to provide input. When making adjustments in the plan based on this input, the planning committee can be enlarged or replaced by an implementation committee whose task it becomes to put the plan into action.

Implementation involves recruiting and preparing teachers and others who will advise and manage the senior project experience for the target population, introducing the idea to students, developing a method for managing the logistics of the advising and evaluation process, and devising a system to continue to allow and respond to feedback.

Hodgson, after its initial series of faculty–principal conversations, elected to use state grant money to send four teachers to a summer curriculum development institute to draft the specific description of its senior project. This team defined the three parts of the senior project: (1) a shop-based research paper; (2) the design/creation of a product; and (3) a public, formal, oral presentation (Ancess & Darling-Hammond, in press, p. 7). In the fall, the entire faculty was invited to give feedback to the draft in a continuation of the open discussions with faculty and principal.

Following these informal discussions, a Senior Project Evaluation Committee (SPEC) of eight teachers was formed. The SPEC recruited a sufficient number of teachers to serve as advisors for the first group of seniors and wrote a student Senior Project Manual, which outlined the objectives, expectations, and requirements for students. The SPEC also managed the overall senior project process, responding to unexpected problems, such as questions about the appropriate scope of proposed student topics, final presentation scheduling, and how to keep the faculty informed of any developments or changes (Ancess & Darling-Hammond, in press).

One of the most difficult decisions to make in implementing a senior project is when to begin. Schools and planning committees must remember that unanimous support is usually impossible to procure, but that the commitment of "a critical mass" of teachers is essential. Further, the decision to begin should not be equated with the end of planning or of developing the senior project process. A certain amount of resistance and confusion are a part of every reform effort, and the unexpected problems that arise do not indicate that it was too soon to begin implementation. Instead, solutions to these early snafus must be sought as quickly as possible. The implementation committee must be supported by the overall consensus on the importance of the senior project concept, and guided by the objectives defined for the senior project and for the student outcomes that are desired.

MANAGING THE DEVELOPMENT OF THE PROCESS

Once the senior project process is in full swing, the nature of interactions among all of the people involved, from students to vocational and academic teachers, changes. While many of these changes focus on the positive aspect of increased teacher communication and the identification of shared educational goals for students, some of them also bring out the difficulties teachers face when forced to give up a certain amount of independence and control over the student's learning process.

Teachers will need to: (1) share information and communicate regularly with many people they may never have had to include in their classroom instructional plans before; and (2) be more flexible about working with topics in which they may not have expertise. Not only will vocational and academic teachers share their resources but others, like the librarian or outside experts, may need to be involved to help students more fully research certain topics. Project advisors must spend a great deal of time seeking and providing new information resources for students. In addition, each student's teacher-advisors must devise systems of sharing information and communicating regularly about students' progress and/or problems throughout the senior project experience.

At TJHSST, laboratory scientists from the firms that are included among the many business partners of the school often supervise student research experience outside the classroom and serve as project teacher-advisors through a mentorship program. These mentors must work closely with the student's technology laboratory teacher to determine project goals, timelines, and evaluation criteria, and to periodically review the student's progress. To assist in these reviews, students are also required to keep a daily log or notebook of their work (TJHSST, 1993).

■
RETHINKING STUDENT PREPARATION FOR THE SENIOR PROJECT

While the majority of the difficulties facing teachers involve new ways of communicating with others about their students, the difficulties students face have to do with being adequately prepared for the requirements of the senior project. Because this problem results from the way the curriculum is designed for students in the ninth through eleventh grades, teachers and schools generally find that the senior project leads to a complex process of schoolwide curriculum changes.

Particularly when the senior project is defined to require independent research and writing skills, it is often too late to wait until the senior year to find out whether or not the student has the necessary skills. Therefore, both vocational and academic classes in the first two or three years of secondary education may need to incorporate miniproject assignments to introduce and develop these skills. For example, vocational-technical or science classes can introduce students to various pieces of laboratory equipment or machinery. English classes can give students experience in technical writing and research skills. Any vocational and academic classes can introduce students to different ways of analyzing and solving problems, and they can also require students to do some kind of oral presentation in front of the class.

South Medford teachers talk about a "trickle-down" effect on the entire curriculum. The oral presentation component encouraged teachers to provide instruction and practice in speech arts to students before senior year. Freshman English teachers began introducing the parts of the research paper (citing sources, paper organization, etc.) by telling their students: "Of course you need to learn to write a 500-word paper now. When you're seniors, you'll have to write a 3,000-word paper to graduate, so let's get started" (Chadwell, 1991). English teachers needed to discuss the technical aspects of students' papers with the technical teachers, and the vocational-technical teachers began to think of the academic relevance of their subjects and teaching methods (Chadwell, 1992).

At Hodgson, the senior project led to many curriculum changes throughout the school, and for students in all grades. The senior English classes were revised to include one semester of technical writing to ensure student success in the research paper component of the senior project. Ninth graders were introduced to research papers and oral presentations in both English and shop classes. The project concept has also been expanded, and all teachers have been encouraged to integrate their content with other subjects. The eleventh grade American history and American literature classes were combined into one American Experience course. The math teachers were given a period to work with shop classes, teaching theory in application to students at all grade levels. As a result of this schoolwide embrace of the concept of integration, Hodgson has moved from a five-track curriculum to one that is increasingly non-tracked, with heterogeneous classrooms and interdisciplinary/interprogrammatic courses (Ancess & Darling-Hammond, in press, pp. 22–24).

GROWTH OF THE SENIOR PROJECT MODEL

The kind of schoolwide curricular accommodation to, and growth of, the integration concept inherent in the senior project just described should be expected of any successful implementation of the senior project model. However, more important than recognizing this growth is the ability to track and evaluate it according to the desired student outcomes defined in the early planning stages. Program evaluation is essential not only to identify problems that can be solved with existing resources but also to solicit potential funding sources that will enable the senior project concept to reach more students, provide more resources in the form of equipment or materials to enable students to choose a wider range of topics to investigate, and provide some compensation or release time for teachers who serve on the planning or implementation committees.

The evaluation should look both at the process and the product and allow feedback from teachers and students. Obtaining and responding to teacher comments should be one of the ongoing tasks of the implementation committee. That is, teachers should respond to teachers, and teachers should be made to feel supported and encouraged, even when facing the difficulties inherent in managing senior projects.

Evaluating student outcomes and changes is also critical to supporting and expanding the senior project. One way to anticipate this aspect is to define the student outcomes in measurable terms at the beginning of the planning process. For example, measures of increased learning-task engagement can include the amount of time students spend working on the senior project in class and at home, or the number of days late or absent, or the strength of positive feelings (excitement about learning, a sense of accomplishment) about work completed for the senior project. Other measures might include the strength of confidence in new skills and knowledge gained, expectations of the relevance of skills gained to future plans, or expectations about the ability to achieve postsecondary employment or educational goals.

Many schools use student and teacher surveys to get at this kind of information. At Hodgson, students reported that they spent more time on home and classwork, that they felt their written and oral communication, as well as research skills, improved (Godowsky, Scarbrough, & Steinwedel, 1992, p. 3), that their sense of being knowledgeable increased, and that they improved their time management capacity and organizational skills. Teachers reported that students developed improved analytical skills and were better able to follow through with long-term goals (Ancess & Darling-Hammond, in press).

A side benefit to encouraging teachers and students to reflect on their senior project experiences and provide feedback is that it encourages them to look for and acknowledge the changes in their own attitudes toward the integration of vocational and academic knowledge, independent exploration and learning, and the roles that teachers and students play in a collaborative learning process. While there may have been initial resistance to the idea of a senior project requirement, the feelings of accomplishment at the end of the process, shared by teachers and students alike, make a powerful marketing tool for incoming seniors and teachers who are potential senior project committee members or advisors.

CONCLUSIONS

In one sense, senior projects can be considered a modest reform. They focus on only part of the student's school experience for part of the senior year. For this reason, senior projects are popular with many schools that might not otherwise consider more substantial reforms. As this chapter has shown, however, the flexibility inherent in senior projects can lead to far-ranging and substantial changes in all those who have a stake in changing the way education is delivered—students, teachers, and the community.

Student-selected topics encourage the development of discipline and of the independent problem-solving, logical-thinking, and presentation skills required to complete projects successfully. The price for this kind of freedom is that students must take far more responsibility for what and how they learn than do students in traditional classrooms. They are not able to simply reproduce the same answers to the same questions that every other student does. In fact, senior projects often produce questions and solutions that neither the teachers nor the students predict, making the learning process that much more compelling for both.

Teachers (and workplace supervisors, when the senior project involves a work experience component) find their roles and relationships redefined by the senior project. The student's successful management and completion of the project require fairly high levels of coordination and communication on the part of project advisors. Where the senior project integrates the work done in an academic and a vocational-technical class, these teachers are brought together by necessity. Although this collaboration may be difficult at first, teachers in schools that require senior projects point to it as one of the most rewarding outcomes of the senior project experience.

Where the student fulfills part of the senior project requirements in the workplace, classroom teachers, both academic and vocational, are forced to provide real-world purpose for the content they teach, while the business community takes an active role in the preparation of its future employees and leaders.

Change with the senior project can begin slowly and in small ways but, allowed to expand, it leads to the transformation of the entire school community. No longer are students allowed to receive a high school diploma without demonstrating mastery of certain skills that the school deems necessary. Far from creating irrelevant hoops that only certain students leap through, senior projects provide steps that allow all students to achieve success.

9

THE VOICES OF STUDENTS AT MAGNET SCHOOLS

AMY HEEBNER

The New York City public high schools offer 133 different programs that integrate academic and vocational education (Crain et al., 1992, iii). The 133 schools in this *educational options program* give students a two track education, preparing them both for college and for entry-level jobs upon graduation. A central purpose of this program is to allow enterprising students to avoid the difficult choice between college and an entry-level job by preparing them for both possibilities (Crain et al., 1992). Although this two track approach to secondary education is a double challenge, nearly a third of public school students in New York City enroll in the educational options program.

Intensive interviews were conducted with 70 students from four high schools in the educational options program.[1] In the interview excerpts in this chapter, students describe in their own words the benefits and problems of combining academic and vocational education. Many students spoke with enthusiasm and seriousness about expanding their options for the future. The students in these high schools reflected a range of socioeconomic strata and academic ability levels because the schools were required by mandate to admit half the student population by lottery among all applicants, with the remaining half admitted by school administrators (students referred to as "school-selected").

■
COMPARISON OF CAREER MAGNETS AND TRADITIONAL HIGH SCHOOLS

The lottery admission requirement created an unusual research opportunity. We interviewed young people who applied to a career magnet (that is, to an educational options high school) and were accepted because of the luck of the draw, not because of a good academic record or political connections. Our interview sample included students who ordinarily would be considered at risk of delinquency or dropping out of high school. In order to provide a basis for comparison, we also interviewed young people who lost the career magnet lottery and instead attended traditional neighborhood high schools that did not offer any vocational courses.[2]

Students from low income and minority families are often at risk of school failure, regardless of the kind of high school they attend, because of economic limitations and a lack of familiarity with middle class role models, attitudes, and communication patterns. However, most at-risk students who stayed in the educational options high schools described ways in which they had benefited, both directly and indirectly, from these schools. The use of ethnographic interviewing allowed students to speak candidly and in depth about their experiences in school, their lives outside school, and their thinking about the future.

NEW YORK'S CAREER MAGNET HIGH SCHOOLS

The educational options program is focused in eight high schools, referred to in this chapter as *total career magnets* (including all enrolled students in some part of the vocational education program, as well as in academic classes) or *career magnets*. Each of these eight schools is organized around a career area, such as business, communications, criminal justice, or medicine. Students from any district in New York City are eligible to apply to the career magnets. If accepted, a student is exempt from the requirement to attend the academically oriented high school in his or her home attendance zone. The career magnets became very popular because they enjoyed excellent reputations, offered vocational education along with college preparation, and gave many students a chance to escape the terrors of zoned high schools in ghetto neighborhoods.

The growth of the New York City career magnets began in 1977 with the opening of John Dewey High School. According to some observers, including adults interviewed in this study, the traditional neighborhood high schools declined while the career magnets flourished because the latter were "creaming" the better students, who tended to choose magnet high schools, away from the neighborhood high schools. Many neighborhood high schools fought back by creating their own magnet programs, referred to in this chapter as *magnet-within-school programs*. Some neighborhood high schools were forced to close because of declining enrollment. Some critics of magnet schools have observed a similar trend in other American cities when selective magnet schools were introduced into public school systems (Blank, 1989; Moore & Davenport, 1988). According to these critics, magnet schools drew many of the more able students from middle income families away from the less advantaged neighborhood schools. Thus, the overall quality of education at neighborhood high schools tended to decline as the magnets gained recognition within the school district.

The New York educational options program began as a plan to balance the appeal of magnets with concerns for educational equity. In 1987 the New York City Board of Education issued a mandate requiring each career magnet to admit half of its students through a computerized lottery. The lottery winners were selected at random, in ratios corresponding to reading levels gauged by their scores on a city-wide test given at the end of junior high school: that is, the Board distributed lottery admission among different ability levels by selecting, for each educational options program, one sixth students with above average reading scores, two thirds with average reading scores, and one sixth with below average reading scores.

The districtwide mandate changed the composition of the student population at the career magnets. Beginning with the entering class of autumn, 1987, the career magnets included a higher proportion of students with average and below average test scores, students with attendance problems, and, according to some teachers, students from low income families. Based on the interviews with school adults, it appeared that at least one established career magnet experienced an uncomfortable transition because the faculty, counselors, and administrators were unprepared for the new mix of students. However, another site, which opened as a new career magnet in 1987, adapted to the lottery mandate readily, perhaps because it had no prior history as a selective career magnet with no lottery requirement. The mandate did provide special funds for "redesign" schools—that is, schools that were forced to close and to reopen as career magnets. Established career magnets were offered no similar financial support to aid the schools' adaptation to the new student population.

<hr />

THE STUDENTS' DESCRIPTIONS

The overall impression created by interviews with 70 students was that they wanted vocational education to play a part in their high school experience, regardless of what kind of high school they attended. Most of the students attending neighborhood high schools were concerned about the relevance of school for getting and keeping jobs. The career magnet students came from four schools, each with a different career emphasis. Two schools were total career magnets. These two schools are referred to in this chapter as the Business Magnet and the Communications Magnet. A third school was a neighborhood high school with a magnet-within-school program that combined career education in criminal justice with academics, including college preparation. The Business Magnet, the Communications Magnet, and the Criminal Justice Magnet were all part of the educational options program, so that each of these magnets admitted half of its students by lottery each year. The fourth site was a neighborhood high school with a magnet-within-school program that offered specific vocational training in cosmetology along with some academics, but that de-emphasized college preparation. The Cosmetology Magnet began as a part of the educational options program, admitting 50% of its students by lottery, but was exempted from the lottery system after the first year (1987–88).

BENEFITS OF CAREER MAGNETS

Students who attended the Business, Communications, and Criminal Justice career magnets were generally positive about their school experience, and described specific ways in which the career magnets aided their preparation for the future. According to these students, the main benefits of integrating vocational education with college preparation were:

1. Participating in situated learning experiences, including jobs
2. Learning about many aspects of a profession or field through a vertical curriculum
3. Active planning for the future, often for multiple job and career possibilities.

However, the schools did not serve all students equally well. Sometimes the two track education was a double burden for both students and school adults. These and other problems at career magnets are highlighted in the section of this chapter entitled Criticisms of Career Magnets.

Selected interview excerpts are included here to elucidate how these young people thought about and experienced the positive aspects of career magnets. Some background information is provided for each student so that his or her comments are understood in the context of the individual's life circumstances. Names and identifying details have been changed to protect the students.

Situated Learning
Students described with enthusiasm internships, after-school programs, and jobs obtained through the school's Cooperative Education (Coop) program. These programs gave students the opportunity to practice skills in real or simulated workplace environments, an approach called *situated, anchored,* or *contextual* learning by cognitive psychologists (Brown et al., 1989; Cognition and Technology Group at Vanderbilt, 1990; Hamilton, 1990; Resnick, 1987a). Another form of situated learning took place in classes that taught practical skills, such as keyboarding, stenography, and computer applications. At the Business and Communications magnets, students said

they believed that these skills would help them get entry-level jobs. The student profiles of Jeremie and Rosa illustrate how at-risk students responded to opportunities for learning practical and communication skills.

JEREMIE.   A junior at a career magnet, Jeremie appeared to be a well adjusted student with diverse interests. He was interested in computers, was majoring in one of the school's computer specializations, and was also interested in the arts. He definitely planned to go to college. But his family background suggested potential for school failure. His extended family circle included alcoholics, drug abusers, and fathers of illegitimate children. Under the guiding influence of his mother and aunt, Jeremie spoke of consciously turning away from the delinquent habits of some male family members. The career magnet offered him situated learning experiences such as tutoring, which eventually led to a paid job tutoring other students in computer applications. The excerpt below gives his description of the tutoring in his own words.

> JEREMIE: I enjoyed working there, in the computer room, you know. All of a sudden I would go there every day and help somebody with class....
> INTERVIEWER: What were you teaching them? What kinds of things?
> JEREMIE: They learned Basic. They learned different commands. How to write a program. If they had a question, they would say, "Hey Jer." I'd be like, "press return, what do you mean?"
> INTERVIEWER: So like the teacher was giving instructions or lectures?
> JEREMIE: Yeah, he was teaching a lesson and, you know, he'd talk about this and I would load the program from the disk and write, save it, whatever.
> INTERVIEWER: And you were the expert who went around and helped everybody individually?
> JEREMIE: Yeah!...
> INTERVIEWER: You mentioned summer work and I was wondering if you had internships or jobs during the year too, while classes were going on?
> JEREMIE: Yeah.... I worked as a tutor from October to June. Yeah. It helped me.
> INTERVIEWER: What did you do as a tutor?
> JEREMIE: I tutored math. I tutored, um, all the math except calculus. And it feels good. And people will come to the classroom and I'll tutor them, and they will either come out learning something or nothing here.
>
>> In October we had about 12, in January we had 10 tutors, December we had about 9 tutors, February we got 2 more, and then 2 of them just stopped coming after a while and then we only

had 7 at the year end. But, yeah, they all came for the pictures though, at the end of the year. Like, "I tutored for a week, so I'm in the picture, right?" "Yeah, cause you wanna be." They came for the party too. They only come for the good stuff. They don't come for the work. I'm the one that stays.

Jeremie's description illustrates that the school's support for his tutoring strengthened his communication skills as well as his commitment to the work. Commitment and communication have been identified as important skills in a variety of workplaces (Levin & Rumberger, 1989).

ROSA. Friendly and warm, both in groups and in individual interviews, Rosa was a committed student who attended regularly and did her homework. From a low income, minority family, she was admitted by lottery to a career magnet with a record of cutting classes in junior high school. However, she pulled herself together in high school and made grades that fluctuated between 70 and 90, by her own report. She said she applied to the magnet because she was interested in the career specialty.

In her first interview, she discussed her desire to participate in a school program sponsored by a telecommunications company. This telecommunications program is one example of a link between a career magnet and a local firm. Rosa succeeded in meeting the admission requirements for the program. After the program was completed, she reported that she learned something about basic telephony, met some people in the company, and had fun. "It was a very nice experience," she concluded, but was disappointed that she had not yet obtained a job offer. She offered the following comments.

> On the first day of the program they met us and we went to the conference room ... and we had lunch with the representatives of the company. We talked with them, had some association with them. There was a lady who connected telecommunications technology with the school work.... We learned things like how to connect one line to another.... They did talk about jobs but we never got to an arrangement about it. I talked to my teacher, and I talked to the students. She told me she could get me with the right people and get me a job. Some people called me but they already gave the jobs away. They said they will call me. I heard that they took boys, not girls.

CAROL. Carol, a junior, liked her skills classes at her career magnet high school. She had grades in the 80s, came from a two-parent, minority family, and generally seemed self-confident. Even with these advantages, she liked the security of having strong secretarial skills as a starting point for entering the business world, where she wanted to make a career.

INTERVIEWER: What's been your best experience in high school over the past three years, including any course or internship or job?

CAROL: Well, my major is, I like it very much ... my major is secretarial and they teach you shorthand.... So, you get, it's like a whole different, it's like, you could say a different language. You learn different symbols and stuff. And they teach you office skills so when you get out of high school, you're at ease in an office, you won't feel uncomfortable. That's, yeah, my major's the best thing I like.

INTERVIEWER: What are your favorite courses this year? What's your favorite class?

CAROL: Well, I don't have that many courses. I have, well ... Business English cause that teaches you where to put the commas in and your grammar and stuff and it's important for a job.

INTERVIEWER: What is that like? What kinds of work do you do in that class?

CAROL: Well, we proofread. There's a lot of proofreading, for the commas, and we learn, um, to catch errors in words. And we use the dictionary a lot.

Carol's comments suggested that she liked the combination of specific and general skills in her Business English class. She seemed interested in comma placement, for example, because she would have to use it in an office job, not because she was interested in English grammar for its own sake. Other students made similar comments about Business math, suggesting that they were interested in math that had workplace applications rather than in math for its own sake. On the other hand, Carol was not the only student to express interest in stenography because it was like learning "a different language," a comment that suggests a more abstract, academic interest. But, in general, students at the Business and Communications magnets said they prized their skills in keyboarding, stenography, and computer applications because these skills would be useful in competing for entry-level jobs. The students' interest in workplace application was clear and enhanced their interest in college preparatory classes that included some connection with general or specific workplace skills.

Vertical Curriculum

Students, particularly those still enrolled at career magnets, showed us that they often thought about the future. Like most adolescents, their thoughts about career direction fluctuated, sometimes focusing on how to get an entry-level job after high school or college, at other times imagining a long-range future in responsible jobs with intrinsic interest and moderate to high salaries. Courses at the Business, Communications, and Criminal Justice magnets were organized as vertical curricula, presenting students with an array that reflected the levels of the respective career specialties. The vertical curricula seemed to enhance not only the motivation but also the career sophistication of the students. These factors contributed to a more positive, flexible view of the possibilities within a career, as exemplified by the following interview.

MELISSA.   Melissa, a school-selected senior from a minority family attending a total career magnet, was on the school leadership committee. Her parents were in favor of higher education. An above-average student, Melissa had chosen to apply to the magnet because of the two track focus that combined vocational education and academics. She expressed this clearly in her own words:

> They prepare you for a job or college. I think it's great! It's like a prep school. You get in step with the corporation early. It works!

RICHARD.   Richard was one of the above average readers admitted by lottery to a career magnet. Richard, like Melissa, was a bright student who preferred to attend a career magnet because of its dual emphasis on career and academics, rather than go to a neighborhood high school. Both Richard and Melissa probably would have excelled in traditional college preparatory programs but chose instead to go to career magnets.

Richard, whose wavy blond hair extended beyond his shoulders, liked visual art and computers. He also liked math, he said, because it "explains a lot of things." At the time of the interviews, he was a junior in the computing major and had taken several programming courses. In his senior year he planned to take an Advanced Placement course in computer programming, the highest level computing course that the career magnet offered at the time.

Richard criticized the career magnet for engaging in some "false advertising," citing the still incomplete video conferencing facility as an example. Still, he was pleased by his progress in the computer programming classes and by the possibility that these courses might fulfill college credits, making it possible for him to take advanced mathematics courses when he got to college.

LAUREL AND TRACY.   As African American females, Laurel and Tracy would be considered by some experts to fall into one of the most potentially risky categories in our society in terms of both educational achievement and employment opportunities. The following interview excerpt suggests that their exposure to a vertical curriculum in criminal justice allowed them to think realistically about jobs at all levels of the legal profession, not only entry-level or clerical positions.

> INTERVIEWER: In the time that you've been in the magnet, what's your best experience? Best class? Best work? Best internship?
>
> LAUREL: Well, I would say the Civil Law course I took … and Mock Trial competition against other schools.

INTERVIEWER: Oh, really. What was that like?

LAUREL: It was interesting. We got to go in the ... Federal Court, something like that ... it was a nice experience....

INTERVIEWER: Tracy, what's your best experience?

TRACY: I think it was in Criminology. I like Criminology. Yeah, cause it's interesting, cause you study why criminals do stuff. And we had a lot of police officers and stuff comin' in and explain different things to us. We had a lot of guest speakers.

INTERVIEWER: So, do you think that this training is gonna help you when you get out of school?

LAUREL: Well, it can only help you if, unless you're goin' into that profession. If you're not goin' to, it's not gonna.... Well for me it's gonna help me, cause it gives me a more open idea of what I have to face.

INTERVIEWER: What do you wanna do when you get done with high school?

LAUREL: I'm goin' into paralegal studies in the fall.

INTERVIEWER: And how did you come to that decision? When did you decide you wanted to be in paralegal studies?

LAUREL: Well, since I came to this school I always wanna do something dealing with law. But being that I had an experience in March ... I knew, know what's expected of a lawyer. I figure paralegal is more important cause of research. And most lawyers don't have enough research when they go into the court room, so....

INTERVIEWER: When did you discover that you like research?

LAUREL: When I had to try to do it. When I had to do it for my case. It was hard, cause just to see all of us crammed in one room for hours and hours tryin' to get information together....

Interviewer: So you're talking about research that you did for your mock trial at the ... Court. And what do you think you'll do when you get done with your studies at college?

LAUREL: Then I'll push on and try to go into the full legal studies as being an attorney lawyer. But I figure this is a stepping stone for me just to try paralegal studies first. It's also givin' me a open idea on what an attorney have to go through....

INTERVIEWER: So you are thinking of going to law school?

LAUREL: Yeah.

Parallel Career Planning

Career magnet students spoke of creating multiple plans for the future, considering different combinations of jobs and higher education. Some were considering careers in two or more fields, while others envisioned themselves in a variety of jobs within a single field. For some low income students who were planning to attend college, the ability to get an entry-level job after high school was a crucial element in the plan. We gave this pattern of creating multiple alternatives the name *parallel career planning,* and found that it contributed to the students' confidence in themselves and in the future.

RITZA.   Ritza described her parallel plans for college and for a backup job in cosmetology. A female member of a minority family, she was a senior in the Cosmetology magnet-within-school program. She did not work in cosmetology during high school because she had not yet earned her license, but she intended to work in the business part-time while going to college the following year. At the time of the interview, she had been accepted to two local colleges and was deciding which she would attend. The magnet's two track education gave her the ability and confidence to consider two different occupations. She stated, "This is my last year, and I'm going to get my cosmetology license. After I get my license, I'll just go to college for business. If one don't work out, I'll go to the other."

CARL.   Carl was a student from a minority family, enrolled at a career magnet, and a junior when interviewed. He began high school as an at-risk student, cutting classes, pulling some low grades, and getting into fights outside school. His experiences with adults and peers at the career magnet seemed to help him turn in a more positive direction. Carl's story illustrates that he was actively planning his future.

INTERVIEWER: What do you want to do when you get done with high school?

CARL: Well, I want to go to college. I definitely know that. Where? That's something else. Well, I really want to go away to college. Well, I been talking with my dean, she's not my counselor, but she's my dean, but I trust her more than my counselor.... So I speak to her. She feels it's better for me to go away, too. Because I know myself, if I stay here, I don't think I would really learn. I'm constantly being distracted by this person and that person. So if I go away, I think I'll do better. I'll apply myself. I'm not one of those average guys....

INTERVIEWER: Think a little further. Supposing you're through college, what kind of job would you like to have, if you could have any job you wanted?

CARL: I want to manage my own business. Something that makes money. It has to be something that makes money. Because I don't think I could take working in an office. I don't like how the office atmosphere is. Everybody just talks behind each other's back. Everybody. No matter where you go, they talk behind each other's back. I can't take that. And I just hate sitting down at a desk, typing, taking calls, filing this, doing that. I can't take that. I always have to be on the go. I'm a very busy person.

MAGGIE.   Maggie, a warm, shy girl from a minority family, who is struggling to develop more self-confidence, benefited from her experience in a
career magnet. She came from a single-parent household, since her parents
were divorced. Her interest in her major and the practical skills she had
developed in stenography and typing gave her confidence in her ability to
earn a living after high school. When she was interviewed as a junior, Maggie was not sure that she wanted to go to college. However, she said she
would consider it if she found secretarial work unfulfilling; thus, she had
created a parallel plan for herself. She spoke of teaching as another career
alternative. In this passage, she described her career goals and fantasies.

> INTERVIEWER: What would you like to do when you get all done with
>   your schooling? What's your fantasy?
> MAGGIE: My fantasy?
> INTERVIEWER: Your ideal.
> MAGGIE: To tell you the truth, my ideal is to become a teacher. (She
>   laughed nervously) ... but like so many people tell me, some peo-
>   ple tell me, like my mother, she's like, "Go for it, go for it. That
>   would be so great." But then other people, "That's no money. There's
>   no money in teaching." So I'm like, I want money. I wanna be com-
>   fortable wherever I work. I want money. So it's like, I'm like, "oh
>   God." I don't know....
> INTERVIEWER: How much would you guess that a full-time teacher
>   makes, say, somebody who's been teaching five years?
> MAGGIE: Maybe $28,000 ... I have no idea. I'm tryin' to go by what my
>   mother makes, but she's not a teacher.... My teacher, my Ameri-
>   can history teacher told me that when he started, awhile back, I
>   think it was in the 60s, '66, I don't know when, he was just making
> $6,000 a year.
> INTERVIEWER: What other ideas do you have about what you might
>   become?
> MAGGIE: Um, going into my major.
> INTERVIEWER: Which is? Becoming a secretary?
> MAGGIE: Yeah.
> INTERVIEWER: Any special kind of secretary?
> MAGGIE: I'm taking sten, mostly because my teacher says that you get,
>   like they'll pay you extra, like say, OK, you're gonna start with $10
>   an hour, "Do you know sten?" "Yes." "OK, we'll start you at $13."
>   That's how she says it is. So. I'm scared, because we take sten in
>   class and I feel comfortable because she's my teacher, but if I was
>   like maybe to go into an office and start working for somebody
>   who says, "Come in, take this," I would be so nervous. I don't
>   know. She says, "Of course you have to get used to the person."

But I know I would be nervous, because I'm like that. So that would be good to go into my major.

Interviews with Maggie and other students suggested that vocational skills were an important factor in the development of confidence, particularly for low income, minority, and female students. According to the interviews, students who have a clear sense of a job opportunity after high school are more likely to aspire to college, knowing that there is a way to earn a paycheck during college and to get a backup job after college.

CRITICISMS OF CAREER MAGNETS

In addition to discussing the benefits of integrated academic and vocational education, career magnet students also offered criticisms. The most frequently heard criticism was, "They expect too much." This comment was heard consistently from students who won the lottery and enrolled in the career magnet of first choice, but later transferred to another school or dropped out of high school entirely.

The negative factors affecting career magnets that emerged from students' criticisms fell into three main categories: (1) inadequate academic preparation, especially among those students who would not have been admitted without the lottery; (2) overworked teachers; and (3) a lack of role models and mentors to help students from low income and minority families.

Inadequate Academic Preparation

The two track combination of college and vocational preparation was also, in a practical sense, a double workload for students. Some students, particularly those with below average academic records and/or truancy habits, had difficulty keeping up with the work. At the time of the interviews, the career magnets' efforts to provide remediation for these students seemed inadequate.

MARIA. Maria was a student from a working-class family who was accepted by lottery to a career magnet and transferred quickly. She said she was unhappy because she was overwhelmed by the workload and did not make new friends at the school.

> INTERVIEWER: So you were in tenth grade at the career magnet. You said
> it was easy at first.... Did the school do anything to make you feel
> at home?
> MARIA: Yeah, like you know, there were all nice people there and every-
> thing. It's just that it wasn't my neighborhood and I wasn't com-
> fortable with, you know, the surroundings, so I thought I'd go

somewhere in my neighborhood. And besides I couldn't wake up for school neither. I have to travel....

INTERVIEWER: What got harder in school?

MARIA: Well, they had me in all Regents classes and I didn't think I was in Regents level. I have a very hard time in English and they ... they would put me in Regents classes that I couldn't pass. And I was telling, I kept tellin' them that I can't pass it so.... But they wouldn't change me. They said that's my own, that's my level....

INTERVIEWER: When did you first start thinking about transferring?

MARIA: Oh, as soon as I got there ... because it was like, it was like a race with school if you really wanna, you know, if you didn't stay with the work sort of people and they would like look at you, the other sort.

EVELYN. Evelyn won the lottery and entered her first choice career magnet, but later left high school. She cut classes frequently and dropped out after three years that included many failed classes. At the time of the interviews, she had a job, was living with relatives in a ghetto neighborhood, and was planning to take the GED exam. When asked about her experience at the career magnet, she said:

> They expect too much.... They're expecting too much, more than you're offering.... It was so easy just to walk out the door. It was hard to walk out the door in junior high school.... I learned my lesson but if I had to do it over I don't think I would cut. I had fun in my cutting days. But if I'd known I was gonna get my GED, I probably wouldn't have done it. I think the career magnet is a very good school. I wish I woulda stayed there. But I don't think I'm messed up. I messed up but I don't think I'm messed up.

Although Evelyn did not complain that she needed money, it seemed that this may have contributed to her lack of motivation at the career magnet. She explained that she was looking for a job while she was studying at the career magnet. After dropping out she entered a GED program, and she reported that she had completed the classes. She said she wanted to go to a college, having investigated both 2-year and 4-year colleges. In fact, she had made an appointment with the admissions office of a large private university. She said, "I want to go to school now before I lose the desire."

Overworked School Adults

The faculty of the career magnets also suffered at times from the workload at the two track career magnets. According to the interviews, some teachers were required to teach courses for which they were not trained. In addition, some teachers, administrators, and counselors protested against a change in the student population that, they believed, resulted from the 1987 lottery admission mandate. They claimed that there were significantly more students who could not keep up with the work, behaved in disorderly ways, or simply did not attend class. Teachers said they were unprepared to teach the new kind of student they faced in the classroom. Complaints were also heard from counselors, who said that they were overwhelmed with paperwork and could not deal adequately with the problems of students.

The following group discussion among school-selected students at a career magnet centered on the problem of teachers being forced to teach courses for which they were not trained. The group included three seniors and one junior.

INTERVIEWER: Who are some of the worst teachers here?

JOEY: Well, there are certain teachers who I can't stand, but do teach. Mr. Restrepo I had once. Mr. Restrepo is a Spanish teacher in the school. I've heard about him, but I had him for economics my last term here, which is a requirement which I'm taking in college next, which I learned nothing about. He could not even spell economics right.... I enjoyed it because I did not have to even earn my grade, I got a very easy grade. I was always there, but like, I have to do something for the school, let me do it now. But it's just not right because I would sit there, and when a sub came in, you didn't know the difference because you learn the same thing, and that's just not right. The way the school sets it up, they try to get teachers, like ... a business teacher that teaches computers, they know computer accounting.... They have to like, rotate them, get them to at least teach something. Most of them are not qualified to teach subjects that they're forced to teach. And there's no purpose in how they rotate the teachers. If you have enough teachers for every subject as it is, don't try to expand them if they don't know what they're doing. And there's a lot of teachers that I've had. My accounting lab class was a business law teacher, my economics class was a Spanish teacher....

INTERVIEWER: Let me see if I'm understanding what you're saying. I think what you're telling me is that the teachers are asked to teach too many different things.

JOEY: Right.

INTERVIEWER: Do you think they, the teachers, ought to be concentrating on their specialties more?

JOEY: Unless they come into the school knowing that they're going to teach more. Some teachers want to teach more than one subject, that's different. But these teachers are forced into....

INTERVIEWER: Against their will?

JOEY: By contract ... that's how I ended up with an accounting lab teacher that didn't know about computers.

JEREMIE: Like my business math teacher is a music teacher.

MELISSA: Kind of like sixth grade, when you have one teacher who teaches everything.

HANNA: Yeah. And then you have teachers that have a degree for one thing, and they're teaching another.

Role Models and Mentors

Often, students from low income and minority households showed a special need for people to model the kind of behavior, and help them acquire the kind of workplace contacts, that their families and friends did not possess. In some cases, a personal relationship with an adult on the school staff, or with a peer, made an important difference in the life of such a student. But too many students drifted through career magnets and neighborhood high schools without connecting with a mentor who could help them learn the attitudes and communication patterns they would need in higher opportunity workplaces. Some have given the name *cultural capital* to these attitudes and communication patterns (Bourdieu & Passeron, 1977; Claus, 1990).

LISA. The following profile of a girl from a low income, minority family who attended a career magnet (and for whom English was a second language) illustrates both successes and failures. On the positive side, she was earning course credits in her chosen major. However, she reported negative experiences with school adults. In the first interview, she discussed her major at the career magnet.

INTERVIEWER: Do you like it?

LISA: Not really.... I'm not good at it.... You know, I have low grades. That's why.

INTERVIEWER: What kind of grades do the teachers give you?

LISA: 70, 65, 75 ... that's all.

INTERVIEWER: Do you think the grades are fair?

LISA: No ... because when I took the test I got 85, sometimes I got 88, I had 80, right, and then on the report card we had—75. And then sometimes I only have 65. And then I went over and asked my teacher, right, and he said that, see, I don't speak up in class. That's why I got low grades.... I'm kinda shy in the class....

Lisa's descriptions of other classes revealed her struggles with the teachers, language, and communication patterns. Although she admitted that she needed to improve her English, she described several incidents that suggested problems with communication, not language use. She usually spoke in short utterances of one or two sentences. This inhibited her performance in classes in which group discussion participation was important for success. Also, she reported some trouble with getting a turn to talk in class when she was ready. She said that, in one class, "When I raise my hand he never calls on me, and when I put down my hand, he calls on me." She said she "hated" an administrator who insisted she take a language class she did not want to take. By her report, the administrator said that, because of her ethnic background, "you have to take this class."

In the first interview, Lisa expressed a tentative interest in going to college, although she was concerned about her grades. She reported that her GPA was in the 70s.

> INTERVIEWER: Have you thought about what you're going to do when you get done with high school? You get done in about a year and a half, right?
> LISA: (after a pause) I don't know what to do.
> INTERVIEWER: What do you think you might do?
> LISA: I want to go to college but … but I don't think … you know, I don't think I'll get into college because my low, I mean my grades was low, right? And I wanna get my Regents diploma also, but … I'm scared that I'm not gonna … pass the Regents class.
> INTERVIEWER: Say you could get into the college you wanted, what college would you go to? (Lisa listed three possibilities.) What would you have to do to get into a college?
> LISA: Study more.
> INTERVIEWER: Have any teachers or counselors talked to you about going to college?
> LISA: Yeah, once, but not really, not really talk about college. Only a little stuff. They asked me where I want to go and that's it.
> INTERVIEWER: Did anybody talk to you about applying to college?
> LISA: No.

The above excerpt suggests that Lisa had received little information or encouragement from school adults regarding the possibility of college. She also had career aspirations that no school adults had recognized.

> INTERVIEWER: If you could do anything you want, what would you do?
> LISA: I wouldn't be a cashier. I wanna be a secretary … uh, fashion designer. I wanna go to fashion designer school.… That's it. I don't know.

In a later interview, it became clear that Lisa's commitment to school had increased during her junior year, as she was beginning to think seriously about going to college. She explained that she had decided to stop cutting classes. "If I want to go to college, I better do good this year," she said.

Instead of finding a mentor at school, Lisa had repeated experiences with school adults that ended in discouragement, suppressed anger, and no recognition of her more ambitious aspirations. An average student, Lisa might have become an above-average student if she had found a sympathetic adult to listen to her and help her cope with communication problems at school.

■

CONCLUSION: THE STRENGTHS OF CAREER MAGNETS

The positive attitude of students at the Business, Communications, and Criminal Justice magnets seemed to originate with their interest in the career specialties. Of the students who made first-choice application to the career magnets we studied, more than three fourths said that the decision came from an interest in the school's career specialty. In the interviews, career magnet students spoke confidently about the practical skills they learned, expecting that their skills would help them get jobs. Most had made plans beyond entry-level jobs after high school. It was especially encouraging to find sophisticated career awareness among low income, minority, and female students, about whom educators and policymakers have expressed special concern.

Of the four career magnet programs, the Communications Magnet seemed to be most successful and provided some clues regarding ways to integrate academic and vocational education effectively. The success of the Communications Magnet began with the fact that it was a "redesign" effort, which means that it replaced a neighborhood high school closed by the Board of Education. As a redesign school, the Communications Magnet had several advantages. The principal had the right to hire as many new teachers as he deemed necessary. Also, the principal negotiated a cap, or maximum limit, of 1,200 students, and this stipulation was written into the school's contract. This cap could not be changed by the Board of Education without renegotiating the entire contract. Another advantage was special funding the school received during its first 5 years as a redesign school. Finally, the school faculty and staff knew from the outset that they would be working with a student population of which half were admitted by lottery, not by the school's admissions committee.

When we began interviewing at the Communications Magnet, we were curious about the quality of vocational education. We were somewhat surprised to find that this magnet seemed to provide a high level of career education in comparison with other sites. Although the principal had no specific professional experience in the communications specialty, he hired other administrators and teachers who did. During the 2-year planning period before the redesigned school opened its doors to students, the principal and the new faculty constructed a curriculum that began with core courses in media, literature, public speaking, reporting, and writing, as well as in basic skill training in keyboarding. The curriculum progressed to specific studies in areas such as computer applications, computer programming, and television. Like students at the other career magnets, the Communications Magnet students told us repeatedly they liked learning skills that they believed would be useful in workplaces. They unanimously accepted the keyboarding course, seemingly the most mundane of the core courses, and several said they enjoyed it.

The principal had forged an excellent working relationship with the faculty and support staff. School adults consistently said that they liked working at the school, and that the principal actively sought and often implemented their ideas. For example, the case management program, described below, originated with a counselor. Also, the principal generated regular opportunities for staff development according to the interests of the faculty and staff.

According to the principal, the cap on the number of students was crucial. For a high school in a large American city, 1,200 students is relatively small. The small size created more opportunities for interaction between students and school adults. The counselors at this school had a caseload of about 250 students per counselor, a ratio that was considered a standard caseload by the counselors interviewed. However, this was the lowest counselor caseload among the four sites.

The Communications Magnet also increased student–adult contact through informal programs. One original and inexpensive scheme for providing mentors was the case management program. Any adult at the school could volunteer for this program and would be assigned a few students. Usually, there was a preexisting rapport between the students and the adult, who might be a teacher, counselor, parent, secretary, or security guard. The same small group of students met regularly with the adult case management worker to talk about school experiences and to help solve problems. If there were problems beyond the scope of a nonprofessional, a counselor or the school psychologist could be consulted.

The counseling, case management groups, and other schemes at the Communications Magnet, increased opportunities for students to develop informal mentoring relationships with adults. In the interviews with students, we learned that at-risk students needed mentors and role models to help them learn about what constitutes appropriate behavior in school and in workplaces. Regular attendance, punctuality, and appropriate dress are examples of such behaviors. More complex behaviors, such as cooperation and communication, are necessary in order to work well with both authority figures and colleagues, as investigators have suggested (Levin & Rumberger, 1989). The career magnets represented a last chance for at-risk students to learn the behavior, values, and attitudes needed to succeed in higher level workplaces. If the schools did not help at-risk students, it seemed unlikely that they would be able to overcome the effects of the negative situations and circumstances in which they grew up.

There were, thus, several benefits offered to students by New York City's career magnets. The appeal and effectiveness of a magnet originated with the choice of a career specialty in a promising occupational field. Through jobs, internships, and vertical curricula, the magnets gave students a two track education that linked their high school experience with work as well as with higher education. The inclusion of vocational skills training in career magnet classes increased the students' confidence in themselves and in the future. In both direct and indirect ways, career magnets encouraged students to make plans for a productive future.

■

NOTES

1. The interview study was part of an umbrella project that included a large-scale analysis of statistical data concerning students in the educational options program and a survey of school administrators (Crain et al., 1992). The statistical study documented the impact of the educational options program on standardized test scores, dropout rates, attendance records, number of credits earned, and other outcomes. This research was supported by a grant from the National Center for Vocational Education. Statements do not necessarily reflect the position or policy of this agency.

2. For this study, 70 students and 60 school adults (teachers, counselors, and administrators) were interviewed. The students and adults were interviewed for at least thirty minutes and for as long as three hours; in many cases, individuals were interviewed more than once. Additional small-group interviews with students were often conducted in order to enhance rapport, observe the students' interaction, and document peer group patterns more effectively. The students came from four high schools that admitted young people from the same three middle schools in adjoining neighborhoods. The sample was taken only from these four high schools, thus reducing sample variance and increasing the possibility of generalizing about the school experience of the students. This sampling strategy also ensured that a proportion of the students interviewed would come from low income and minority families, so that we could study the reaction of this kind of student to the career magnets. The students were selected through a combination of stratified random sampling and theoretical sampling (Glaser & Strauss, 1967). Lottery winners and lottery losers were sampled at random for each of the two total career magnets. In addition, a theoretical sample of students who were "hand-picked" by the two total magnets was constructed.

PART III

THE PEDAGOGY
OF CURRICULUM
INTEGRATION

10

TEACHING GENERIC SKILLS

CATHY STASZ
KIMBERLY RAMSEY
RICK EDEN

There is growing consensus that American education needs fundamental reform. The widespread dissatisfaction with secondary education in particular is partly based on two concerns about skill demand in the workplace. One is that America is losing its competitive edge over other nations that educate and train a higher skilled work force (Commission on the Skills of the American Workforce [CSAW], 1990). The second is that changes in the workplace will continue to demand highly skilled and more flexible workers (Bailey, 1991).

Two questions hold center stage for school reformers:

- What kinds of skills should be taught and learned?
- How should schooling be reorganized?

This chapter examines the intersection of one answer to the first question—i.e., teach generic skills—with one answer to the second—i.e., integrate vocational and academic education.

The suggestion that students be taught generic skills—problem solving, communication, teamwork, higher order thinking—in addition to subject-matter knowledge was made by a widely cited commission report sponsored by the Secretary of Labor (Secretary's Commission on Achieving Necessary Skills [SCANS], 1991). That report also notes that students' attitudes toward work need improvement.

The *how* question must be addressed at both the program and classroom levels. At the program level, one sees the development of many models to improve the school-to-work transition (cf. Bodily, Ramsey, Stasz, &

169

Eden, 1993; Stern, 1990). These models often require changes in curriculum, pedagogy, and organizational structure in addition to new relationships between secondary schools and institutions that provide postsecondary education and training. The integration of academic and vocational education is one of these approaches.

Program-level changes often entail changes in the classroom as well. At the classroom level, one way that teachers can accomplish integration is to specifically teach generic skills and attitudes. Thus, although integration and teaching generic skills are in theory independent—that is, you can have one without the other—the two are mutually reinforcing. This chapter will illustrate how teaching generic skills can facilitate integration. The authors studied the teaching and learning of generic skills in both academic and vocational classrooms.[1] Our efforts to understand these classrooms focused on answering several questions:

- What practices do vocational and academic teachers use to teach generic skills and work-related attitudes?
- How do elements of the broader schooling context support or hinder these teaching practices?
- How can the context be changed—for example, through a policy change—to improve support of these teaching practices?

We found that generic skills and positive work-related attitudes can be taught in both academic and vocational classrooms. We developed a framework for designing classrooms that support the learning of both generic and subject-specific skills. By applying the components of this framework systematically, academic and vocational teachers can collaborate to create new programs that teach a variety of generic and subject-specific skills and that actively engage students in learning.

GENERIC SKILLS AND WORK-RELATED ATTITUDES

We distinguish two broad categories of generic skills:

- *Basic or enabling skills* include such abilities as reading, doing simple mathematics, and such life skills as reading a schedule or filling out an application. Rudimentary prosocial behaviors can also be considered basic skills. Basic skills are often used in the service of more complex tasks requiring higher skill levels.
- *Complex reasoning skills* comprise the second category of generic skills. Some tasks require formal reasoning: The problem to be solved specifies all premises or given information in advance. Other tasks require informal, or everyday, reasoning: Premises are not completely supplied for the problem, and everyday thinking activities must be invoked

(e.g., planning, making commitments, evaluating arguments, choosing options— see Galotti [1989] for a detailed discussion). Complex reasoning skills are the types of skills needed in "flexible" work arrangements (U.S. Congress, Office of Technology Assessment [OTA], 1990; SCANS, 1991; CSAW, 1990).

These generic skills can be applied in a variety of domains or vocations and in combination with subject-specific knowledge and skills that define competence in a particular area.

A third component of our conceptualization identifies work-related skills and attitudes that individuals bring to a task. These can influence how any skills are acquired and learned.

- Work-related skills and attitudes include: cooperative skills; personal qualities, such as individual responsibility, self-esteem, self-management, and sociability (cf. SCANS, 1991); "habits of thought" that can lead individuals to engage in higher order thinking (cf. Resnick, 1987a); and psychological factors that influence a person's motivation to respond to a task in either adaptive or maladaptive ways (cf. Dweck & Leggett, 1988).

These three categories of generic skills and attitudes overlap and it is difficult to determine exactly what proportion of different skills or attitudes contribute to skilled performance. It is known, however, that individuals faced with school-related, work-related, or everyday life tasks bring a constellation of knowledge, skills, and attitudes to bear in accomplishing them.[2] Knowledge, skills, and attitudes interact with one another and with the task in complex ways to produce degrees of success or failure. While skills define a person's competence or ability to do a task, attitudes influence willingness and the effort expended to perform a task (Stasz et al., 1990).[3]

■
THE STUDY FINDINGS

To observe the learning and teaching of generic skills in vocational and academic settings, we conducted intensive field studies of both kinds of classrooms. We used a combination of research approaches that included case study, ethnographic, and survey methods. We selected eight classrooms in Los Angeles County, including both academic and vocational classrooms, in which teachers claimed to (1) teach problem-solving skills, (2) value students' cooperation and responsibility for their own learning, (3) provide opportunities for project and group work, and (4) hold high expectations for students' performance. Characteristics of the eight classrooms are summarized in Table 10.1. Four teachers taught these eight classes; their backgrounds are summarized in Table 10.2.[4]

TABLE 10.1.   Site Characteristics

Type of Classroom	Type of High School	Location	Socio-economic Status	Ethnicity
Interior design (vocational)	Comprehensive	Urban	Mixed	Anglo, increasing African-American, Latino, Asian
Landscape (vocational)	Comprehensive	Suburban	Middle to high	Primarily Anglo
English (academic)	Comprehensive	Suburban	Middle to high	Primarily Anglo
Electronics (vocational)	Comprehensive	Suburban	Middle to high	Primarily Anglo
Architecture (vocational)	Comprehensive	Suburban	Middle to high	Primarily Anglo
Manufacturing (vocational)	Comprehensive	Suburban	Middle to high	Primarily Anglo
Chemistry (2 classes) (academic)	Academy within comprehensive high school	Urban	Mixed	Primarily African-American and Latino

Our systematic comparison of the eight classrooms, following a year of sequential study, reveals that they fall into two groups, five that enjoyed a strong measure of success in imparting generic skills and attitudes (interior design, electronics, manufacturing, architectural drawing, and English), and three that were markedly less successful (landscape and two chemistry classes). The successful and unsuccessful groups contained both vocational and academic classrooms. The similarities that we observed among the five successful classrooms permit us to identify key categories for describing successful classrooms (these are summarized as column headings in Table 10.3). From these similarities we derive several themes regarding how to design and conduct a classroom that works, and we organize these into an instructional model for teaching generic skills and work-related attitudes (the components of this model are summarized in Table 10.3). Teachers who wish to include generic skills and attitudes among their instructional goals can draw on this model to help them design and conduct their classes.

TABLE 10.1 (CONT'D.).

Grade Levels	Gender Mix	Special Needs	Academic Level
Tenth to twelfth	Both	Some limited English proficiency (LEP) and special education	Mixed
Eleventh and twelfth	Both	Many with emotional and behavioral problems, some LEP	Most in lowest third academically
Twelfth	Both	Some LEP	College-bound
Ninth to twelfth	All male	Some LEP, some with emotional, behavioral problems	Some in lowest third academically
Ninth to twelfth	Both	Some LEP, some with emotional, behavioral problems	Some in lowest third academically
Ninth to twelfth	Primarily male, one female	Some LEP, some with emotional, behavioral problems	Some in lowest third academically
Tenth	Both	Some LEP and special education	Mixed, with most in middle and lowest thirds

Although we present our findings in these categories separately, they are linked in practice: Instructional goals influence classroom design and teaching techniques; classroom design and teaching techniques influence each other; and school context influences goals, design, and techniques. Because of these interactions, the categories must be considered in an integrated fashion in order to design classrooms that work.

INSTRUCTIONAL GOALS

Teachers' planning, instructional activities, and teaching techniques are organized around their instructional goals—the particular kinds of knowledge, skills, and attitudes that teachers want students to learn (Collins & Stevens, 1982; Leinhardt, 1983; Leinhardt & Greeno, 1986; McArthur, Stasz, & Zmuidzinas, 1990; Putnam, 1987). Instructional goals can be either subject-specific or generic (i.e., applying to more than one subject area). For

TABLE 10.2. Characteristics of Teachers in the Sample

Teacher	Courses	Degrees and Credentials	Teaching Experience	Vocational Experience
Ms. Adams	Interior design	Vocational teaching credential	7 years	Interior designer
Mr. Price	Landscape/ horticulture, English	Bachelor's degrees in botany and English, professional writer certificate	12 years	—
Mr. Benson	Industrial arts, algebra	MS in industrial technology, MA in fine arts	Over 20 years	Hobbyist in furniture design and home construction
Mr. Stone	Chemistry	MS in seismology	3 years	Seismology lab worker

example, a subject-specific instructional goal is learning certain chemistry facts; another is learning how to wire a circuit. An example of a generic work-related attitude is taking responsibility for one's own work.

The teachers in our sample had a mix of instructional goals for students that included subject-specific knowledge and skills, complex reasoning skills and problem-solving strategies, work-related attitudes, and cooperative or group skills. Each teacher placed a different emphasis on these goals.

Complex Reasoning Skills
In five of eight classrooms, generic problem-solving and thinking skills were included as instructional goals. The vocational classes—interior design, electronics, manufacturing, and architectural drawing—all provided opportunities for students to learn and practice several generic problem-solving skills, including problem analysis, generation of solution paths, evaluation of solution paths, repair, and troubleshooting. The use of these skills was implicitly built into project work (designing a house or an electrical circuit, and designing and manufacturing a wooden truck), such that students had to exercise the skills while solving problems. Similarly, students in Mr. Price's English class learned complex thinking skills that resemble these problem-solving skills. Mr. Price also taught specific heuristics and strategies to aid students in idea generation and evaluation, and was quite explicit in discussing a particular composition process that he wanted students to learn.

In contrast, students in the landscaping and chemistry classes had lit-

TABLE 10.3 Components of an Instructional Model for Teaching Generic Skills and Work-Related Attitudes

Instructional Goals	Classroom Design	Teaching Techniques	School Context
Complex reasoning skills	Situated learning	Modeling	Access to knowledge
Work-related attitudes	Culture of expert practice	Coaching	Press for achievement
Cooperative skills	Motivation	Scaffolding	Professional teaching conditions
Subject-specific knowledge, skills	Cooperation, teacher roles	Articulation, reflection exploration	

tle opportunity to practice complex reasoning or problem-solving skills, since teachers emphasized skills that were specific to the course and organized activities around discrete, unconnected tasks rather than evolving projects. In landscaping, for example, students worked at specific short-term tasks, such as pruning roses, weeding, or watering. Chemistry students worked in pairs to complete laboratory experiments, each of which presented a well-defined but decontextualized problem that students had to solve by following a prescribed sequence of steps.

Work-Related Attitudes

Ms. Adams, Mr. Benson, and Mr. Price (English class) stressed the importance of students taking responsibility for their own learning and for completing their assigned tasks. As a result, they all gave students opportunities to work on their own and to solve their own problems, and often exhorted students to "take responsibility" or "figure it out." Ms. Adams, as a practicing interior designer, made the strongest and most frequent links between classwork and schoolwork. Mr. Price and Mr. Benson—perhaps because they lacked actual work experience in their domains—did not use workplace-based examples to support the development of work-related attitudes. Mr. Price appealed to the notion of lifelong learning. He reinforced a disposition toward reading and thinking that he believed would help students in college and beyond.

In his landscape/horticulture class, however, Mr. Price failed to impart any work-related attitudes. He spent a great deal of class time "managing" inappropriate behavior, including instances of leaving the school grounds, fighting and arguing among students, and persistent nonperformance of required tasks. He had little opportunity to teach generic skills and attitudes to the remaining students who at least attempted to carry out assigned tasks. Work-related attitudes also were not stressed in the chemistry classes. In the laboratory exercises, Mr. Stone encouraged students to learn to trust their observations and to record the data associated with those observations, or to observe safety precautions. But this learning seemed task-specific and not linked, for example, to actual work in a laboratory or related scientific work. Although Mr. Stone had work experience in a seismology lab, he did not use that experience to place classroom assignments in a broader, work-related context.

Cooperative Skills

In five classes, teachers had enhancing cooperative skills as an instructional goal. Ms. Adams had students work in groups on their design project and explicitly taught a consensus process that students used to make a design decision (e.g., selecting fabric) and to justify a decision (the rationale). In electronics, Mr. Benson wanted students to become "contributing partners"; in manufacturing, he expected students working in groups to learn to resolve differences on their own. Mr. Price wanted students to learn how to use each other as "resources," and designed several group exercises where students assumed different roles (e.g., reader or critic).

In contrast, Mr. Price had a difficult time fostering cooperation in his landscape class. For many students, he focused on improving appropriate individual behavior in class—for example, reducing disruptive behavior. Mr. Stone did not face behavior problems that worked against cooperation, but also did not make cooperation between lab partners or among class members an objective of the learning process. His only inclination toward promoting cooperation was to have lab partners submit one report for the pair.

Subject-Specific Skills

Ms. Adams and Mr. Price were both more concerned with teaching students how to engage in a process than on having them acquire or demonstrate specific skills out of context. While Ms. Adams valued subject-specific skills and, for example, gave detailed lectures on fabrics in her interior design class, she never directly tested students on subject area knowledge. Rather, the students' knowledge was tested in their performance of the design process. Similarly, Mr. Price's instruction was geared primarily toward teaching processes that would help students engage in reading and writing, promote understanding of the novels, and aid in producing a final paper. Mr. Benson paid more attention to subject-specific skills but still focused instruction on application of knowledge and skills to solve problems.

Whether dealing with ill defined or well defined problems, these teachers defined their instructional subject area in broad terms that went far beyond subject-specific knowledge.[5] Their view of relevant class content was not constrained by curriculum frameworks, learning objectives, standardized tests, textbooks, or specific bits of subject-area knowledge. Another factor contributing to a broad conceptualization of a subject is teacher expertise. These three teachers, Ms. Adams, Mr. Price, and Mr. Benson, had deep knowledge and understanding of their respective subjects, in addition to professional experience and/or an avocation for the subject area that contributed to their expertise.

In contrast, Mr. Stone's vision of chemistry instruction in the academy program exceeded his ability to execute that vision. His instructional goals focused on learning terminology, certain principles (e.g., oxidation reduction), and basic laboratory procedures—what he referred to as "chemistry facts." Mr. Price's landscape class included relatively low-level subject area knowledge (e.g., how to water deeply to encourage deep root systems) or basic botany (e.g., the parts of plants). While Mr. Price had a botany degree and substantial practical experience and knowledge about landscaping that might have shaped a more sophisticated curriculum in landscape/horticulture, the needs and abilities of this particular group of students—or his perceptions of those needs and abilities—appeared to work toward simplification of the curriculum and overall classroom design.

CLASSROOM DESIGN

Ideally, teachers design classrooms to support their instructional goals, and it is expected the designs will vary to reflect alternative emphases among goals. We compared our eight classrooms along several dimensions of classroom design, based on the instructional model elaborated by Collins et al. (1989). These features include situated learning, culture of practice, motivation, cooperation, and competition. Each of these is discussed below. Because competition was not a factor in these classes, we do not elaborate on this aspect of classroom design. We also compare the roles that teachers adopted to support classroom design and instructional goals.

Situated Learning

Many practitioners and researchers posit that learning through the work process itself is an effective method for acquiring work-related knowledge. In the absence of direct experience, new instructional models support *situating* learning in the context of real-life problems suggested by a culture of expert practice. This requires teachers to take different roles in teaching and for students to take a more active role in learning. In situated learning environments, students carry out tasks and solve problems that are realistic or "authentic" in the sense that they "reflect the multiple uses to which their knowledge will be put in the future" (Collins et al., 1989, p. 487). By working on authentic problems, students come to understand the uses of the knowledge they are learning and different conditions under which that knowledge can be applied. It is thought that this authentic environment increases both learning efficacy and motivation. They also learn how to transfer knowledge and skills learned in one context to new problems or domains (Resnick, 1987a; Singley & Anderson, 1989). Students are actively engaged in a process that requires them to interact with the environment and to deal with new problems that result from that interaction.

In five classrooms, teachers had students carry out tasks and solve problems in environments that reflected the multiple uses to which their knowledge will be put in the future. Teachers designed project work that students carried out individually, in teams, or both. These projects were complex enough to challenge students to use new subject-specific skills as well as many generic skills. For example, over the course of 6 weeks, Ms. Adams' students designed a contemporary interior for a Victorian-era house. Working in teams for the most part, students researched the original house and its design tradition, drew the house, drafted floor plans, selected furnishings and colors, and prepared boards to display their proposed design. At the end of the semester, each team presented their design orally to the class.

In contrast, Mr. Price organized his landscape/horticulture class on the model of a road crew, a work unit devised as much for disciplinary and control reasons as for productivity. This classroom environment produced minimal work from most students, who were expected only to complete their tasks while maintaining appropriate classroom behavior. Similarly, Mr. Stone's chemistry labs were "cookbook" exercises that required students to simply follow directions, collect data, and use the data to solve math problems. These labs epitomized the kind of decontextualized learning experience that many reformers criticize.[6]

Culture of Practice

A second characteristic of classroom design is the creation of a culture of expert practice in which participants "actively communicate about and engage in the skills involved in expertise, where expertise is understood as the practice of solving problems and carrying out tasks in a domain" (Collins et al., 1989, p. 488). Coupled with the authentic activities pursued in situated learning, a culture of practice helps students acquire the knowledge, skills, and attitudes typical of practitioners who work within that particular subject area. Ideally, interactions between learners and experts will reveal underlying cognitive processes that experts engage in as they solve problems.[7] In an interior design class, for example, the teacher can relate a story from her own experience as a designer to explain why a particular fabric is a poor choice for drapes (Stasz et al., 1990). Such expert anecdotes ("war stories") appear to aid learning by providing students with concrete, memorable stories that communicate valuable knowledge or lessons (Orr, 1986).

Some classrooms in our sample implicitly or explicitly promoted different cultures of practice; some reflected the adult world of work in the particular subject area. Ms. Adams' class invoked the practice of interior design professionals. Mr. Price's English class embodied several cultures of practice, including that of the reader, the writer, and the college student. His students most frequently identified with the latter. Mr. Benson's classes supported cultures where "hobbyists" with interest in the subject and varying degrees of expertise could work on projects and learn from each other or where workers on the "shop floor" collectively produced a real product.

Three classes failed to establish either situated learning environments or to foster effective cultures of practice that would provide opportunities for learning high-level skills. Mr. Price's landscape class, for example, successfully supported the culture of the road crew, but few would argue that high school is the place for teaching the low-level skills associated with basic gardening and landscaping. In spite of Mr. Stone's past employment in a seismology lab, his chemistry classes offered standard, decontextualized science exercises and did not support any recognizable culture of practice beyond that of the college-bound high school student.

Motivation

While schools often use extrinsic factors to enhance student motivation (e.g., grades and teacher praise), intrinsic factors (e.g., challenge, interest, and degree of student control) are often more effective (Malone, 1981; Malone & Lepper, 1987). The main motivational feature in the five successful classrooms—interior design, electronics, manufacturing, architectural drawing, and English—was the teachers' emphasis on intrinsic over extrinsic motivational factors. Teachers deemphasized grades and did not discuss performance criteria in terms of grades. Rather, they focused on finding ways to engage students to exert effort, recognizing that every student could learn and make a contribution to the class if he or she applied effort. All three teachers saw individual interest as the key to mobilizing effort. Mr. Price and Mr. Benson, for example, encouraged students to follow their interests in identifying themes for critical essays or for choosing electronics projects.

In addition to teacher strategies for motivating students, students identified specific teacher characteristics as motivating factors. In every class we visited, even the less successful ones, students mentioned teacher enthusiasm for the topic, or genuine concern for students, as having motivational appeal.

Although the landscape and chemistry classes were taught by enthusiastic and caring teachers, other factors seemed to hamper student involvement and motivation. In the landscape class, students who were at all inclined to work typically faced menial, uninteresting tasks, like watering a flower bed or digging a ditch. In this case, the design of the classroom activities seems at fault. Few students in Mr. Stone's class seemed motivated to go beyond minimum performance. Students were focused on just "getting the work done" needed for at least a C grade, because the academy demanded at least C performance.

Cooperation

Learning to work cooperatively with others is an important skill for the workplace, where group work and collaboration among team members or individuals is increasingly becoming the norm. In most classrooms in our sample, students learned to work together in self-managing groups in which cooperation was important. Sometimes they worked in teams and were graded on team effort. Other times they worked alone, but engaged other students to help solve problems, sound out an opinion, or ask advice. Or they worked in pairs to do electronics labs or on a project of their own choosing. Importantly, the teachers behaved and were accepted as contributors to cooperative effort, whether they worked hands-on with the students (Mr. Benson) or more as facilitators and guides on the sidelines (Ms. Adams, Mr. Stone, and Mr. Price).

The landscape class supported coacting groups that report to a teacher/supervisor and where each student has an individually defined task, like picking weeds or pruning a rose bush. In the chemistry class, student pairs divided lab activities on their own but were basically just following a set of step-by-step instructions. In neither class did students have authority to proceed as they saw fit to generate a group product, service, or decision.

Even where teachers had students work in teams, we saw some negative effects that diminished cooperation. For example, we observed some student pairs in electronics where one student was the learner and the other was the assistant. Students who stayed in the assistant role, for whatever reason, lost opportunities to become more independent thinkers and problem solvers.

Teacher Roles

Different classroom design characteristics imply different roles for the teacher and different expectations about what students should and can learn. Specifically, a teacher who designs a classroom that embodies these characteristics is likely to establish a *master-apprentice* relationship with students, or act more as the students' coach or guide in the learning process. This teacher will expect students to be actively engaged in learning and to come to the classroom with knowledge, skills, and experience that the teacher can build upon. Teachers and learners can participate together in the learning process. In contrast, a teacher adopting a more traditional role would use lectures, teacher-directed discussion, and closely guided review techniques to impart knowledge and skills to students. The implicit expectation in this approach is that students lack necessary subject area knowledge and skills and the teacher's job is to direct learning in ways that transfer knowledge from teacher to student.

Relationships we observed arising between students and teachers in classrooms that worked well were not the typical student–teacher relationships, but resembled those of masters and apprentices. The teacher was regarded as the expert or "model" practitioner of the craft, and he or she also possessed greater factual knowledge or skill. Teachers did little lecturing. One-on-one tutoring or master–apprentice interactions were the main methods by which Ms. Adams, Mr. Benson, and Mr. Price (in English class) distributed information and shaped the students' progress. These teachers often circulated throughout the classroom, stopping to visit each group. Teachers took advantage of student skill variation, and the fact that cooperative work was the norm, by encouraging more advanced students to help less advanced ones. This policy permitted teachers to spend more time with students needing the most help.

Teacher roles in the other classes were quite different. Mr. Price was more like a therapist than a teacher to some landscape students. With working students he infrequently guided them and more frequently supervised them—gave specific instructions, checked their work, admonished them for faulty work. Mr. Stone was the oracle to whom students came for answers. His missionary attitude or role was one of giving constant help and protecting students from their own failings (e.g., collecting papers so students would not lose them). Unfortunately, this kind of teaching prevents students from learning important skills, such as initiating and problem solving.

TEACHING TECHNIQUES

Teaching techniques refer to actual teacher instructional behaviors or tactics used to implement instructional goals. The techniques that teachers adopt are embedded in the context of instructional goals and the particular learning environment, and are best understood within that context. Collins et al. (1989) provide a useful formulation of teaching methods that they believe are designed to give students "the opportunity to observe, engage in, and invent or discover expert strategies in context" (p. 481). That is, these techniques are designed to support situated learning and authentic practice, as discussed above. The six methods that they identify fall roughly into three groups:

- *Modeling, coaching,* and *scaffolding* are designed to help students acquire an integrated set of cognitive and metacognitive skills (e.g., learning strategies) through processes of observation (via modeling), and of guided and supported practice (coaching and scaffolding). In addition to observable behaviors, teachers can model mental activities; for example, when a teacher models the use of heuristics, the general rules of thumb that subject area experts use to guide their problem solving.
- *Articulation* and *reflection* are designed to help students both focus their observations of expert problem solving and gain control of their own problem-solving strategies.
- *Exploration* is designed to encourage learner autonomy in carrying out problem-solving processes and in formulating the problems to be solved.

Generally speaking, all of these techniques are suited to a project-centered classroom where students are given considerable freedom to carry out individual and group tasks. Since students have different degrees of skill and are not proceeding in unison, teachers must be ready for flexible interactions, where students place unpredictable demands on them. They tend not to follow lesson plans but instead follow individual student progress. This student-centered approach results in opportunistic, not planned teaching.

Teachers in successful classrooms relied heavily on modeling how experts carry out a task. In Ms. Adams' class and Mr. Benson's class, this often involved manipulating physical objects and demonstrating correct procedures. In English class, Mr. Price often modeled internal cognitive processes and activities as well (e.g., articulated his own thinking to generate themes in a novel and provided heuristics for terminating a library search).

These teachers also used coaching, scaffolding, and fading. Mr. Benson primarily used highly interactive coaching to help students through particular problems they faced when carrying out a task. Mr. Price provided scaffolds in the form of physical supports (e.g., diagramming three ways to structure a paper) and suggestions or help (e.g., reminding students to use personal events in their lives as a stimulus for identifying themes). He also provided emotional scaffolds, by acknowledging and accepting students' discomfort with *negative capability* —the notion that temporary confusion is preferable to quick judgments about the meaning of text.

These teachers also employed techniques to get students to articulate or reflect on their knowledge, reasoning, or problem-solving processes. Mr. Price had students assume the critic's role in cooperative activities, thereby leading them to formulate and articulate their own thoughts about the novels. Ms. Adams had students reflect on their own performance as a group and discuss how group performance might have been improved.

In the other three classes, teachers and students did not assume master–apprentice roles and, for the most part, did not use the methods discussed above. While Mr. Price did use modeling techniques in his landscape class to, for example, demonstrate the proper use of a tool, most of his time was consumed by managing inappropriate behavior—fighting, shirking work, truancy, and heated confrontations. Mr. Price's genuine feeling for students, and his intense interaction with them, suggested a therapist–patient relationship. With those students who made some attempt to work, his role was more of a supervisor to workers. Mr. Stone spent much of his time lecturing or reviewing homework problems or laboratory exercises with the whole class. He made it clear to students that he was there to answer questions and help students, and said that he used student questions to gauge their learning. Mr. Stone used similar techniques in both chemistry classes, despite the fact that students in one class had higher math ability than students in the other. Mr. Stone acted as though his students should not be pressured or challenged too much, because they needed care and nurturing.

SCHOOL CONTEXT FOR TEACHING AND LEARNING

Teachers and classrooms operate within a particular context, beginning with the school and community environment and expanding to district, state, and federal levels. The broader context affects teaching and learning through such factors as resources allocated, policies, organizational structures, and processes (Oakes, 1989). Study of this context is needed, particularly at the school level, to understand the conditions or constraints that teachers and students face because these help shape the teaching and learning we observe in the classroom. We focus on three indicators of school context that can promote high-quality teaching and learning: student access to knowledge, press for student achievement, and professional teaching conditions (Oakes, 1989).

Access to Knowledge
Access to knowledge refers to the extent to which schools provide students with opportunities to learn various domains of knowledge and skills. Access is influenced not only by basic resources—such as time, materials, staff, and facilities—but also by curricular emphasis and structure—such as classroom or course assignment practices (ability-grouped or mixed instructional groups) and the curriculum associated with each group—and by teacher qualifications or opportunities for staff development.

All three high schools in our study tracked students, and tracking practices influenced who enrolled in the classrooms we observed. In the classes we studied, the mix of students depended on the type of class (academic or vocational) and the kind of credit attached to it.[8] For example, the vocational classes taught by Mr. Benson and Ms. Adams were elective courses and attracted a mixed group of students who were interested in the subject area, and, in some cases could use the class to fulfill a graduation requirement. College-bound students may actually have less access to these classes simply because these students need a certain number and type of credits for college enrollment. Thus, they lose a potential opportunity to learn generic skills taught in vocational classrooms.

A second factor affecting access is resources. Teachers generally felt that they lacked adequate resources but, because their classes were sponsored by the state's Regional Occupational Program (ROP), Ms. Adams (interior design) and Mr. Price (landscape), for example, received extra funds to purchase materials.

Press for Achievement

Press for achievement is indicated by institutional pressures that the school exerts to get students to work hard and to achieve. The schools and teachers in our sample communicated different expectations and values about achievement to their students. Obviously, any school that tracks students does not hold the same achievement standards for all students. But it appears that individual teacher standards can make a difference for students.

Although vocational classes were less valued than were academic classes in the schools where Ms. Adams and Mr. Benson taught, their personal views about students explicitly challenged the schools' views. Both of these teachers had high expectations for student achievement, which they believed was linked to effort. They worked with and supported any student who tried. They "designed in" interesting and meaningful learning activities, employing high-level cultures of practice. Mr. Price had similarly high expectations for his English students.

Mr. Price's learning expectations for the landscape students were quite different. In landscape he wanted students to maintain a level of *behavior* that did not interfere with the class; this attention to behavior led to highly structured activities and boring tasks, in service of avoiding mischief, and seemed to override any expectations about achievement per se.

Similarly, the academy program, though it required teachers to work with students who failed until they had mastered the material, did not appear to foster individual thinking, higher achievement, or effort for most students.

Professional Teaching Conditions

Teaching conditions can support or constrain teachers as they attempt to create and implement instructional programs, and they define how schools function as a workplace for teachers. Although professional teaching conditions have not been directly linked to student outcomes, there is evidence that a professional staff will work toward implementing strategies and programs to improve results (Bodilly et al., 1993; Oakes, 1989). In schools where professional teaching conditions exist, teachers have some autonomy and flexibility in implementing curriculum and instruction, in participating in schoolwide decision making, and in spending time on such activities as goal setting, staff development, program planning, curriculum development, and collaboration.

Teachers in our sample experienced varying teaching conditions, but these differences did not strongly affect teaching practices, except in one respect: Teacher autonomy appeared to contribute to the ability to design classrooms that imparted generic skills and attitudes. Among the teachers studied, vocational teachers were given more autonomy because the administration considered them outside the school mainstream. For example, Ms. Adams' interior design class was basically ignored by the school administration, but this neglect proved advantageous to the teacher because it left her wide berth to experiment.

■

RECOMMENDATIONS

It appears that generic skills and work-related attitudes can best be taught in classrooms and programs that blur the traditional distinctions between learning in school and out of school (cf. Resnick, 1987b). Classified from a traditional perspective, such classrooms and programs may be either vocational or academic. Regardless of the content area, the successful teaching of generic skills requires a common instructional model. Teachers need to adopt instructional goals that include generic skills in addition to subject-specific skills. They must create classrooms where students can acquire and apply knowledge and skills to real-world problems, learn to work with others in a community of learner-practitioners, and develop intrinsic motivation for learning and working. It requires teachers and schools to adopt the view that all students are entitled to and can benefit from learning opportunities. All students need to acquire not only knowledge and skills but also a positive perspective on learning that includes their own responsibility for it. Finally, this approach requires schools to provide a context that enables, encourages, and rewards the effective teaching and learning of generic skills and attitudes.

For reformers who believe that students can benefit from instruction in generic skills and useful work-related attitudes, our study has implications that can stimulate and inform their efforts.

DESIGNING CLASSROOM INSTRUCTION

Once a teacher decides to incorporate teaching of generic skills and attitudes, he or she must design classroom activities to support this instructional goal. Our data indicate that one successful approach is to design classroom instruction around project work that situates learning in a specific context and provides opportunities for authentic practice in a subject area. The project that students engage in should permit them to apply subject-specific knowledge and skills to real, complex problems. Students should begin with enough basic knowledge to get started and should be permitted to work on their own. Teachers should guide and facilitate learning while encouraging students to experiment and to work through emergent problems the students may encounter.

Situated learning can be enhanced by creating a culture of practice in the subject area. Depending on the goals of the class, the culture of practice may or may not need to mimic a culture of expert practice in the adult world of work. If the class is part of a program that intends to prepare students for work directly out of high school, then creating a relevant culture of practice might be an important teacher goal. In the classrooms we studied, however, few students saw the class as training for immediate employment. Except for Ms. Adams, teachers in classrooms that *worked*—i.e., that were effectively designed to impart generic skills and attitudes—were not experts (e.g., a professional writer or an electrical engineer) and had no actual work experience in the relevant culture of practice. But they were skilled and experienced adult practitioners with enough expertise to create a situated learning environment where students could acquire high-level skills, including subject-specific and generic skills.

ENHANCING STUDENT LEARNING AND ENGAGEMENT

Many educators and members of the general public voice concern over students' disengagement from learning. While we did not formally evaluate learning, the students we observed in classrooms that worked were on-task and involved with their learning. Focus group discussions and survey responses reinforce this view; students clearly articulated what they had learned, how their attitudes about learning had changed, and so on. By contrast, students in other classrooms were clearly less motivated and less challenged. They either did not appear to learn much at all (as in the landscape class) or they focused their energy on just getting a task done (as in the chemistry classes).

An important outcome of classrooms that worked was that students became "encultured." While many came into the class with vague or nonexistent learning goals, they came to accept and become a part of a culture of practice. In our view, the situated learning approach, coupled with the teachers' emphasis on appealing to intrinsic motivation (interest and challenge), were most influential in engaging students' participation. While student abilities and interests undoubtedly affect learning, effective classroom design can make a difference in students' attention and engagement in the learning process.

HOLDING HIGH EXPECTATIONS FOR STUDENTS

A clear difference between classrooms that work and those that did not rests with performance expectations that teachers and others held for students. This difference was especially startling in the two classes taught by Mr. Price, English and landscape. Mr. Price ably demonstrated skills for designing an English class that offered students a challenging and rewarding experience that went beyond requirements outlined in the state curriculum framework. In contrast, the class for landscape students provided menial, often boring work and few academic lessons, despite the science credit that came with it. Mr. Price's expectations for these students—that some would behave badly, not cooperate, not work very hard—influenced the decisions he made about what to teach and how to organize the class.

Ms. Adams and Mr. Benson stand out as teachers with uniformly high expectations for students, in spite of the low view of vocational students (and even of vocational teachers) in their schools. Unlike Mr. Price's landscape class, Mr. Benson's and Ms. Adams' classes had a more heterogeneous group of students who took the class for various reasons. This mix—of both skill and interest—was anticipated by these teachers, who designed classroom activities to both accommodate and take advantage of student differences, and who viewed each student as an individual for evaluation purposes. This mix, coupled with the teachers' high expectations, differentiated these classes from the others. The heterogeneous mix of students may be beneficial both because it enhances the learning of all students and because it circumvents institutionalized labeling and the stigma often associated with vocational education (Oakes , 1986). One example of how this difference affected classrooms is the contrast between Mr. Price's and Mr. Benson's views of how to structure the class. Mr. Benson believed the class should be structured to enhance students' motivation by teaching basic skills needed for more complex tasks, and by incorporating technology to capture students' interest. Mr. Price structured the landscape class more to control students than to motivate them: He developed a point system for student performance on well defined tasks—a divide-and-conquer strategy to separate and contain consistent troublemakers from the rest of the class—and gave students a choice of menial tasks.

GRANTING TEACHERS AUTONOMY AND ADDITIONAL RESOURCES

Teachers in classrooms that worked had a great deal of autonomy in developing their curricula and classroom activities. This freedom to innovate, however, was more a byproduct of other school policies than a belief that teacher autonomy would lead to improved instruction. As vocational teachers, Ms. Adams and Mr. Benson taught elective courses to primarily non-college-bound students. Their courses were not prerequisites for any others. The schools in which they taught placed value on college-bound students, which tends to create the standard of worth both for students and for teachers (cf. Little & Threatt, 1992). In contrast, Mr. Benson spoke of how his teaching differed in his algebra class because the required content constrained what and how he could teach.

The policies that influence autonomy have to do with course prerequisite requirements, graduation requirements, and credit standards set by the state college and university system: All are tied to the college-preparatory curriculum. If teachers don't teach college-prep courses, these policies don't constrain what they teach and how they teach it. Mr. Price had to fight for permission to teach his English composition class as he did. One can easily surmise that a teacher's *failure* to innovate may in fact be a wise choice in a constraining regulatory environment, particularly in traditional academic disciplines, where there is a trend toward more proscribed curricula.

In addition to regulatory constraints associated with accrediting courses, teachers often lack the resources they need to design classrooms that work. Except for Ms. Adams, teachers complained about the lack of basic materials, like dictionaries and books, let alone the more sophisticated tools needed in electronics and manufacturing classes. Without the promise of additional resources, there is little incentive for teachers to design more innovative instructional activities of the type described earlier. If adequate funds become available, teachers must be attuned to the materials and equipment required by "authentic" activities.

IMPROVING TEACHER TRAINING AND STAFF DEVELOPMENT

Traditional teacher training and staff development practices pose a barrier to widespread adoption of the classroom design principles and teaching practices defined in classrooms that impart generic skills and attitudes. New teachers are rarely trained to acquire the skills they will need to design classrooms that work. Much of teacher education involves perfecting the skills of writing behavioral objectives, lesson plans, and worksheets. Once graduated and working, newcomers are likely to receive staff development that deals with schoolwide issues, i.e., drug and alcohol problems and changes in state policy. This leaves them largely unprepared to experiment with mixing subject-specific and generic skills, designing situated learning opportunities, or taking on innovative and flexible teacher roles.[9]

Another implication of our study is that teachers may benefit from entirely new forms of staff development, beyond the typical 1- or 2-day workshops, on topics such as cooperative learning techniques or new curriculum frameworks. Ms. Adams' experience in the world of work, for example, clearly contributed to her desire and ability to teach work-related attitudes. Although vocational teachers often have occupational experience—sometimes as a requirement for teacher certification (cf. Lynch & Griggs, 1989)—academic teacher training typically follows the baccalaureate model, which emphasizes subject-matter preparation, with the addition of courses in teaching methods. Further staff development for teachers might include, for example, summer internships in firms that would broaden teachers' understanding of work outside of school in their chosen subject.

ASSESSING GENERIC SKILLS LEARNING

Assessment strategies employed at most schools do not serve the needs of generic skills instruction. Popular forms of assessment test students' knowledge of facts, concepts, and processes in a particular subject. They rarely assess students' ability to solve problems, reason, cooperate with others, or demonstrate other capabilities and skills learned in situated learning environments. Currently, new assessment standards, and the influence that such standards might have on improving curriculum, are being widely debated nationwide (National Council on Education Standards and Testing, 1992; Learning Research and Development Center and the National Center on Education and the Economy, 1992). While these new standards encompass the types of assessments needed to evaluate generic skills instruction, new tests are just in the process of being developed and piloted in schools. While testing reforms appear to be going in the right direction, it will be several years at best before new measures are widely available. In the meantime, a patchwork of teacher-made, nonstandardized assessments could be adopted, but such a move is unlikely. For a variety of reasons, schools rely on standardized testing regimes or qualitative assessments to evaluate program goals associated with student outcomes.

◼ CONCLUSION

We found that generic skills and positive work-related attitudes can be taught in both academic and vocational classrooms. While every attempt to incorporate generic skills teaching into classroom instruction will be faced with a unique set of barriers, the nature of the subject area itself should not be one of them. This finding has an important implication, namely, that a focus on instruction in generic skills and attitudes can be viewed as a "model" for integrating academic and vocational education (Grubb et al., 1991; Bodily et al., 1993).

One prominent feature of integration—and one of the significant barriers to its success—is the (often forced) collaboration between academic and vocational teachers. As a vocational education reform mandated by the 1990 Perkins Amendments, the thrust of integration has been to enhance the academic content of vocational programs by having academically certified teachers teach "applied" academics that, for example, correlate math instruction with a specific occupational focus. Because academic teachers lack relevant vocational training and because vocational teachers are typically not certified to teach academics, the solution has been for these teachers to pool their knowledge and skills in designing curriculum. This is an uneasy collaboration: Vocational and academic teachers, curriculum, and students have been separated in our educational institutions for decades (for further discussion see: Bodily et al., 1993; Little, 1992; Little & Threatt, 1992; Oakes, 1989).

Our study of teaching generic skills offers a different perspective. The instructional goals of classrooms that work aim to integrate the teaching of a variety of subject-specific and generic skills in a situated learning environment that actively engages students in learning. These goals mirror the spirit of integration of academic and vocational education. But this model does not require the teacher-to-teacher collaboration that creates a stumbling block for implementing many other models of integration. Rather, it requires a teacher to enter the company of experts, become a learner, and then translate a culture of practice into the design of classrooms that work. This focus has the advantage of bridging schooling with working and, thereby, improving the school's ability to prepare high school students for a future beyond school.

Thus, our notion of teaching generic skills as a model of integration is consistent with other reforms now underway (see Chapter 3), including school-to-work programs and efforts to reform teaching. Teaching generic skills, then, is a crucial and integral part of the reshaping of American education at a critical juncture in its economic and educational history.

■
NOTES

1. This study was conducted by RAND under the sponsorship of the National Center for Research in Vocational Education (NCRVE), University of California, Berkeley. In addition to the authors, members of the project team included Joan DaVanzo, Hilary Farris, and Matthew Lewis. Preparation of this chapter was supported in part by RAND's Institute on Education and Training.

2. Our definition of generic skills is similar to the three-part foundation skills identified by SCANS (1991). We place a stronger emphasis on work-related attitudes and focus more on the interplay between skills and attitudes.

3. See Stasz et al. (1990) for a review of the literature on changes in the nature and structure of work that underlie the demand for generic skills and on school reformers' rationale for teaching them. See also Berryman, 1991; Capelli, 1992; Raizen, 1989; and Resnick, 1987b.

4. To ensure anonymity, teachers and students have been given pseudonyms throughout this article.

5. A problem is well defined if a test exists that determines whether a proposed solution is in fact a solution. Ill-defined problems need further specification before they can be solved (see Hayes, 1981; Newell & Simon, 1972).

6. Effective work design has been linked to the satisfaction of the worker (Hackman & Oldham, 1980). For example, the ways in which groups are organized (e.g., self-managing vs. coacting teams) and work is designed (e.g., boring, repetitive tasks vs. meaningful, challenging tasks) can affect the amount of effort that workers choose to devote to a task (Bailey, 1991).

7. It is unclear whether an expert is needed to cultivate what Collins describes as a "culture of expert practice." It may be that a competent and experienced adult practitioner is sufficient. This question has important implications for teacher training and certification.

8. A heterogeneous mix of students may tend to raise the level of teaching and can also counteract negative affects associated with tracking students: Individual achievement and aspirations are lower among students in low-ability and nonacademic tracks at the secondary level (Oakes, 1986; 1989).

9. For example, in a recent study of integrating academic and vocational education (Bodilly et al., 1993) a 1990 teacher education graduate reported that her former university instructors were surprised to learn that her first teaching assignment (as a math teacher) required her to correlate math with occupational lessons. Despite the fact that integration of academic and vocational education was a statewide reform mandated by the State Department of Education, the faculty in the teacher training program at the state's major public university had not even heard of curricular integration and could offer their former student little practical advice.

11

Apprenticeship as a Paradigm of Learning

SUE E. BERRYMAN

Knowledge without the skill to use knowledge is, in Alfred North White-head's language, "inert." Regardless of the domain—mathematics or machining—learning consists of both knowledge and skill, requiring not just content but also the capacity to use knowledge appropriately as a tool. Developing skill requires content, acquired under the conditions of use, within learning situations that model the cognitive, social, and technological conditions where knowledge of that kind is used. Similarly, acquiring knowledge by using it makes visible, and therefore susceptible of correction, the places where the learner is still making mistakes.

As Norton Grubb shows in Chapter 4, models of academic and vocational integration are first and foremost models of *curricular* integration—in other words, models of content, not of how content is acquired. Curriculum always implies something about pedagogy, and some of the integration models, such as the senior project as a form of integration, have explicit pedagogic implications. However, the focus of integration policy and practice is curricular, not pedagogic, and the lack of systematic attention to how content is taught remains a substantial hole in integration policy and practice. Relative to academic education, good vocational education tends to use some of the strategies identified by cognitive science[1] as characteristic of more effective learning environments. However, the vocational field has not really formalized these as pedagogic principles, or systematically refined them in light of cognitive science knowledge about effective learning. Thus, vocational educators are not as able as they should be to bring their potential pedagogic advantage to the integration table, and thus are less able to work with their academic counterparts to push the integration movement beyond curriculum to pedagogy.

Relying heavily on cognitive science, this chapter addresses the pedagogic side of the equation. Specifically, it develops four arguments.

1. The learning paradigm that prevails in K–12 education routinely and profoundly violates what much of our experience, and a century of formal thought and research, tell us about effective learning, whether for the college-bound or the non-college-bound.
2. Apprenticeship, understood as a way of setting up the learning situation, is an alternative paradigm that promises to generate more effective learning for both the college-bound and non-college-bound.
3. Traditional apprenticeship, usually organized around visually observable practices that need to be learned, has to be modified to make available for modeling and discussion the nonvisible, cognitive components of modern activity, including work. It also needs to be modified to help individuals accommodate the nonroutine and changeable nature of modern work activity.
4. Apprenticeship as a paradigm for learning needs to be distinguished from the location for apprenticeship. Apprenticeship normally occurs in the workplace, but as a paradigm of learning, it can and should also occur in schools. The optimal location for apprenticeship as an organization of learning depends on issues such as the educational richness of the situation, whether it be school or work.

THE PREVAILING K-12 PARADIGM OF LEARNING

Although this discussion is couched in K–12 terms, it is important to recognize that K–12 practices tend to permeate all levels and sectors of American education and training, from elementary school to corporate training. Traditionally, these practices maintain distinctions between:

- Head and hand
- Academic and vocational education
- Knowing and doing
- Abstract and applied learning
- Education and training
- School-based and work-based learning

The standard practices in K–12 classrooms are based on four flawed paradigms: passive learning; fragmented learning; fact-based/right-answer learning; and noncontextual learning.

PASSIVE LEARNING

In a typical schoolroom, Congressional hearing, or corporate training session, the teacher—or "expert"—faces the learners in the role of knowledge source. The learner is the passive receiver of wisdom—a glass into which water is poured. This instructional arrangement arises from an implicit assumption that the basic purpose of education is to transmit the society's culture from one generation to the next. The concept of transmission implies a one-way flow from the adult members of the society to society's young (Lave, 1988) or from the expert to the novice. Education thus becomes the conveying of what experts know to be true rather than a process of inquiry and discovery. This view of education leads naturally to viewing the student as receiver of the "Word," to the teacher as the controller of the process, and to a lecture mode of teaching.

These arrangements have several unhappy consequences. If schools present what is to be learned as a delineated body of knowledge, students come to regard the subject being studied—mathematics, for example—as something received, not discovered, and as an entity to be ingested rather than as a form of activity. However, students need chances to engage in choice, judgment, control processes, and problem formulation; they need chances to make mistakes. The saying, "experience is the best teacher" is borne out by the research—you learn when you do. Not sufficient for effective learning, doing is nonetheless necessary.

Passive learning also creates learners dependent on teachers for guidance and feedback, thus undercutting the development of confidence in one's own sense-making and problem-solving abilities, and discouraging displays of initiative. As Lave (1988) observes, people experience themselves as both subjects and objects in the world. In the supermarket, for example, they are subjects, seeing themselves as controlling

> their activities, interacting with the setting, generating problems in relation [to] the setting, and controlling problem-solving processes.... In contrast, school ... create[s] contexts in which children ... experience themselves as objects, with no control over problems or choice about problem-solving processes. (Lave, 1988, pp. 69–70)

Passive learning, in addition to (and just as important as) its effects on learning, also undercuts the development of certain higher order cognitive skills called *knowing how to learn, cognitive self-management,* or *executive thinking* skills. These are simply the skills that we use to govern our problem-solving attempts. They include goal setting, strategic planning, checking for accurate plan execution, monitoring our progress, and evaluating and revising our plans. As Pea (1989) observes, passive learning is disastrous for developing these skills. They seem to get developed when the learning situation is structured to shift control from the teacher to the student, the teacher gradually removing the support that students need initially as they begin to show the ability to work autonomously.

Passive learning also creates motivational and crowd control problems. Jordan (1987) describes a Mexican public health training program designed to improve the practice of Mayan midwives. Her analysis spotlights behaviors that American teachers constantly complain about in their students.

The teaching is organized as straight didactic or instructive material in a minilecture format. When these lectures begin, the midwives shift into what Jordan calls their "waiting-it-out" behavior. "They sit impassively, gaze far away, feet dangling, obviously tuned out. This is behavior that one might also observe in other waiting situations, such as when a bus is late or during sermons in church" (p. 3).

We see the same behaviors in American third graders. Hass (n.d.) found the students deeply engaged in team problem solving during their drill and practice time but investing little attention or involvement in the teacher's instruction sessions. In the three weeks of observation, the children had not adopted any of the specific strategies demonstrated by the teacher during general instruction time.

As teachers know so well, motivational problems end up as crowd control problems, as illustrated by the behaviors of different groups of school children at a Metropolitan Museum display of Ice Age art and artifacts (Farnham-Diggory, 1990). Most of the school groups were moved from one exhibit to the next, pausing before each to hear a guide's or teacher's lecture. Since the children were bunched in front of an exhibit, they could not all hear the lecture, and, even when they could, they lacked understanding of the time frames involved or the archaeological significance of bits of bone. Teachers had not set up the museum visit to prepare students for and involve them in what they were going to see. Groups were therefore restless and crowd control became the teacher's primary concern. One junior high school class behaved very differently, exhibiting a quiet intensity as they moved through the exhibit. They had packets of work sheets with questions about issues and problems that they were expected to use the exhibit to solve. Some questions were factual, but most required inference and thought. The students had to figure out for themselves where and what the evidence would be concerning particular questions.

FRAGMENTED LEARNING

American education reflects a behaviorist theory of learning—a view that conceives of learning as the strengthening of bonds between stimuli and the learner's responses to those stimuli. Based on his animal experiments, Edward Thorndike (1898) developed a new theory of learning, presuming that learning was the association of a specific response with a specific stimulus through a physiological bond in the neural system. The stimulus (S) then regularly called forth the response (R). The bond between S and R was created by being continually rewarded; an undesired bond was extinguished through punishment or failure.

This psychological theory had several effects. It led to the breakdown of complex tasks and ideas into components, subtasks, and items ("stimuli") that could be separately trained. It encouraged repetitive training ("stamping in"). And it led to a focus on the right answer ("successful response") and to the counting of the number of correct responses to items and subtasks, a perspective that ended up in psychometrically elegant tests considered the scientific way to measure achievement.

The result was fractionation, or splitting into pieces: having to learn disconnected subroutines, items, and subskills, without an understanding of the larger context into which they fit and which give them meaning. Farnham-Diggory (1990) notes that fractionated instruction maximizes forgetting, inattention, and passivity. Since children and adults seem to acquire knowledge from active participation in complex and meaningful environments, he noted, "school programs could hardly have been better designed to prevent a child's natural learning system from operating" (p. 146).

The phrase "a child's natural learning system" goes to the heart of why the usual school programs do not meet their own learning objectives well. Human beings are quintessentially sense making, problem solving animals; even small children are absorbed by the *why* of things. Fractionated and decontextualized instruction fails to mobilize this powerful property of human beings in the service of learning.

The point about subtasks is not that learners do not have to do simple operations. Studies of traditional apprenticeships in tailoring show that novices start with simple tasks. However, they conduct simple tasks in the context of being able to observe the master's execution of complex tailoring, which involves the integration of different subskills. Observation lets learners develop a conceptual model, or cognitive map, of what it means to be an expert tailor. This model gives learners an advanced "organizer" for their initial attempts to execute a complex skill; it provides an interpretive structure for making sense of the feedback and corrections from the master; it provides a guide to which the learner can refer during times of relatively independent practice (Collins et al., 1989).

Fact-Based/Right-Answer Learning

Both the transmission and behaviorist views of learning place a premium on getting the right answer. A transmission view stresses the ability of the learner to "reproduce" the "Word"; a behaviorist view, the ability of the learner to generate the correct response. The end result is the same: students and teachers focus on the right answer, jeopardizing the development of real understanding. This focus plays out in several ways.

Students learn to sound and test "right" within the school system. They figure out what answers the teacher or the test seem to want, but often at the cost of real learning. These surface achievements have been called "veneers of accomplishment" (Lave, Smith, & Butler, 1988). Again, Jordan's (1987) analysis of a Mayan midwives' training program illuminates basic truths about the learning and testing of American students. She found that midwives who had been through the training course saw the official health care system as powerful, in that it commanded resources and authority. They came to distinguish "good" from "not good" things to say. Specifically, they learned new ways of legitimizing themselves, new ways of presenting themselves as being in league with this powerful system, but with little impact on their daily practice. Although they could converse appropriately with supervisory medical personnel, their new knowledge was not incorporated into their behavioral repertoire. It was "verbally but not behaviorally fixed" (Jordan, 1987, pp. 10–12).

The same behaviors show up with Hass's (n.d.) American third graders. He observed that in mathematics lessons, the students got much practice in problem-solving methods that they had brought into the classroom with them—methods that were not being taught and that were not supposed to be used. The children used these methods to produce right answers, which the teacher took as evidence of their having grasped the formal procedures that she was teaching them. *In fact, all that had happened was the appearance of learning.*

We end up with appearances of learning because, in their search for right answers, teachers often fail to check behind answers to understand what assumptions students have brought into the learning situation. The evidence shows that learners carry into the learning situation conceptions and constructs that they have acquired elsewhere—Hass's students are an example. Thus, the teaching challenge is not to write on a clean slate, but to confirm, disconfirm, modify, replace, and add to what is already written there.

Since they are looking for right answers, teachers tend to consider student errors as failures rather than as opportunities to strengthen students' understanding. In their observations of urban and suburban Chicago (U.S.A.), Taipei (Taiwan), Beijing (China), and Sendai (Japan) first and fifth grade mathematics classes, Stigler and Stevenson (1991; also Stevenson & Stigler, 1992) found a marked difference in how American versus Asian teachers treated student mistakes. American teachers place little emphasis on the constructive use of errors as a teaching technique, a practice that Stigler and Stevenson attribute to the strong influence of behaviorism in American education.

In contrast, for example, a teacher in a Japanese fifth grade class introduced the problem of adding fractions with unequal denominators. The problem was simple: adding 1/2 and 1/3. The teacher called on one of the students to give his answer and explain his solution. The student answered, 2/5. Pointing first to the numerators and then to the denominators, he explained that one plus one was two and three plus two was five, giving him two fifths. Without comment, the teacher asked a second student his solution. This student said that 2.1 plus 3.1 added up to 5.2. When changed into a fraction, he got two fifths. The teacher, unperturbed, asked a third student for her solution, and she answered 5/6. She showed how she had found the common denominator, changed the fractions so that each had this denominator, and then added them. Instead of emphasizing the correct solution and ignoring the incorrect ones, the teacher next capitalized on the errors that the first two students had made to help them, and the other students, confront two common misconceptions about fractions. She helped the first student test how sensible his solution was by asking which was larger, two fifths or one half? When it was acknowledged that one half was larger, she asked whether it didn't seem strange that adding something to one half gave you an amount less than one half. In working with the second boy, she helped him to see that he had confused decimals with fractions, but that, *given that error,* he had arrived at a sensible solution (Stigler and Stevenson, 1991).

Perhaps the most serious consequence, in fact, of a right-answer emphasis is that, as in the example above, it excludes a focus on how to approach the problem to be solved or on different ways to solve the same problem. It emphasizes facts, which are important but which, by themselves, constitute an impoverished understanding of a domain. A fact focus does not develop students' abilities to think about the domain in different ways. Cognitive analyses of a range of jobs show that being able to generate different solutions to problems that are formally the same is a hallmark of expert performance (Scribner, 1988).

Again, Asian teachers differ markedly from American teachers. They seem to focus more on concepts, conceptual understanding, and, at least in mathematics, on the notational system needed to represent concepts and their relationships. Stigler and Stevenson (1991) found that teachers ask questions for different reasons in the United States and in Japan. In the United States, the purpose of a question is to get an answer, but Japanese teachers pose questions to stimulate thought. In fact, they consider questions to be poor if they elicit immediate answers because this indicates that students were not challenged to think.

A common type of lesson in Asian classrooms is one that asks the students to invent and evaluate different ways of solving the same problem without worrying about specifying an answer. A videotape of typical Asian classrooms (Stevenson, 1989) shows a fifth grade teacher who started her class by showing the students a trapezoid drawn within a rectangle. She divided the class into small groups, asking each group to figure out one or more ways to determine the area of the trapezoid. She stressed that it did not matter which method they used. "You don't need to show us your calculations; just show us your method. It is your method that matters, not simply getting the correct answer." The groups came up with several different and ingenious solutions.

Lessons like these have several effects. First, they give control over problem solving to the students, both in terms of generating the solutions and of evaluating their mathematical validity. The teacher guides the process and ensures that mathematical values are respected, but her role, in the words of one American teacher, is that of "guide on the side," not "sage on the stage."

Second, lessons such as these reproduce the actual processes in which mathematicians themselves engage—the processes of mathematical argument, discourse, and proof. By doing mathematics, students come to understand how mathematics got put together over the centuries, to see that they can engage in the same processes, and, by virtue of participating in mathematical argument, develop a deeper understanding of mathematical concepts. Finally, by being encouraged to generate multiple solutions to the same problem, students can regard the problem from multiple angles, thus developing a fuller understanding of its properties. They come to realize that problems can usually be solved in several ways, freeing them from a constraining hunt for the "one right way."

NONCONTEXTUAL LEARNING

Schools often teach skills and knowledge outside their contexts of use. This problem is often called *decontextualized learning,* which simply means learning in the absence of context or meaning. The rationale for decontextualized learning is that, if fundamentals are learned independent of specific context, they become available for application to a wide range of specific situations.

Almost three-quarters of a century earlier, John and Evelyn Dewey (1915) wrote about the learning costs of decontextualized education.

> A statement, even of facts, does not reveal the value of the fact, or the sense of its truth—of the fact that it is a fact. Where children are fed only on book knowledge, one "fact" is as good as another; they have no standards of judgment or belief. Take the child studying weights and measures; he reads in his textbook that eight quarts make a peck, but when he does examples he is apt, as every schoolteacher knows, to substitute four for eight. Evidently the statement as he read it in the book did not stand for anything that goes on outside the book, so it is a matter of accident what figure lodges in his brain, or whether any does. But the grocer's boy who has measured out

pecks with a quart measure *knows*. He has made pecks; he would laugh at anybody who suggested that four quarts made a peck. What is the difference in these two cases? The schoolboy has a result without the activity of which it is the result. To the grocer's boy the statement has value and truth, for it is the obvious result of an experience—it is a *fact*.

In other words, practical activities do not have only, or even mainly, a utilitarian value in the schoolroom. Context turns out to be critical for understanding and thus for learning. We are back to the issue of meaning making and sense making, discussed earlier. The importance of context lies in the meaning that it gives to learning.

When teaching mathematics, American teachers tend to introduce mathematical concepts and rules abstractly, only later (if ever) turning to real-world problems that involve these ideas. For example, they often start the lesson on fractions by defining the term *fraction* formally and naming the elements of fractional notation (denominator and numerator). Asian teachers, on the other hand, tend to introduce new mathematical ideas by first "interpreting and relating a real-world problem to the quantification that is necessary for a mathematical solution" (Stigler & Stevenson, 1991, p. 20). For example, a teacher might start the lesson by asking students to estimate how many liters of colored water a beaker contains, the amount always being some part of a whole liter, such as 1 1/2 or 1 1/3 liters. He then helps them translate their visual appreciation of "parts of" into fractional notations. The terms *fraction, denominator,* and *numerator* are mentioned only at the end of the lesson, these formal words now being connected to real-world experiences. In other words, these teachers understand that concrete experiences are not sufficient for learning—they have to be linked to formal notation and abstract concepts. However, real-world experiences provide the intuitive meaning that lets students "hook into" and take possession of abstract ideas.

Confusion surrounds the idea of *teaching in context*. It is not about making learning *relevant*, as that term came to be used in American education in the 1960s, defined as "teaching subject matter directly applicable to students' lives" rather than teaching the traditional academic disciplines. This is not the same as using students' experiences to help them learn the disciplines. Teaching in context does not necessarily refer to a vocational or applied curriculum. The fact that well-designed vocational curricula use real-world problems and objects does not mean that teaching in context is vocational teaching. As was illustrated above, Asian teachers make use of context in the form of concrete objects and real-world problems for teaching a distinctly academic subject (mathematics).

There is only limited research on the outcomes of learning in context versus out of context. For example, Brazilian street vendor children were found to be able to successfully solve 98% of their marketplace transactions—such as calculating total costs and change—but when presented with the same transactions in formal word arithmetic problems that provided some descriptive context, the children correctly solved only 74% of the problems (Carraher, Carraher, & Schliemann, 1985). Their success rate dropped to 37% when asked to solve the same types of problems presented as mathematical operations without descriptive context. Sticht (1989) found that marginally literate adults in a job-related reading program gained in job-related reading twice what they gained in general reading—that is, they did better when a meaningful context was provided for the text.

TRADITIONAL APPRENTICESHIP AS A PARADIGM OF LEARNING

In their search for more effective learning strategies, analysts have researched two particular areas: what has been called the "spectacular" learning of young children; and apprenticeship programs in developing countries. They noted that children's learning situations had certain characteristics (Bransford, Stein, Arbitman-Smith, & Vye, 1985; Pea, 1989). First, learning took place in context. During their first 5 years, children were learning in the midst of culturally meaningful, ongoing activities, and receiving immediate feedback on the success of their actions. Second, learning was often guided. Parents, friends, and peers not only served as models for imitative learning but also helped the children learn by providing structure for and connections between their experiences. These mediators highlighted information in the situation that helped the child carry out a task. Third, learning was useful. Learning in context and with adult guidance gave children an understanding of the role of information in problem solving. Concepts and skills were acquired as tools with a range of purposes. And fourth, the uses of new knowledge were not only shown but often explicitly stated—in other words, the need for and purpose of the learning were explained.

In the area of apprenticeships, researchers found that, although traditional apprenticeships can certainly be structured in educationally sterile ways, anthropological observations have identified several pedagogically interesting characteristics of this form of learning (Jordan, 1987).

1. Apprenticeship happens as a way of, and in the course of, daily life and may not be recognized as a teaching effort at all. In other words, there is likely to be almost no separation between the activities of daily living and the learning of "professional" skills. This aspect of traditional apprenticeship recalls how very young children learn in contemporary families.
2. "Work" is the driving force. In apprenticeship, the activities in which masters and students engage are driven by the requirements of the

work to be accomplished. As a consequence, the progressive mastering of tasks by the apprentice is appreciated not so much as a step toward a distant, symbolic goal (such as a certificate), but for its immediate use value. Apprentices are not so much practicing for the real thing as doing useful and necessary tasks.

3. There is a temporal ordering of skill acquisition. Apprentices start with skills that are relatively easy, and with which mistakes are least costly.

4. Traditional apprenticeship learning focuses on actual performance and embodied knowledge, while the verbalization of general principles is secondary, ill-developed, and not well rehearsed.

5. Standards of performance and evaluation of competence are implicit—in fact, they are embedded in the work environment in which the novice participates. The success or failure of a task that has been performed is obvious and needs no commentary. To a large extent, the person who judges the apprentice's performance is the apprentice himself or herself rather than the expert. The apprentice, having observed the work sequence many times, knows what remains to be learned and tends to "own the problem" of moving on to learning the next skill.

6. Teachers and teaching are largely invisible. In apprenticeship learning—and during informal, on-the-job training in modern American workplaces—it looks as though little teaching is going on.

In sum: An apprenticeship situation consists of a community of experts and novices. Apprenticing is a process of being inducted, or "entrained," into the community of expert practice, whether the practice is that of tailoring, weaving, or farming. In the case of learning accomplished by very young children, the child is being inducted into the broader community—into the "way" of his or her native culture. Critical to this learning situation is the fact that whoever assumes the role of the teacher continuously engages in, and is a master at, the practice being learned. His or her performances constitute the standards of performance for the apprentice.

THE NEED TO MODIFY TRADITIONAL APPRENTICESHIP

Traditional apprenticeships are not entirely transferable to a modern society for two reasons. First, practices such as tailoring or weaving are visually observable to the novice and embodied knowledge—the knowledge of the "hand"—is important. However, in many modern work and work-related practices—whether it be reading, machine repair, management, mathematics, law, or computer-based machine operation—cognitive skills complement embodied knowledge, and are equal in importance. These cognitive components of activity are ordinarily not visible and therefore are unavailable to students and teachers for observation, comment, refinement, and correction, unless ways are found to externalize processes that are usually carried out internally.

Second, traditional apprenticeship presumes relative constancy in the activities being learned. Thus, it does not focus on developing the skills and knowledge that are needed when change and nonroutine events are what characterize the workplace. Workers such as tailors, midwives, and rug makers do encounter nonroutine events, but their incidence would seem to be much lower than they are in the modern, technological workplace, especially in those sectors characterized by substantial international or domestic competition.

The greater volatility of the modern workplace should increase the importance of two types of skills. One is higher order cognitive skills, such as problem defining, problem solving, and knowing how to learn. The other is facility with the principles that govern a domain, and that can be used to handle variations in the situation-specific manifestations of those principles.

■

COGNITIVE APPRENTICESHIP AS A PARADIGM OF LEARNING

At the same time, traditional apprenticeships show what contextualized, effective learning looks like. Given the images of traditional apprenticeships, cognitive scientists have been able to invent analogies appropriate for learning less visible practices, and those subject to change. Collins et al. (1989) have proposed what they believe to be key elements of these analogous situations, calling the emergent strategy "cognitive apprenticeship."

Cognitive apprenticeship modifies traditional apprenticeship to teach symbolically based, and therefore less observable, activities, such as reading, writing, and mathematics. The term *cognitive* should not be read to mean *academic*. The cognitive apprenticeship model ignores the usual distinctions between academic and vocational education in that its objective is to entrain the novice into communities of expert practice, whether that practice is what is generally termed academic (for example, mathematics) or vocational (for example, interior design).[2] In this sense, cognitive apprenticeship provides a pedagogic strategy for reducing tracking and increasing equity *without* resorting to the mechanism of least common denominator.

Collins et al. (1989) argue that the most important difference between traditional schooling and apprenticeship is that, in schooling, skills and knowledge are abstracted from their uses in the world; in apprenticeship, they are continually used by skilled practitioners and are instrumental in accomplishing meaningful tasks. For these authors, "apprenticeship embeds the learning of skills and knowledge in their social and functional context" (p. 454). Thus, their focus is on learning through guided experience, but emphasizing cognitive skills and processes, not just the physical ones that characterize traditional apprenticeship.

CHARACTERISTICS OF COGNITIVE APPRENTICESHIP

Collins et al. (1989) identify characteristics of ideal learning environments. These authors' ideas retain the power of traditional apprenticeships but modify it for contemporary activity, at the same time eliminating the flawed characteristics of the standard K–12 paradigm of learning. Four elements are crucial to this approach: content, teaching methods, sequencing, and the sociology of learning.

Content

Target knowledge for an ideal learning environment includes conceptual, factual, and procedural knowledge associated with a particular subject, such as physics, and three types of strategic knowledge. Schools and traditional apprenticeships usually focus only on the first three but the three strategic types are needed to operate effectively in, on, and with domain-particular knowledge. They are:

- *"Tricks of the trade":* Although often formally called *heuristic strategies,* these are problem-solving strategies that experts pick up with experience. They do not always work, but when they do, they are quite helpful.
- *Cognitive management strategies:* These govern the process of carrying out a task and are also known as *executive thinking* or *metacognitive* skills. They include goal setting, strategic planning, checking for accurate plan executive, goal-progress monitoring, plan evaluation, and plan revision.
- *Learning strategies:* These are strategies for learning any of the kinds of content described above. Knowledge about how to learn includes general strategies for exploring a new domain. It also includes strategies for obtaining more knowledge in an area already somewhat understood, and reconfiguring the knowledge already possessed.

Methods

Teaching methods should be designed to give students the chance to observe, engage in, invent, or discover expert strategies in context. The important elements include:

- *Modeling:* For students to model expert performance, the learning situation must include an expert's performing a task so that the students can observe and build a conceptual model of the processes that are required to accomplish it.

- *Coaching:* This means observing students as they carry out a task and offering hints, support, feedback, modeling, reminders, and new tasks to bring their performances closer to expert performance.
- *Scaffolding and fading:* "Scaffolding" refers to the supports that the teacher provides to help the student carry out the task. Supports can take the form of suggestions, help, or actual physical supports (for example, in learning to ski, the short skis that are used to teach novices). Fading is the gradual removal of supports until students are on their own; it encourages autonomous and independent functioning.
- *Articulation:* This includes any method to get students to articulate their knowledge, reasoning, or problem-solving processes in a domain. It makes visible otherwise invisible cognitive processes. It also makes explicit assumptions that students bring to the learning situation.
- *Reflection:* This is any technique that lets students compare their own problem-solving processes with those of an expert, of another student, and, ultimately, with an internal cognitive model of expertise.
- *Exploration:* This refers to any device that pushes students into a mode of problem solving on their own. Forcing them to explore is critical if they are to learn how to frame questions or problems that are interesting and that they can solve. This part of the model provides opportunities for the experiential feedback that is so much a key to learning.

Sequencing

Learning should be "staged" so that the learner builds the multiple skills required in expert performance and discovers the conditions to which they generalize.

- *Increasing complexity:* Tasks and task environments are sequenced to require more and more of the skills and concepts necessary for expert performance.
- *Increasing diversity:* Tasks are constructed so that they require a wider and wider variety of strategies or skills. This strategy helps students learn to distinguish the conditions under which they do (and do not) apply. (This principle is key to students' seeing transfer possibilities, and their limits.)
- *Global before local skills:* This simply means staging the learning so that students first develop a "feel" for, a conceptual map of, the overall terrain before attending to its details. (In tailoring, apprentices learn to put together a garment from precut pieces before learning to cut out the pieces themselves.) Having a mental image of the overall activity helps the student make sense of the subactivity that he or she is carrying out. It also acts as a guide for the learner's performance.

Sociology of Learning

The learning environment should reproduce the technological, social, time, and motivational characteristics of the real world situations in which what is being learned will be used. Several practices are important:

- *Situated (contextualized) learning:* This refers to students' carrying out tasks and solving problems in a way that reflects the nature of such tasks in the world. For example, reading and writing instruction might be situated in the context of an electronic message system that students use to send each other questions and advice.
- *Community of expert practice:* This refers to the creation of a learning environment where participants actively communicate about and engage in the skills evidenced by experts. In other words, the learning situation needs to include experts and learners; experts performing tasks and learners being drawn into the community of expert practice by watching experts, working with experts to solve problems and to carry out tasks, and coming to assume autonomous control over problems and tasks.
- *Intrinsically motivated learning:* This refers to the incentives that govern the learning situation. Intrinsic motivation arises when students are engaged with interesting, or at least coherent, goals, rather than goals aimed at some extrinsic reason, such as pleasing the teacher.
- *Cooperative learning:* This refers to having students work together to solve problems and carry out tasks. Learning through cooperative problem solving is both a powerful intrinsic motivator and a way to extend learning resources. For example, in contemporary computer clubs nonexperts were able to use each other as scaffolding for increasing their command of computers. They pooled their fragments of knowledge about computers to bootstrap themselves toward expertise (Levin, 1982).
- *Competitive learning:* This refers to giving students the same task to carry out and then comparing their performances to focus their attention on strengths and weaknesses. Learning in today's classrooms is competitively, and usually destructively, structured. For competition to be constructive, comparisons should be made, not among the products of student problem solving but among the processes that generate the products. The learning objectives for students should be defined; they should not be based on making no errors but on learning to spot errors and on using an understanding of them to improve. Combining cooperative and competitive learning can mitigate the destructive aspects of competition. For example, students might work together in teams to compete with other teams, thus allowing them to use team members as scaffolding, and to use comparisons of team performances to focus attention on better ways to carry out a task.

EXAMPLES OF COGNITIVE APPRENTICESHIP

There are instances of cognitive apprenticeships, not just in the annals of cognitive scientists but also in actual school courses and projects designed by school teachers. Although these examples come from schools, this does not mean that work-based apprenticeships cannot incorporate cognitive apprenticeship principles as well.

Redesigning the American Constitution

Salomon (1990) describes a project for studying the American Constitution. Recognizing that studying constitutions is not very exciting for eighth graders, the designers created a purpose. The students took the positions of different stakeholders—the federalists, the loyalists, representatives from the different colonies (New York, Pennsylvania, Virginia, etc.), and plantation owners. Working in teams of three, the students treated the Constitution as a draft, the study teams proposing changes in it according to their stakeholder perspectives. This gave them a reason and framework for dealing with the Constitution, inviting them to reclassify its legal clauses, compare them, and draw out implications for their political positions. They then formulated proposed changes in the Constitution to be introduced in subsequent interteam debate. In other words, the Constitution was treated, not as the "Word," but as a document that was originally built from dynamic political forces and that students can rebuild in the same spirit.

The project culminated in a recreation of the Constitutional Convention, where the teams, as delegations under the guidance of George Washington (the teacher), debated the changes that they wanted adopted. Three students became clerks of the convention to count votes and announce decisions, and other students served as an audience. Creating a position to take to the convention generated opportunities for the students to articulate their positions, knowledge, reasoning, and problem solving. It also allowed them to reflect on their efforts by letting each student compare his/her own problem-solving processes with those of other students in the team. The constitutional convention itself created more opportunities for articulation, reflection and, because it embodied important elements of competition and public comparison, more opportunities for focusing the teams' attention on the strengths and weaknesses of their performances.

Building and Racing a Solar-Powered Car

Students from Conval High School in Peterborough, New Hampshire, built and raced a solar-powered car as an applied science project (National Council on Vocational Education, 1990). The project required the students to acquire and use a wide variety of skills spanning many academic and practical disciplines, including physics and mathematics, basic solar engineering, hydraulics, electronics, drafting, model fabrication, metal working, and welding. Ten models were built and tested before the students finally decided on a production design, and this decision process required the students to articulate and reflect on the strengths and weaknesses of each model.

The students quickly learned the necessity for other skills as well. They had to acquire the business skills necessary to manage some grant funds. They also had to learn the English, journalism, and graphics skills needed for a public relations effort about the project. Perhaps most surprising to the students, they had to acquire the leadership, management, and interpersonal relations skills necessary to construct a rational division of labor to keep the project moving forward. Among the more significant outcomes of the management process was a negotiated decision to build the car for racing safety at the sacrifice of speed, a decision that forced students to articulate their positions, to reflect on the merits of those positions, and to cooperate with one another.

WHERE SHOULD APPRENTICESHIPS BE LOCATED: THE WORKPLACE OR THE SCHOOL?

The current explosion of interest in apprenticeship programs in the United States (and in the popularity of school-to-work programs incorporating work-based learning) has, for several reasons, been concerned with a conception of these activities as more work-based than school-based. To begin with, the German (and Austrian and Swiss) work-based apprenticeship system is better known here than are the school-based systems of Sweden, Denmark, or France. In addition, the U.S. Department of Labor saw the traditional, work-based apprenticeship programs under its jurisdiction as a base for a work-based system that could be extended to younger aged students and to a wider range of occupations. It was also generally acknowledged that many school-based programs—even many vocational ones—are divorced from the needs of the workplace.

Thus, a work-based system appears to be an appealing solution. It suggests the possibility of eliminating the problem of coordinating work-oriented schooling with the workplace because learning and the workplace are coincident with one another. It seems to reduce the school-to-work transition problem for youth for the same reason.

Work-based apprenticeship presumes: (1) an apprenticeship learning situation; and (2) the workplace as the locus of that situation. However, these represent two separable assumptions; one does not logically require the other. The previous section argued for apprenticeship forms of learning modified to reflect the greater cognitive and theoretical demands of contemporary activities, especially in restructured workplaces. Although apprenticeship is usually associated with the workplace, it remains essentially a paradigm of learning that can be implemented in diverse settings—in schools, in workplaces, or in some combination of the two.

The location issue can be approached by considering the use of specific criteria to determine optimal locations under various conditions. We propose evaluating alternative locations utilizing the following criteria.

1. *Is the location organized to deliver effective and efficient learning?* Work-based apprenticeship has tended to assume that school-based programs are inappropriate learning places for work and that, therefore, workplaces must be appropriate ones. Workplaces may be more appropriate learning places under some circumstances, but one assumption does not necessarily follow the other. Observations of informal, on-the-job training of the less educated raise questions about the workplace as a learning place. Informal, on-the-job training can be catch-as-catch-can. Its quality depends heavily on who happens to be doing the training. In work groups with high turnover, individuals who are almost novices are doing the training; they are often underequipped and too inexperienced to accomplish effective training, a situation that violates all models of good apprenticeship. (This problem is analogous to "out of field" teaching in schools, i.e., when an athletics coach is drafted to teach chemistry.) Even experienced members of a work group can do little more than pass on their understanding of the job, and of the corporate context in which it is embedded, as they themselves learned it. This understanding is rarely monitored and can vary wildly (Scribner & Sachs, 1990).

The key issues for the workplace as a learning place are no different than those for school-based learning (Scribner & Sachs, 1991). The way in which work or school activities are set up is the determining factor in what enhances or inhibits learning. For example, a company that organizes work, or a school that organizes learning, as a set of segmented tasks will limit what its workers or its students learn. (Companies with mass-production organizations of work will be more apt to structure learning as segmented tasks.) Whether in the workplace or in the schoolroom, what is emphasized and encouraged in the setting helps learners develop either a conceptual understanding or a highly routinized, inflexible set of responses. Since most companies follow a mass-production organization of work, we may face a Hobson's choice between two worlds (schools and the workplace), neither of which is routinely well designed for powerful learning.

The inherent power of the location to motivate the learner also affects learning effectiveness. Researchers have shown that a work-based option is motivating.

Apprentices are encouraged to quickly learn skills that are useful and therefore meaningful within the social context of the workplace. Moreover, apprentices have natural opportunities to realize the value, in concrete economic terms, of their developing skill: well-executed tasks result in products that can be sold (Collins et al., 1989).

At the same time, actual school-based trials of cognitive apprenticeships show that intrinsically motivating learning situations can also be set up in the school (Schoenfeld, 1988; DeWitt, 1991). A motivational key seems to be whether or not the learning situation is organized around the natural learning system of human beings—around the fact that we are naturally sense making, problem solving, and environmentally interactive.

In terms of the efficiency of learning, the school-based option may have an edge over the work-based option. Collins et al. (1989) point out that the problems and tasks given to learners in standard, work-based apprenticeships arise not from pedagogical but from workplace concerns. Cognitive apprenticeship instead selects tasks and problems that illustrate the power of certain techniques, to give students practice in applying these methods in diverse settings, and to increase the complexity of tasks slowly, so that component skills and models can be integrated. Tasks are sequenced to reflect the changing demands of learning. Letting job demands select the tasks for students to practice is one of the great inefficiencies of traditional apprenticeship (Collins et al., 1989).

Since a highly motivating, work-based apprenticeship means that individuals learn whatever they are trying to learn quickly, the inefficiency of a work-based option seems to reside not in the initial speed with which learning occurs, but in the potential of that speed for creating "learning holes" and unnecessary repetition.

2. *Does the learning location reflect the knowledge demands of the workplace and the work contexts in which knowledge and skill have to be used?* A workplace location seems to be a winner here, with two caveats. First, in considering sites for a work-based apprenticeship, a normal sample of workplaces will include many with traditionally organized work contexts. If one objective is to prepare individuals for a restructuring economy, the nature of the work contexts has to be monitored carefully, and workplaces should be carefully selected.

Second, a key principle of cognitive apprenticeships—which were developed as school-based—is that they mirror the nonschool conditions under which knowledge and skill are used. Thus, a school-based option *can* meet this second criterion, but not as automatically or as easily as can the work-based option.

3. *Does the learning location develop knowledge and skills that are broadly applicable?* We noted earlier that modern work activities are relatively change-

able and nonroutine, requiring an arrangement of learning that develops higher order cognitive skills and an understanding of the principles that govern the domain under study. A school-based option would seem to have the edge here. A work-based option can be set up to develop higher order cognitive skills in the context of the domain being learned. However, the embeddedness of the learning within a work situation makes it harder to ensure that learners grapple with issues and problems outside the limits of that particular situation. This is especially a problem with the low-skill jobs available to most teenagers.

At the same time, a work-based option can be designed to develop broader skills and knowledge. Without extensive academic, professional, or even on-the-job training, people can achieve conceptual understanding on the job. Again, the issue is the nature of the individual's job responsibilities—how the work situation is set up. Some work activities, in and of themselves, are educationally rich. The question is the probability of finding such arrangements in the workplace versus the school.

4. *Does the location blur the division between academic and vocational?* This criterion revolves around allaying parents' fear that vocational programs of any kind will rob their children of the hope for a better economic future. Parents, poor and rich alike, have clearly understood society's message: College—and the high school academic track that gets a student there—is the most desirable destination for ensuring their children a shot at an economically viable future. In the absence of a national system organized around preparing students for middle/higher skill jobs, many parents may feel that anything other than the academic track and college amounts to no preparation at all, which at best translates into low skill and poorly paid jobs.

Thus, parents resist reforms that appear to preclude college for their children. They are willing to settle for the so-called "general track" curriculum, a virtual wasteland, only because it purports to give weaker students academic, albeit applied academic, training. The terms *vocational, workplace,* or *applied* are all heard by parents as warning bells. In fact, early returns from the work-based apprenticeship demonstrations show that parents are reluctant to place their children in these programs. They see them as something that forecloses the option of college, whether or not this, in fact, is true. A school-based cognitive apprenticeship, even if focused on an occupational domain such as interior design, is better able to blur the division between academic and vocational.

There is a final reason to think carefully about the location of apprenticeship learning. A fundamental impetus for work-based apprenticeships is that schools generally have done a poor job of preparing the non-baccalaureate-bound. The question is whether or not we will let the schools off the hook of taking educational responsibility for this large group of students. If the workplace turns out to be the learning place of choice for this group, well and good. However, we need to be careful that we do not resort to work-based apprenticeships to finesse problems with the schools. We are already paying for second-chance programs and for remedial college programs to accomplish what the K–12 system should have gotten done in the first place.

Finally, what emerges in this assessment of alternative locations for learning is that all settings—be they work, school, mixed work–school arrangements, and, by extension, family and community settings—face similar problems. With few exceptions, it is hard to argue that one location is intrinsically or automatically better than another. Relative to the four criteria listed above, all settings fail under some conditions and succeed under others. *The implication is that our criteria for selecting locations—but not the locations themselves—are matters having to do with policy.* Location decisions will vary, depending on circumstances, and, once made, must be monitored.

SUMMARY

Models of academic and vocational integration are essentially models of curricular integration—in other words, models of content, not of how content is acquired. The lack of systematic attention to how content is taught remains a substantial hole in integration policy and practice, in part because the prevailing K–12 pedagogic paradigm will undercut the achievement of the purported objectives of the integration movement. As identified by the cognitive sciences, poor pedagogic practices are probably more characteristic of academic than of vocational education. However, the vocational field has not really formalized its sometimes better pedagogic practice as principles, or systematically refined them in light of the cognitive science knowledge base on effective learning. Thus, both parties to the integration effort are handicapped in efforts to extend the integration movement beyond curriculum to pedagogy.

The principles of cognitive apprenticeship constitute a pedagogic model for integration efforts. At abstract levels, they also constitute a content model. Regardless of the domain being studied, cognitive apprenticeship identifies the types of content that should be learned and the pedagogic strategies that support the acquisition and appropriate use of content. Our experience with cognitive apprenticeship is still partial and limited. However, unlike proposed innovations in education, it is unusually well grounded in a century of thought and in research of high quality. It codifies and refines principles that good teachers, whether academic or vocational, implicitly use and will recognize.

Although apprenticeship implies work-based learning, cognitive apprenticeship can and has been used in both work and school settings. Relative to criteria such as the educational richness of the environment, neither setting is automatically or intrinsically preferable to the other. Depending on particular circumstances, both fail and both succeed. Prior to and determinant of location decisions are our learning goals for students.

■
NOTES

1. Cognitive science is an interdisciplinary field that encompasses psychologists, linguists, anthropologists, computer scientists, philosophers, and neuroscientists. The word *cognitive* refers to perceiving and knowing, and cognitive science is the science of the mind. Cognitive scientists seek to understand perceiving, thinking, remembering, understanding language, learning, and other similar phenomena. Their research is very diverse, ranging from observing children learning mathematics to observing experienced workers handling the cognitive demands of their jobs—programming computers, doing complex problem solving, or analyzing the nature of meaning (Stillings et al., 1987).

2. The subtitle of the Collins et al. (1989) paper on cognitive apprenticeship is revealing in this respect. It reads, "Teaching the Craft of Reading, Writing, and Mathematics." The subjects might be seen as academic but their practice is defined as a craft.

THE PROMISES OF
CURRICULUM INTEGRATION

W. NORTON GRUBB

Integrating academic and vocational education is a reform rich with possibilities precisely because there are so many purposes it can serve. Since there have been many independent sources of support for the idea of curriculum integration, both historical and current—as outlined in Chapter 1—there are many different goals for these changes. Some are modest, though they are still changes in the right direction; others are more thorough; and some promise to reshape all of American education around distinctly different approaches to content and teaching.

At the most basic level, integrating academic and vocational education has been a way of enriching vocational programs—or, more broadly, a way of reforming secondary education for the majority of students who are not part of the college track. The efforts to incorporate more academic content in vocational courses (described in Chapter 4) and to include generic and higher order skills (examined in Chapter 10) are good examples of increasing the rigor and sophistication of programs that have often been emptied of content. Similarly, even though some applied academic courses have their own limitations (particularly when they are used "off the shelf," without the active collaboration of local teachers), they are often used to replace courses in the general track with more applied teaching of somewhat greater rigor. Even when integrated programs are used for frankly remedial purposes, they at least have the potential of being more effective because they provide a context for instruction and a purpose that conventional academic courses lack—as is argued in Chapter 11. Reversing the separation of academic instruction from vocational programs can therefore create programs of greater intellectual sophistication for students who, for various reasons, have been labeled academically incompetent and presumed "manually minded," and then segregated from the high-status academic programs.

In the process, programs of integration have promoted a new conception of vocational education—one that prepares students either for employment after high school, for postsecondary education, or for that combination of postsecondary education and employment that has become increasingly common. This two-track strategy emerges especially clearly in magnet schools and in academies (as examined in Chapters 5 and 7, and in the voices of students themselves in Chapter 9). The link between integrated programs and postsecondary education through tech prep programs (examined in Chapter 10 of Volume II) has further solidified this kind of two-track strategy. In addition, preparation for a broad variety of occupations, as happens in most academies, clusters, and magnet schools, also broadens the goals of vocational education. This conception of the *new vocationalism* stands in stark contrast to the conventional goals of vocational education, which prepared students only for employment after high school, and very often for narrowly defined occupations.

However, enriching vocational courses and broadening the goals of vocational programs can, by definition, improve the education only of those students who self-consciously elect a vocational program—and that number has been dwindling over the past decade. A somewhat broader goal of integrated programs, therefore, is what we might term the guidance and counseling role of integrated programs—their role in getting students to think about their occupational futures, about the curricular choices they make in high school, and about the relationship between school-based learning and future work life. As the chapters in Part II argued, and as the statements of students in Chapter 9 further illustrated, a crucial role of integrated curricula has been to indicate to students the ways in which learning in schools is later applied. And, as Chapter 6 clarified, most schools adopting clusters, or majors, have simultaneously improved their guidance and counseling to enable students to make informed choices—and large districts adopting magnet schools have similarly been forced to confront the need for students and parents to make informed choices. When the default option of the conventional college prep curriculum is abandoned, then schools have come to understand the need for students to be active choosers, and have adopted more active methods with which students can consider occupational alternatives and the capacities they require. This kind of change affects a greater number of students, since even those who do not choose a particular academy, major, or magnet school must weigh the choices and pick a course of study because some alternative to the college prep default seems most appropriate.

But the greatest ambition of these efforts to integrate academic and vocational education is that they can reshape the entire high school, for all students and all teachers. In the first place, the most thorough efforts at integration—the academies, clusters or majors, and magnet schools examined in Part II of this volume—eliminate the "shopping mall high school" (Powell et al., 1985), replacing the aimless choice of electives with a more coherent set of academic and elective courses unified by a broadly defined occupation, an industry, or some other intrinsically important theme. In the process, these schools can become what some have called "focus schools" (Hill et al., 1990), and what others have tried to create in *charter schools*—schools with distinctive identities. Such schools are not anything like the common schools of the nineteenth century: They do not presume to meet the needs and interests of all students, or to hold to the dictum that: "Every subject which is taught at all in a secondary school should be taught in the same way and to the same extent to every pupil so long as he pursues it, no matter what the probable destination of the pupil may be" (National Education Association, 1893, cited in Chapter 1). Instead, they provide an image of formal schooling in which heterogeneity exists among alternative curricula, each of which is itself coherent—a heterogeneity that is important because students vary in their interests and in the kinds of capacities (or intelligences) they seek to develop (Gardner, 1983).

In creating educational alternatives that are different but still equally attractive to various students, curriculum integration also provides a way to reduce the tracking and segregation that permeates the high school. In the shopping mall high school, the vertical curriculum—the differentiation of core academic subjects by ability levels, in turn related to the "evident and probable destinies" of students—is the primary form of differentiating among students, and it usually leads to segregation by class, by gender, and by race. In its stead, those schools that have adopted broadly defined majors—or academies or magnet schools based on broad occupational or industry clusters—have devised a very different way of differentiating among students, one that can bring together students who otherwise might not mix—the would-be doctor and the nurse, the future engineer and the presumed assembly-line operative. To be sure, the extent of such integration depends on the care with which integrated programs are devised, and efforts to concentrate on at-risk students can undermine the entire effort—as Chapter 5 illustrates in the context of academies. Still, even with the recent interest in "de-tracking" schools (Oakes, 1985), there are few other curricular and structural innovations that allow this to happen. Just as it reverses many other elements of the high school established around the turn of the century, the integration of academic and vocational education can reverse the segregation originally reinforced by vocational education.

The notion of responding to student interests and capacities is also a powerful change in the approach to education—away from one that dictates content to students through omnipotent teachers, texts, and administrators, and toward one in which students are more active in deciding the course of their schooling, and ultimately in constructing for themselves the kind of education they receive. This is yet another powerful aspect of curriculum integration: that it can, in its most thorough forms, change not only the content of schooling, but the way that content is taught. The incorporation of generic or higher order skills, explored in Chapter 10, is yet another aspect of that change, as is the opportunity that integrated curricula provides for the kind of contextualized instruction described in Chapter 11. The ability to explore the moral and political aspects of education examined in Chapter 6 of Volume II—especially those dimensions of history and social studies that are among the most widely loathed parts of the conventional curriculum—is yet another illustration. To be sure, such shifts in approaches to teaching are not universal components of integrating academic and vocational education: The teaching of integrated curricula can still follow the fragmented and didactic strategies associated with skills and drills, particularly because teachers without extensive training are prone to sliding back into techniques that are familiar and ubiquitous. But at least the underlying assumptions of curriculum integration are more consistent with constructivist learning and teaching in the tradition of meaning making: that disciplines are less important than applications; that the school must help students to make connections among different disciplines and skills rather than forcing them to integrate various capacities on their own; that there are different perspectives from different disciplines and occupations, and by extension many interpretations of important issues; and that there is a context and rationale for most learning. Changes in teaching methods may come slowly, especially to the high school (Cuban, 1993)—but integrating academic and vocational education is one of the powerful ways of doing so.

In the process, integration can enhance the engagement of high school students—particularly the large number who understand the high school to be related to their futures (as mentioned in the Introduction) but who fail to see exactly how schooling is important. The classes described in Chapter 10, where teachers have changed their teaching, and the students quoted in Chapter 9, from occupational magnet schools, are quite different from most other classes and students—they possess a greater sense of purpose and submit to fewer distractions from educational goals. The elements that enhance the engagement of students are varied, but the changes in teaching methods, the self-conscious links between schooling and its future application, and the smaller scale of most academies, majors, and magnet schools all contribute to the overall effect.

Finally, curriculum integration provides a way for high schools to establish connections to institutions outside their walls. In particular, schools with integrated curricula usually find it easier to establish connections to a variety of postsecondary institutions—as Chapter 10 of Volume II illustrates at greater length—and to employers, as Chapter 9 of Volume II shows. In the current interest in school-to-work programs that include work-based components, schools with integrated curricula can establish natural ties to employers—ties that are neither opportunistic nor forced because they are often ties with academic high schools. Indeed, without such integration, school-to-work programs threaten simply to replicate the independent work-experience programs devised during the 1970s (Grubb, 1994)—programs that ended up simply by devising low-quality work placements that were little better than the jobs students could find on their own, programs that failed utterly to reshape high schools.

In the end, the thorough reform of the high school is both the most hopeful aspect of integrating academic and vocational education and the most daunting prospect. All the benefits illustrated in this volume can be realized—the benefits that caused John Dewey to proclaim that "Education *through* occupations consequently combines within itself more of the factors conducive to learning than any other method" (Dewey, 1916, p. 309). But the changes necessary to do so are substantial, as Dewey also recognized. As he acknowledged 90 years ago:

> In spite of all the advances that have been made throughout the country, there is still one unsolved problem in elementary and secondary education. That is the question of duly adapting to each other the practical and the utilitarian, the executive and the abstract, the tool and the book, the head and the hand. This is a problem of such vast scope that any systematic attempt to deal with it must have greater influence upon the whole course of education everywhere.... In this attempt [to fuse hitherto separated factors] we shall need your sympathetic intelligence (Dewey, 1904, p. 14).

In light of this insight, the chapters in Volume II will widen our discussion by illustrating the kinds of changes that are necessary for this kind of fusion or integration. The changes are not simple because they are pervasive and because the integration of academic and vocational education can be misinterpreted and misapplied. But with a clear vision and the "sympathetic intelligence" that Dewey called for, the changes can be powerful, and beneficial to all students.

REFERENCES

Academy for Educational Development (1990). *Employment and educational experiences of Academy of Finance graduates.* New York: Author.

Adelman, N. E. (1989). *The case for integrating academic and vocational education.* Washington, DC: Policy Studies Associates, Inc., for the National Assessment of Vocational Education, U.S. Department of Education.

Adler, M. (1982). *The Paideia proposal: An educational manifesto.* New York: Macmillan.

Advisory Committee on Vocational Education (1968). *Vocational education: The bridge between man and his work.* Washington, DC: U.S. Department of Health, Education, and Welfare.

Agee, J. (Ed.) (1992). *Second to none: A vision of the new California high school.* Sacramento, CA: California State Department of Education.

Ancess, J., & Darling-Hammond, L. (in press). *The senior project at Hodgson Vocational Technical High School: A case study of authentic assessment.* New York: Teachers College Press.

Anrig, G. (1992, June). A very American way: Everybody's getting into the act. *Education Week Special Report, 11*(38), S7–8.

Association for Supervision and Curriculum Development (1990). *Public schools of choice.* Alexandria, VA: Author.

Bailey, T. (1989). *Changes in the nature and structure of work: Implications for skill requirements and skill formation.* Berkeley, CA: National Center for Research in Vocational Education, University of California at Berkeley.

Bailey, T. (1991). Jobs of the future and the education they will require: Evidence from occupational forecasts. *Educational Researcher, 20*(2), 11–20.

Bailey, T. (1992). *School/work: Economic change and educational reform.* Berkeley, CA: National Center for Research in Vocational Education, University of California at Berkeley.

Bailey, T. (1993). *Discretionary effort and the organization of work: Employee involvement and work reform since Hawthorne* (report prepared for the Sloan Foundation). New York: Institute on Education and the Economy, Teachers College, Columbia University.

Berryman, S. (1991). *Cognitive science: Indicting today's schools and designing effective learning environments.* Washington, DC: National Council on Vocational Education and the Employment and Training Administration, U.S. Department of Labor.

Berryman, S., & Bailey, T. (1992). *The double helix of education and the economy.* New York: Institute on Education and the Economy, Teachers College, Columbia University.

Blank, R. (1989). *Educational effects of magnet schools.* Washington, DC: Council of Chief State School Officers.

Blank, R. (1990). Educational effects of magnet schools. In W. Clune & J. Witte (Eds.), *Choice and control in American education, Vol. 2: The practice of choice, decentralization, and school restructuring.* New York: Falmer Press.

Blank, R., Dentler, R. A., Baltzell, D. C., & Chabotar, K. (1983). *Survey of magnet schools: Analyzing a model for quality integrated education.* Washington, DC: James Lowry and Associates for the U.S. Department of Education.

Bodilly, S., Ramsey, K., Stasz, C., & Eden, R. (1993). *Integrating academic and vocational education: Lessons from eight early innovators* (Report R-4265 NCRVE/UCB). Santa Monica, CA: Rand Corporation.

Bottoms, G., Presson, A., & Johnson, M. (1992). *Making high schools work.* Atlanta, GA: Southern Regional Education Board.

Bourdieu, P., & Passeron, J. (1977). *Reproduction: In education, society and culture.* Beverly Hills, CA: Sage.

Boyer, E. L. (1983). *High school: A report on secondary education in America.* New York: Harper & Row.

Bransford, J. D., Stein, B. S., Arbitman-Smith, R., & Vye, N. J. (1985). Three approaches to improving thinking and learning skills. In J. W. Segal, S. F. Chipman, and R. Glaser (Eds.), *Thinking and learning skills: Relating instruction to basic research, 1*(pp. 133–200). Hillsdale, NJ: Erlbaum.

Brooks, J., & Brooks, M. (1993). *The case for constructivist classrooms.* Alexandria, VA: Association for Supervision and Curriculum Development.

Brown, J. S., Collins, A., & Duguid, P. (1989). Situated cognition and the culture of learning. *Educational Researcher, 18* (1), 32–41.

Caine, R. N., & Caine, G. (1991). *Making connections: Teaching and the human brain.* Alexandria, VA: Association for Supervision and Curriculum Development.

Capelli, P. (1992). *Is the "Skills Gap" really about attitudes?* EQW working paper. Philadelphia: National Center on the Educational Quality of the Workforce.

Carraher, T. N., Carraher, D. W., & Schliemann, A. D. (1985). Mathematics in the Streets and in Schools. *British Journal of Developmental Psychology, 3,* 21–29.

Chadwell, D. R. (1991). Show what you know: The senior project requires students to prove their skills and knowledge. *American School Board Journal, 4,* 34–35.

Chadwell, D. R. (1992). The senior project: South Medford High School—Medford, Oregon. *Exemplary Practices in Education, 4,* 8–9.

Chubb, J., & Moe, T. (1990). *Politics, markets, and America's schools.* Washington, DC: Brookings Institute.

Claus, J. (1990). Opportunity or inequality in vocational education? A qualitative investigation. *Curriculum Inquiry, 20* (1), 7–39.

Clune, W., & White, P. (1988). *School-based management: Institutional variation, implementation and issues for further research.* Rutgers, NJ: Center for Policy and Research Education, Rutgers State University of New Jersey.

Clune, W. H., White, P., & Patterson, J. (1989). *The implementation and effects of high school graduation requirements: First steps toward curricular reform* (Center for Policy Research in Education Research Report Series RR-011). New Brunswick, NJ: Rutgers University.

Cognition and Technology Group at Vanderbilt (1990). Anchored instruction and its relationship to situated learning. *Educational Researcher, 19* (6), 2–10.

Collins, A., Brown, J. S., & Newman, S. (1989). Cognitive apprenticeship: Teaching the craft of reading, writing, and mathematics. In L.B. Resnick (Ed.), *Knowing, learning and instruction: Essays in honor of Robert Glaser* (pp. 453–494). Hillsdale, NJ: Erlbaum.

Collins, A., & Stevens, A. L. (1982). Goals and strategies of inquiry teachers. In R. Glaser (Ed.), *Advances in Instructional Psychology, 2* (pp. 65–119). Hillsdale, NJ: Lawrence Erlbaum Associates.

Commission on the Skills of the American Workforce (CSAW) (1990). *America's choice: High skills or low wages!* Rochester, NY: National Center on Education and the Economy.

Committee for Economic Development (1985). *Investing in our children: Business and the public schools.* New York: Author.

Cox, P., & deFrees, J. (1992). *Work in progress: Restructuring in ten Maine schools.* Augusta, ME: The Regional Laboratory for Educational Improvement of the Northeast and Islands.

Crain, R. L., Heebner, A. L., Si, Y. P., Jordan, W. J., & Kiefer, D. R. (1992). *The effectiveness of New York City's career magnet schools: An evaluation of ninth grade performance using an experimental design.* Berkeley, CA: National Center for Research in Vocational Education, University of California at Berkeley.

Cremin, L. A. (1961). *The transformation of the school.* New York: Alfred Knopf.

Cross, K. P. (1984). The rising tide of school reform reports. *Phi Delta Kappan, 66* (3), 166–172.

Cuban, L. (1988). *The managerial imperative and the practice of leadership in schools.* Albany, NY: State University of New York Press.

Cuban, L. (1990, January). Reforming again, again, and again. *Educational Researcher, 19* (1), 3–13.

Cuban, L. (1993). *How teachers taught: Constancy and change in American classrooms, 1890-1990.* Second Edition. New York: Teachers College Press.

Cushman, K. (1992). Math and science in the Essential School. *Horace, The Coalition of Essential Schools, 8* (3), 1–5.

Darling-Hammond, L. (1988). Accountability for professional practice. In M. Levine (Ed.), *Professional practice schools building a model* (pp. 71–102). Washington, DC: American Federation of Teachers.

David, J. (1991). Restructuring in progress: Lessons from pioneering districts. In Elmore, R. (Ed.), *Restructuring schools: The next generation of educational reform.* San Francisco: Jossey-Bass.

Dewey, J. (1904). Significance of the school of education. *The Elementary School Teacher, 5* (3), 12–16.

Dewey, J. (1916). *Democracy and education: An introduction to the philosophy of education.* New York: Macmillan.

Dewey, J., & Dewey, E. (1915). *Schools of tomorrow.* New York: E. P. Dutton.

DeWitt., K. (1991, April 24). Vermont gauges learning by what's in portfolio. *The New York Times*, p. A23.

Dweck, C. S., & Leggett, E. L. (1988). A social-cognitive approach to motivation and personality. *Psychological Review, 95*, 256–273.

Eaton, A. E., & Voos, P. B. (1992). Union and contemporary innovations in work organization, compensation, and employee participation. In L. Mishel & P. Voos,

(Eds.), *Unions and economic competitiveness.* Armonk, NY: M.E. Sharpe, Inc.

Education Commission of the States (1991). *Restructuring the education system: Consumers guide* (Vol. 1). Denver, CO: Author.

Farnham-Diggory, S. (1990). *Schooling.* Cambridge, MA: Harvard University Press.

Finn, C., Jr. (1990). Why we need choice. In W. L. Boyd & H. J. Walberg (Eds.), *Choice in education: Potential and problems* (pp. 3–19). Berkeley, CA: McCutchan.

Fliegel, S. (1990). A district of choice. *Equity and Choice, 5* (1), 17–18.

Fogarty, R. (1991). Ten ways to integrate the curriculum. *Educational Leadership, 49* (2), 61–65.

Foothill Associates (1992). *Pasadena's project alive: A replication guide.* Pasadena, CA: Pasadena Unified School District.

Freund, W. C., & Epstein, E. (1984). *People and productivity: The New York stock exchange guide to financial incentives and the quality of work life.* Homewood, IL: Dow-Jones-Irwin.

Galotti, K. M. (1989). Approaches to studying formal and everyday reasoning. *Psychological Bulletin, 105*, pp. 331–351.

Gardner, H. (1983). *Frames of mind: The theory of multiple intelligences.* New York: Basic Books.

Gheens Academy (1991). *The professional practice schools.* Louisville, KY: Author.

Glaser, B., & Strauss, A. (1967). *The discovery of grounded theory.* Chicago, IL: Aldine.

Godowsky, S. H., Scarbrough, M. A., & Steinwedel, C. (1992). The senior project: An exhibition of achievement. In J. B. Podl (Ed.). *The process of planning backwards: Stories from three schools* (pp. 2–5). Providence, RI: Coalition of Essential Schools.

Goodlad, J. (1984). *A place called school: Prospects for the future.* New York: McGraw-Hill.

Goodman, K. (1986). *What's whole in whole language?* Ontario, Canada: Scholastic Books.

W. T. Grant Foundation Commission on Work, Family, and Citizenship (1988). *The forgotten half: Pathways to success for American's youth and young families.* Washington, DC: Author.

Grasso, J., & Shea, J. (1979). *Vocational education and training: Impact on youth.* Berkeley, CA: Carnegie Council on Policy Studies in Higher Education.

Grubb, W. N. (1994). School-to-work programs: True reforms or tired retreads? In *The leadership challenge: Accommodating different perspectives toward school-to-work transition in the United States.* Washington, DC: National Governors Association.

Grubb, W. N., Davis., G., Lum, J., Plihal, J., & Morgaine, C. (1991). *"The cunning hand, the cultured mind": Models for integrating vocational and academic education.* Berkeley, CA: National Center for Research in Vocational Education.

Grubb, W. N., Kalman, J., Castellano, M., Brown, C., & Bradby, D. (1991, September). *Readin', writin', and 'rithmetic one more time: The role of remediation in vocational education and job training programs.* Berkeley, CA: National Center for Research in Vocational Education.

Grubb, W.N., & Kalman, J. (1994, November). Relearning to earn: The role of remediation in vocational education and job training. *American Journal of Education, 103*(1): 54–93.

Grubb, W. N., & Lazerson, M. (1975). Rally 'round the workplace: Continuities and fallacies in career education. *Harvard Educational Review, 45* (4), 451–474.

Grubb, W. N., & Stasz, C. (1993). *Integrating academic and vocational education: Progress under the Carl Perkins Amendments of 1990.* Berkeley, CA: National Center for Research in Vocational Education, for the National Assessment of Vocational Education., U.S. Department of Education.

Grubb, W. N., & Wilson, R. (1992). Trends in wage and salary inequality, 1967–88. *Monthly Labor Review, 115* (6), 23–39.

Hackman, R. R., & Oldham, G. (1980). *Work Redesign.* Menlo Park, CA: Addison-Wesley Publishing Company.

Hamilton, S. F. (1990). *Apprenticeship for adulthood: Preparing youth for the future.* New York: Free Press.

Hass, M. (n.d.). *Cognition-in-context: The social nature of the transformation of mathematical knowledge in a third grade classroom.* Irvine, CA: Social Relations Graduate Program, University of California.

Hayes, J. R. (1981). *The Complete Problem Solver.* Philadelphia: Franklin Institute Press.

Heebner, A., Crain, R. L., Kiefer, D R., & Si, Y-P. (1992). *Career magnets: Interviews with students and staff.* Berkeley, CA: National Center for Research in Vocational Education.

Higher Education Research Institute (1994). *The American freshman: Twenty-five year trends.* Los Angeles: Higher Education Research Institute, University of California at Los Angeles.

Hill, P., & Bonan, J. (1991). *Decentralization and accountability in public education.* Santa Monica, CA: The Rand Corporation.

Hill, P., Foster, G., & Gendler, T. (1990). *High schools with character.* Santa Monica, CA: The Rand Corporation.

Hoachlander, E. G. (1994). *Industry-based education: A new approach for school-to-work transition.* Berkeley, CA: MPR Associates.

Jacobs, H. H. (1989). *Interdisciplinary curriculum: Design and implementation.* Alexandria, VA: Association of Supervision and Curriculum Development.

Jenkins, J. M., & Tanner, D. (Eds.) (1992). *Restructuring for an interdisciplinary curriculum.* Reston, VA: National Association of Secondary School Principals.

Jobs for the Future 1992. *From high school to high-skilled health careers: New models of work-and-learning in health care.* Cambridge, MA: Author.

Jordan, B. (1987). *Modes of teaching and learning: Questions raised by the training of traditional birth attendants* (Report No. IRL87-0004). Palo Alto, CA: Institute for Research on Learning.

Kanoy, R. (1992). How do you make the Paideia program work? *Paideia Next Century, 1* (1), 7.

Kantor, H. A. (1988). *Learning to earn: School, work, and vocational reform in California, 1880–1930.* Madison, WI: University of Wisconsin Press.

Kliebard, H. M. (1986). *The struggle for the American curriculum: 1893–1958.* Boston: Routledge & Kegan Paul.

Knapp, M. S., & Turnbull, B. J. (1990). *Better schooling for the children of poverty: Alternatives to conventional wisdo*m. *Volume I: Summary.* Washington, DC: U.S. Department of Education.

Knowles, M. S., & Associates (1980). *Andragogy in action: Applying modern principles of adult learning.* San Francisco, CA: Jossey-Bass.

Lave, J. (1988). *Cognition in practice.* New York: Cambridge University Press.

Lave, J., Smith, S., & Butler, M. (1988). Problem solving as an everyday practice. In *Learning mathematical problem solving.* Report No. IRL88-0006. Palo Alto, CA: Institute for Research on Learning.

Lawler, E., Ledford, G., Jr., & Mohrman, S. (1989). *Employee involvement in America: A study of contemporary practice.* Houston, TX: American Productivity and Quality Center.

Lawler, E., Mohrman, S., & Ledford, G., Jr. (1992). *Employee involvement and TQM: Practice and results in Fortune 500 companies.* San Francisco, CA: Jossey-Bass.

Lazerson, M., & Grubb, W. N. (1974). *American education and vocationalism: A documentary history, 1970–1970.* New York: Teachers College Press.

Learning Research and Development Center (1992). *The New Standards Project: An overview.* Pittsburgh: University of Pittsburgh and the National Center for Education and the Economy.

Leinhardt, G. (1983). Novice and expert knowledge of individual students' achievement. *Educational Psychologist, 18,* 165–179.

Leinhardt, G., & Greeno, J. (1986). The cognitive skill of teaching. *Journal of Educational Psychology, 78,* 75–95.

Leversee, M. (1991, November). *The manual training movement reassessed.* Unpublished M.A. dissertation, School of Education, University of California, Berkeley.

Levin, H., & Rumberger, R. (1989, March). *A taxonomy of generic work skills.* Presentation to the annual meeting of the American Educational Research Association, San Francisco, CA.

Levin, J. A. (1982). Microcomputer communication networks for education. *Quarterly Newsletter of the Laboratory of Comparative Human Cognition, 4*(2).

Levitan, S. A., & Gallo, F. (1993). *Education reform: Federal initiatives and national mandates, 1963–1993.* Washington, DC: The George Washington University, Center for Social Policy Studies.

Levy, F., & Murnane, R. (1992). U.S. earnings levels and earnings inequality: A review of recent trends and proposed explanations. *Journal of Economic Literature, 30* (3), 1333–1382.

Lieberman, A. (1990). Restructuring school: What matters and what works. *Phi Delta Kappan, 71* (10), 759–764.

Little, J. (1992). *Two worlds: Vocational and academic teachers in comprehensive high schools.* Berkeley, CA: National Center for Research in Vocational Education.

Little, J., & Threatt, S. (1992). *Work on the margins: The experience of vocational teachers in comprehensive high schools.* Berkeley, CA: National Center for Research in Vocational Education.

Lynch, R., & Griggs, M. (1989). *Vocational teacher education: A context for the future,* Berkeley, CA: National Center for Research in Vocational Education.

Malone, T. (1981). Toward a theory of intrinsically motivating instruction. *Cognitive Science, 4,* 333–369.

Malone, T., & Lepper, M. (1987). Making learning fun: A taxonomy of intrinsic motivations for learning. In R. Snow & M. Farr (Eds.), *Aptitude, Learning, and Instruction.* Hillsdale, NJ: Lawrence Erlbaum Associates.

Marland, S. P. (1974). *Career education: A proposal for reform.* New York: McGraw-Hill.

McArthur, D., Stasz, C., & Zmuidzinas, M. (1990). Tutoring techniques in algebra. *Cognition and Instruction, 7*, 194–244.

Metz, M. H. (1986). *Different by design: The context and character of three magnet schools.* New York: Routledge and Kegan Paul.

Meyer, R. (1981). An economic analysis of high school education. In *The federal role in vocational education: Sponsored research* . Washington, DC: National Commission for Employment Policy.

Mitchell, V., Russell, E. S., & Benson, C. (1989). *Exemplary urban career-oriented secondary school programs.* Berkeley, CA: National Center for Research in Vocational Education.

Moore, D. R., & Davenport, S. (1988). *The new improved sorting machine.* Madison, WI: National Center on Effective Secondary Schools.

National Academy of Sciences (1984). *High schools and the changing workplace: The employers' view* (Report of the Panel on Secondary School Education for the Changing Workplace). Washington, DC: National Academy Press.

National Center for Education Statistics, U.S. Department of Education (1993). *The Condition of Education, 1993.* Washington, DC: U.S. Government Printing Office.

National Commission on Secondary Vocational Education (1985). *The unfinished agenda: The role of vocational education in the high school.* Washington, DC: U.S. Department of Education, Office of Vocational and Adult Education.

National Council on Education Standards, and Testing (1992, January 24). *Raising standards for American education.* Washington D.C.: Author.

National Council on Vocational Education (1990). *Time for action: A business, industry, and education forum.* Washington, DC: National Council on Vocational Education.

National Education Association (1893). *Report of the committee on secondary school studies.* Washington, DC: U.S. Government Printing Office.

National Governors' Association (1991). *From rhetoric to action: State progress in restructuring the education system.* Washington, DC: Author.

New York City Public Schools (1992). *New York City Public Schools High School Graduation Requirements 1992-1993.* New York: Author.

New York City Public Schools (1994). *New York City Annual and Long Range Plan for Occupational Education: 1992–94, 1993–94 Annual Update.* New York: Author.

New York State Job Training Partnership Council and New York State Department of Education (1992). *Education that works: Creating career pathways for New York State Youth.* Albany, NY: Author.

Newell, A., & Simon, H. (1972). *Human problem solving.* Englewood Cliffs, NJ: Prentice-Hall.

Oakes, J. (1985). *Keeping track: How schools structure inequality.* New Haven: Yale University Press.

Oakes, J. (1986). Beyond tinkering: Reconstructing vocational education. In G. Copa, J. Plihal, & M. Johnson (Eds.), *Re-visioning vocational education in the secondary school.* St. Paul, MN: University of Minnesota.

Oakes, J. (1989). What educational indicators? The case for assessing the school context. *Educational Evaluation and Policy Analysis, 11*, 181–199.

Ohio Department of Education, Division of Vocational and Career Education (1990). *Applied academics: Modernizing vocational education.* Columbus, OH: Author.

Orr, J. (1986, December). *Narratives at work: Story telling as cooperative diagnostic activity.* Proceedings of the Conference on Computer-Supported Cooperative Work, Austin, TX.

Osterman, P. (1994, January). How common is workplace transformation and who adopts it? *Industrial and Labor Relations Review 47*(2), 173–188.

Panel of Consultants on Vocational Education (1963). *Education for a changing world of work.* Washington, DC: U.S. Department of Health, Education, and Welfare.

Passow, H. (1989). Present and future directions in school reform. In T. Sergiovanni (Ed.), *Schooling for tomorrow* (pp. 13–37). Boston: Allyn and Bacon.

Paulu, N. (1989). *Improving schools and empowering parents: Choice in American education.* Washington, DC: U.S. Department of Education.

Pauly, E., Kopp, H., & Haimson, J. (1994). *Home-grown lessons: Innovative programs linking work and high school.* New York: Manpower Demonstration Research Corporation.

Pea, R. D. (1989). *Socializing the knowledge transfer problem* (Report No. IRL89-0009). Palo Alto, CA: Institute for Research on Learning.

Philadelphia Schools Collaborative (1990). *The Philadelphia story, comprehensive high schools: Rethinking and restructuring.* Philadelphia: Author.

Powell, A., Farrar, E., & Cohen, D. (1985). *The shopping mall high school.* Boston: Houghton Mifflin.

Prawat, R.S. (1993, August-September). The value of ideas: Problems versus possibilities in learning. *Educational Researcher 22*(6), 5–16.

Prestine, N., & Bowen, C. (1993 Fall). Benchmarks of change: Assessing essential school restructuring efforts. *Educational Evaluation and Policy Analysis, 15 (3),* 298–319.

Pritz, S. G., & Crowe, M. R. (Eds.) (1987). *Techniques for joint effort: The vocational-academic approach.* Columbus, OH: National Center for Research in Vocational Education.

Putnam, R. T. (1987). Structuring and adjusting content for students: A study of live and simulated tutoring of addition. *American Educational Research Journal, 24* (1), 13–48.

Raizen, S. (1989). *Reforming education for work: A cognitive science perspective.* Berkeley, CA: National Center for Research in Vocational Education.

Reller, D. (1984). *The Peninsula Academies: Final technical evaluation report.* Palo Alto, CA: American Institutes for Research in the Behavior Sciences.

Resnick, L. (1987a). *Education and learning to think.* Washington, DC: National Research Council, National Academy Press.

Resnick, L. B. (1987b). Learning in school and out. *Educational Researcher, 16* (9), 13–20.

Reubens, B. (1974). Vocational education for all in high school? In J. O'Toole, *Work and the quality of life* (pp. 299–337). Boston: MIT Press.

Rochester City School District (1989). *Questions and answers about school-based planning.* Rochester: Author.

Rumberger, R. W., & Daymont, T. (1984). The economics of academic and vocational training acquired in high school. In M. E. Borus (Ed.), *Youth and the labor market: Analyses of the National Longitudinal Study* (pp. 157–192). Kalamazoo, MI: W. E. Upjohn Institute for Employment Research.

Russell, J. (1938). *Vocational education.* Washington, DC: Advisory Commission on Education, Staff Study No. 8.

Salomon, G. (1990). *Studying the flute and the orchestra: Controlled experimentation vs. whole classroom research on computers.* Unpublished paper, University of Arizona, Tucson, AZ.

Schoenfeld, A. H. (1988). *Ideas in the air* (Report No. IRL88-0011). Palo Alto, CA: Institute for Research on Learning.

Scribner, S. (1988). *Head and hand: An action approach to thinking.* New York: Institute on Education and the Economy, Teachers College, Columbia University.

Scribner, S., & Sachs, P. (1990). *A study of on-the-job training.* New York: Institute on Education and the Economy, Teachers College, Columbia University.

Scribner, S., & Sachs, P. (1991). *Knowledge acquisition at work.* New York: Institute on Education and the Economy, Teachers College, Columbia University.

Secretary's Commission on Achieving Necessary Skills (SCANS) (1991). *What work requires of schools.* Washington, DC: U.S. Department of Labor.

SCANS (1992a). *Learning a living: A blueprint for high performance.* Washington, DC: U.S. Department of Labor.

SCANS (1992b). *SCANS in the schools.* Washington, DC: U.S. Department of Labor.

SCANS (1993). *Teaching the SCANS competencies.* Washington, DC: U.S. Department of Labor.

Singley, M., & Anderson, J. R. (1989). *The transfer of cognitive skill.* Cambridge, MA: Harvard University Press.

Sirotnik, K. (1983). What you see is what you get: Consistency, persistency, and mediocrity in classrooms. *Harvard Educational Review, 53,* 16–31.

Sizer, T. (1984). *Horace's compromise: The dilemma of the American high school.* Boston, MA: Houghton Mifflin

Snyder, P., & McMullen, B. (1987). *Allies in education: A profile of Philadelphia high school academies, Philadelphia, Pennsylvania.* Philadelphia: Public/Private Ventures.

Spady, W., & Marshall, K. (1991). Beyond traditional outcomes-based education. *Educational Leadership, 49* (2), 67–72.

Spenner, K.I. (1990). Skills: Meanings, methods, and measures. *Work and Occupations 17*(4): 399–421.

Stasz, C., McArthur, D., Lewis, M., & Ramsey, K. (1990). *Teaching and learning generic skills for the workplace* (Report R-4004-NCRVE/UCB). Berkeley, CA: University of California, National Center for Research in Vocational Education.

Stern, D. (1990, November). *Combining school and work: Options in high schools and two-year colleges.* Paper prepared for the Office of Vocational and Adult Education, U.S. Department of Education, Washington, DC.

Stern, D., Dayton, C., Paik, I., & Weisberg, A. (1989). Benefits and costs of dropout prevention in a high school program combining academic and vocational education: Third-year results from replications of the California Peninsula Academies. *Educational Evaluation and Policy Analysis, 11* (4), 405–416.

Stern, D., Hoachlander, G. E., Choy, S., & Benson, C. (1986, March). *One million hours a day: Vocational education in California secondary schools.* Policy paper no. PP86-3-2. Berkeley, CA: University of California, Policy Analysis for California Education.

Stevenson, H. W. (Author). (1989). *The polished stone* [Film]. Ann Arbor, MI: Center for Human Growth and Development, University of Michigan.

Stevenson, H. W., & Stigler J. W. (1992). *The learning gap.* New York: Summit Books.

Sticht, T. (1989). Adult literacy education. In E. Z. Rothkopf (Ed.), *Review of research in education, 1988-89, 15.* Washington, DC: American Educational Research Association.

Stigler, J. W., & Stevenson, H. W. (1991, Spring). How Asian teachers polish each lesson to perfection. *American Educator,* pp. 12–20, 43–47.

Stillings, N., Feinstein, M., Garfield, J., Rissland, E., Rosenbaum, D., Weisler, S., & Baker-Ward, L. (1987). *Cognitive science: An introduction.* Cambridge, MA: MIT Press.

Tanner, D., & Tanner, L. (1990). *History of the school curriculum.* New York: Macmillan.

Thomas Jefferson High School for Science and Technology (1993). *Mentor handbook.* Alexandria, VA: Author.

Thorndike, E. L. (1898). *Animal intelligence.* New York: Macmillan.

Tomlinson, L. (1989). *Postsecondary developmental programs: A traditional agenda with new imperatives* (ASHE-ERIC Higher Education Report 3). Washington, DC: George Washington University.

Tucker, M. (1992, June). A new "social compact" for mastery in education. *Education Week, Special Report, 11* (38), S3–4.

Tyack, D. (1974). *The one best system.* Cambridge, MA: Harvard University Press.

U.S. Commission on Excellence in Education (1983). *A nation at risk.* Washington, DC: U.S. Government Printing Office.

U.S. Congress, Office of Technology Assessment (1990). *Worker training: Competing in the new international economy* (OTA-ITE-457). Washington, DC: U.S. Government Printing Office.

The University of the State of New York and The State Department of Education (1991). *New York state plan for the administration of occupational education under the Carl D. Perkins Vocational and Applied Technology Act of 1990, 1991-92, 1992-93, 1993-94.* Albany: Author.

The University of the State of New York and The State Education Department, Office of General and Occupational Education, Division of Occupational Education Instruction (1989). *Occupational education curriculum of New York state: A handbook for administrators and counselors.* Albany, NY: Author

Van Sickle, R. (1990). The personal relevance of the social studies. *Social Education 54* (4), 23–27, 59.

Violence in the Schools: A Search for Safety. (1993, December 12). *The New York Times,* p. 1.

Weiss, J. (1982). The advent of education for clerical workers in the high school: A reconsideration of the historiography of vocationalism. *Teachers College Record, 83* (4), 613–638.

Woodward, C. M. (1887). *The manual training school.* Boston: D. C. Heath & Co.

ABOUT THE CONTRIBUTORS

W. NORTON GRUBB is a professor at the School of Education, the University of California, Berkeley. His research interests include the role of schooling in labor markets; the flows of students into and through postsecondary education; the interactions among education and training programs; community colleges; and social policy toward children and youth. In addition to his research, he works extensively with both secondary and postsecondary educators, particularly about the integration of academic and vocational education. He is also a site director for the National Center for Research in Vocational Education at the University of California, Berkeley, and has been instrumental in establishing the Center at Berkeley. He received a Ph.D. in economics from Harvard University in 1975.

ERICA NEILSEN ANDREW is a project manager at the National Center for Research for Vocational Education, responsible for a project sponsored by the Joyce Foundation on the concept of teaching "all aspects of the industry." She coordinates a number of school sites and partner organizations—Jobs for the Future, the Center for Law and Education, and the New Standards Project—participating in this effort. Prior to joining the National Center, Erika worked as a high school teacher and school administrator. She has also been active in the state of California, and recently finished writing state training procedures for teachers and administrators related to *Second to None*, a state report recommending the adoption of career pathways for all high school students. She is a graduate student at the University of California, Berkeley.

THOMAS BAILEY is the director of the Institute of Education and the Economy and an associate professor in the Department of Economics, Education, Philosophy and Social Sciences at Teachers College, Columbia University. He is also a site director and board member of the National Center for Research in Vocational Education. He is an expert on education reform, school to work transition, workplace organization, and the educational and training implications of changes in the workplace. He has served as a consultant to many public agencies and foundations including the U.S. Department of Labor, the U.S. Department of Education, the U.S. Congress Office of Technology Assessment, the Alfred P. Sloan Foundation, the William T. Grant Foundation, and several state and local economic development and educational agencies. His articles have appeared in a wide variety of policy-oriented and academic journals, and he has authored or coauthored books on the employment and training of immigrants and the extent and effects of on the job training. His most recent book, written with Sue Berryman, *The Double Helix of Education and the Economy*, examines the poorly understood link between the needs of the workplace and the contemporary understanding of effective learning. He holds a Ph.D. in labor economics from MIT.

CHARLES S. BENSON was director of the National Center for Research in Vocational Education (NCRVE) at the University of California, Berkeley, from its inception in 1988 until his untimely death in 1994. Dr. Benson was also a professor in the Graduate School of Education at the University of California, Berkeley, where he had been a member of the faculty since 1964. Dr. Benson has conducted research and written extensively in the following fields: economics of education, finance of K-12 education, finance of postsecondary education, distribution of local public services, educational planning, the relationship between education and economic development, educational innovation, teacher policy, family influences on school achievement, public sector bargaining, and vocational education. Dr. Benson has had extensive experience in the management of R & D projects, including the State Committee on Public Education (California Legislature); Pakistan-Berkeley Program in Educational Planning (Ford Foundation); New York State Commission on the Quality, Cost, and Financing of Elementary and Secondary Education (New York State Legislature); Select Committee on School District Finance (California Legislature); Childhood and Government Project (Ford Foundation and Carnegie Foundation); Berkeley-Stanford Seminar in Educational Finance and Organization (National Institute of Education); Berkeley Project on Education and Nutrition (U.S. Agency for International Development); Project on National Vocational Education Resources (National Institute of Education); Children's Time Study Project (Ford Foundation and the National Institute of Education); and Project on Vocational Education (California State Legislature). He received his A.B. from Princeton University and his M.A. and Ph.D., both in economics, from Columbia University.

SUE E. BERRYMAN is an education specialist with the World Bank in Washington, D.C., where she provides technical assistance for the Bank's human capital work in the Middle East, North Africa, Eastern Europe, and the former countries of the Soviet Union. From 1985–92 she directed the Institute on Education and the Economy at Teachers College, Columbia University, a research institute that focuses on the implications for changes in the U.S. economy and workplace for the education and training system. She was a behavioral scientist with the RAND Corporation for 12 years, after serving on the faculty of the University of Minnesota, working as a research associate in the Director's Division of the Oak Ridge National Laboratory, and teaching at the Harvard Business School. She is a member of several national advisory boards, including the Committee on Postsecondary Education and Training for the Workplace of the National Academy of Science, and speaks widely on issues of education and employability in the United States. Her most recent book, coauthored with Thomas Bailey, is *The Double Helix of Education and the Economy.*

RICK EDEN received his doctorate in English from UCLA in 1980. From 1981 to 1984 he was an assistant professor of English at the University of New Mexico, where he taught undergraduate and graduate courses in writing, rhetoric, and composition pedagogy. In 1984 he joined RAND's research staff. He participated in two previous NCRVE studies and has 15 years of teaching experience at the adult level.

AMY HEEBNER conducted intensive interviewing of students and adults in New York City career magnets, as senior research associate for a project funded by the National Center for Research in Vocational Education (Robert L. Crain, Principal Investigator). As a research fellow at the Center for Intelligent Tools in Education, an IBM-funded research and development project at Teachers College, Columbia University, she investigated computer use in writing classrooms. She is currently an assistant professor in the Department of Mass Communications, St. Cloud State University, Minnesota.

LOLA JEFFRIES JACKSON is an associate professor of Career and Technical Education at Wayne State University in Detroit, Michigan. Her faculty responsibilities include teaching graduate courses in career and technical education, teacher preparation, administration, issues and trends, tech prep, integration of academics and diversity in the workplace. In her consulting capacity of outreach coordinator for the National Center for Research in Vocational Education's Urban Schools Project, she provides technical assistance to urban school districts that are planning and implementing programs for tech prep and integration of academic and vocational education. Dr. Jackson was formerly the State Director for Vocational Education in the Michigan Department of Education. She has also taught home economics and consumer education in Detroit Public Schools and has been a home economist for the Potomac Electric Power Company in Washington, D.C. She serves on numerous boards and committees at both the state and national levels. Dr. Jackson holds a Ph.D. in Higher Education Administration from Michigan State University in East Lansing, a master's in Consumer Education from Wayne State University, and a bachelor's degree in Home Economics from Howard University in Washington, D.C.

RUTH H. KATZ is the director of the Urban Schools Network, a project of The National Center for Research in Vocational Education (NCRVE). The Network coordinates teams of educators—academic and vocational instructors, counselors, and administrators, business partners, and state level Department of Education representatives—actively engaged in the development and implementation of programs integrating academic and vocational education, and/or programs of Tech Prep. Ms. Katz has been associated with NCRVE since 1990, and has been involved with the Urban Schools Network since its formation in 1992. Prior to her work with NCRVE, she directed programs for high schools in the San Francisco Unified School District. Ms. Katz holds a B.A. degree from Grinnell College in Iowa, and an M.A. in Communication from Stanford University in California.

MARILYN RABY is currently director of curriculum services in the Sequoia Union High School District (Redwood City, CA). She was the director of the first California Partnership Academies program and presently supervises an Academies national demonstration site. Dr. Raby also serves as a consultant for technical assistance to Academy startups, and is author of several journal articles and coauthor of *Career Academies: Partnerships for Reconstructing American High Schools* (with David Stern and Charles Dayton).

KIMBERLY RAMSEY is a resident consultant at RAND. She has 12 years of experience in educating and training adults in schools, corporations, and community-based organizations. Ms. Ramsey has been involved in National Center for Research in Vocational Education (NCRVE) research at RAND for five years, on studies of academic and vocational integration, skill needs in the workplace, and teaching generic skills. She has conducted several studies of work sites using anthropological methods. Ms. Ramsey holds an M.A. degree from the School of Education, University of California, Los Angeles.

KATHY REEVES is a research associate with the Tech Prep research group at the National Center for Research in Vocational Education (NCRVE). She has conducted research on the linkage between high schools and colleges, the relationship between education and work for community college students, and policy implementation. Ms. Reeves is a doctoral candidate in the School of Education at the University of California, Berkeley, specializing in higher education policy and administration.

CATHY STASZ is a cognitive psychologist at RAND and site director for the National Center for Research in Vocational Education (NCRVE). Her research areas include the development of generic and domain-specific skills and the implementation of advanced computer-based technologies in education, the workplace, and the military. Her current research examines new skill needs in the workplace and develops methods for assessing skills in the context of work. She received a Ph.D. from the University of California, Los Angeles.

MAYO TSUZUKI has a B.A. from Harvard University and has studied piano performance at The Juilliard School in New York City—continuing her musical training which began at the age of four. She has worked in the arts management and marketing fields, and is currently a doctoral student in the Educational Psychology Division of the School of Education at the University of California at Berkeley, studying adolescent development and conceptions of authority. In addition to tutoring minority and at-risk students in English and Journalism at an Oakland public high school, Ms. Tsuzuki is a research assistant at the National Center for Research in Vocational Education, working with teams of educators from 30 urban sites—including secondary and postsecondary institutions—that are integrating vocational and academic education.

INDEX

■